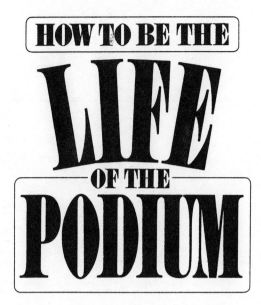

HOW TO BE THE LIFE OF THE PODIUM
OF THE
PODIUM

HOW TO BE THE LIFE OF THE PODIUM

Openers, Closers & Everything In Between to Keep Them Listening

SYLVIA SIMMONS

amacom

American Management Association

This book is available at a special
discount when ordered in bulk quantities.
For information, contact Special Sales Department,
AMACOM, a division of American Management Association,
135 West 50th Street, New York, NY 10020.

Library of Congress Cataloging-in-Publication Data

Simmons, S. H. (Sylvia H.)
How to be the life of the podium : openers, closers & everything
in between to keep them listening / Sylvia Simmons.
p. cm.
Includes indexes.
ISBN 0-8144-5069-5
1. Public speaking—Handbooks, manuals, etc. 2. Wit and humor.
I. Title.
PN4193.I5S493   1991
808.5′1—dc20   91-23684
                                                                                CIP

Printing number

10 9 8 7 6 5 4 3 2 1

CONTENTS

———◆◀●▶◆———

Foreword   ix

Who Is Sylvia?

Introduction   1

Inside Tips From the Author
to Make Your Talk Funnier, Smarter, Better

Openers   5

Off to a Good Start

The Simmons System   27

Your Speech Will Almost Write Itself

Politics   36

Poking Fun at Public Figures or Issues

Youth and Age   49

Bridging the Generation Gap

Business   66

Raising Your Listeners' Blood Pressure

Facts, Figures, and Research   84

Shoring Up Credibility, or Kidding the Statisticians

One-Liners   95

Establishing Yourself as a Sage, Wit, Philosopher

Fables, Tales, and Allegories   112

Making Your Point Without Sermonizing

The World of Advertising   123

Getting Your Audience All Worked Up

Away From Home   136

Out of Town or Out of the Country:
Make It Work for You

Doctors, Lawyers, Industry Chiefs   151

Needling the Untouchables

Proverbs   172

Letting the Sages of the Ages Say It for You

Spellbinders   185

Great Orators . . . Memorable Quotes

Wisdom of the East   206

Worldly Comments on Life From India and China

Closings   220

Getting Off While You're Still Ahead

Audio and Visual Aids 239
Making Them Work Harder for You

Guaranteed Applause 251
The Fifteen Best Speech Bits I've Ever Heard

Rehearsals 265
You're in Show Biz, So Do As the Professionals Do

Extra Mileage From Your Speech 272
Provocative Titles and Good Publicity

Biographical Index 281
How to Authenticate Your Speech

Subject Index 311
How to Track Your Topic

FOREWORD

Who Is Sylvia?

At age 36, I became the president of Young & Rubicam-USA (Y&R), then and now one of the most prestigious and respected advertising agencies at home and abroad. This venerable company was then the second largest advertising agency in the world, with an awesome reputation for creativity and marketing savvy. An industry survey at that time showed Y&R to be the agency where most advertising people would like to work, so my appointment to the top position received considerable coverage in the business press.

Almost immediately after my new title was announced, I was besieged with invitations from the business world and the media, as well as from civic, academic, and social groups, to speak at conventions, symposia, graduations, and the like. Were I to have accepted even a tenth of those invitations, I would have had no time left to do my new job at the agency. It soon became obvious that I would need a speechwriter to work with me in drafting those speeches that I agreed to give.

I became a frequent after-lunch and after-dinner speaker—often the keynote speaker on a program—and occasionally the recipient of some award that called for an appropriately dignified and humble "recipient's acknowledgment," as the programs sometimes list it. Fortunately, the agency had on staff a speechwriter named Sylvia Simmons who wrote speeches for executives in client companies. It wasn't long before I arranged for Sylvia to become part of the team that served as the president's staff.

Sometimes she wrote my talks; in other instances in which I

found time to draft my own rough scripts, she acted as my speech doctor. Her fine pen and quick wit eventually touched every speech I gave—except impromptu ones—and thanks to her talents I soon became a favorite of program chairpersons from London to Rio.

As a matter of fact, even some of my impromptu talks have been enhanced by the material in this book. Half of Madison Avenue knew that Sylvia kept locked in her desk a voluminous file of index cards, each of which carried a single story or line that she or some of her equally accredited ghost friends had used with great results in the talk of some important person to some equally important audience. She was constantly besieged by requests to borrow the file or, when she was willing and available, to doctor a dull script with material from her private collection. I was one of the few people privileged to have access to this file, and often faced with the need to talk on very short notice to some delegation from abroad or perhaps to a college class, I would rummage through Sylvia's material in hopes of finding some appropriate comments with which to enliven the more serious aspects of my message. She never failed me. I always found such a plethora of good stuff that I was sometimes tempted to throw away my script and just flip sophisticated lines at my audience, much as a stand-up comic might do. Fortunately, good sense (usually Sylvia's) prevailed.

On one occasion, "Sylvia's File"—I had more than passing familiarity with it by then—saved the reputation I enjoyed as a raconteur. I had been invited to England to bring a message from the colonies to the London Television Advertising Congress, an audience that was a veritable Who's Who of British businesspeople and their advertising agency counterparts. Many of my own agency's international clients were in the audience. The organizers of the congress had chosen to employ a complicated audiovisual device. They had set up twelve monitors—small TV screens—along the sides of the huge auditorium so that members of the audience, wherever they sat, could get a close-up view of each speaker. Both sound and pictures were transmitted to television trucks (parked three blocks from the auditorium) and relayed back again to the monitors. I thought the setup complicated and unnecessary; but then, I was only a foreign guest speaker.

In accordance with Murphy's Law, which tells us that anything that can go wrong *will*, the equipment broke down, and there was no substitute equipment to project the film, without which my talk was meaningless. To make matters worse (for me), I happened to be the speaker at the mike when all systems wouldn't go. Afraid that this high-powered audience would just get up and leave, the program chairman sent a panic-filled note up to me. It said, "Just talk!"

Well, what in the world can a man say under those circumstances? As a technician hung a temporary mike around my sweating neck, Sylvia's File flashed before my eyes, and without quite knowing where I was headed I followed the chairman's instructions. I talked. "Let me use this waiting time," I said, "to tell you an old Russian fable that is not inapplicable to the situation in which our program chairman now finds himself." And then I told the Russian fable that appears on page 252 of this book. Immodest as it may sound, I must tell you that it brought down the house. Those dignified British executives howled and stamped their feet and shouted for more. I culled my memory, and one after another of Sylvia's anecdotes and one-liners began to come to me. I can't say that I delivered them in very sensible sequence, but the audience had a great time during the fifteen-minute wait upon technology.

When I left Y&R to become president of Kenyon & Eckhardt Advertising, Sylvia came with me as that agency's director of corporate communications and my personal speechwriter. Clients, too, vied for her help in drafting some of their speeches, and she soon became well-known as a ghost for some favored executives at such companies as Bristol-Myers, Chrysler, Warner-Lambert, and others. No doubt about it: I could never have achieved some degree of international fame as a public speaker and platform personality were it not for my extraordinary ghostwriter.

Stephen O. Frankfurt

INTRODUCTION

Inside Tips From the Author to Make Your Talk Funnier, Smarter, Better

In *How to Be the Life of the Podium*, I have drawn upon my many years of experience as a professional "ghost" to give you some inside tips of the trade, along with my private collection of openings, closings, jokes, anecdotes, and philosophical comments with which I have enhanced, enlivened, and illuminated several hundred speeches and, in so doing, earned more than a million dollars during my career as a ghost.

First let me say what this book will *not* do for you. The material that follows is not designed to tell you *how* to deliver a line or improve your phrasing. For that you need a coach or director. Few people, aware that their public performances are not all they would have them be, ever consider engaging the services of a local theatrical director to coach them before a scheduled performance. Yet I have found that, even in New York and London, quite famous stage directors (who are, perhaps, between plays) are willing, if the price is right, to direct a nontheatrical public speaker in advance of a platform appearance.

What this book *will* do for you is supply you with a choice of material that will help you get into your talk, enliven it along the way, and get off while the getting is good. And it will give you, briefly and in simple language, some practical advice about writing a talk that will get you the sort of applause every speaker wants.

Whenever possible, I have indicated where I first heard or read a given piece of material. That is not to say that the source given is actually the first person ever to have said it. It is merely where I heard it. And since the contents of this book were collected over a period of some twenty years—during which time I ghostwrote and doctored several hundred speeches for business tycoons, politicians, doctors, publishers, and paid lecturers—many anecdotal sources have long since been forgotten. In some instances, the source of a line or passage is myself, since I have chosen to include lines of my own creation where they have been tested in successful platform use.

A few words of explanation about my use of the pronoun *I* in this handbook. In all the explanatory copy—wherever I tell how to write something or where I describe a technique or give advice on using this book or some specific material in it—the pronoun *I* refers to me, the author of this book. For example, in the preceding paragraph when I said, "I have indicated where I first heard or read a given piece of material," the first-person pronoun refers to your author.

However, wherever I provide actual material for you to use in preparing your talk—openings or closings, anecdotes, philosophical comments, witticisms—the material, where appropriate, has been written in the first person to make it easy for you to see how it might be used in your own speech. In all those instances, the pronoun *I* is meant to be *you*—you the reader, the person talking to an audience.

Here's an example. In the section entitled "Openers," you will find this item suggested as a throwaway line a speaker can use while adjusting the microphone: "I'm always a little intimidated by a microphone. Of course, a microphone never *made* a fool of anybody. It only shows 'em up!" Should you decide to use that comment in one of your own speeches, you could use it exactly as is—because the first-person copy is written just the way you would deliver the line from the platform. This cuts down the amount of time you would otherwise have to spend in editing suggested material for your own personal use.

In addition, all the items in this book have been selected because they have been successfully platform-tested. They were written for the *ear*, and by presenting them as an audience would hear them, you can get a better idea of how they would actually sound in platform use. (Only the section entitled "Wisdom of the East" contains some material I have not personally tested. Keen interest in India and China is of such recent vintage I have not had the opportunity to use all those items in speeches I've written. But I would stress the timeliness of that material for today's public speaker.)

Let me give you another example. In the section on politics, you will find this opening to a short story: "One of the young men in my office said to me the other day, 'You know, I have half a mind to go into politics.' " In this instance, the *me* means *you*, the reader, the user of this platform bit. If you used this particular anecdote, you would say those very words, "One of the young men in *my* office. . . ." Of course, you might want to make other changes. If, for instance, you are a teacher, you would change the line to say, "One of the young men in my *class*. . . ." But the first-person pronoun would remain—it's *you*.

A few words about the use of *he* and *she*. Most of the material in this book can be used by women or men. Where a masculine or feminine pronoun is used rather than both, it is in the interest of brevity and to enable you to use this material effectively but quickly. Were I to say "he/she," "him/her," and "men/women" in the thousands of places where *he*, *him*, and *man* appear, it would add many pages and slow down your reading. In some instances, it might even make it difficult to understand the punch line of a story.

Here's a word of practical advice concerning publicity and the special material you select for use in your talks: If you speak frequently and especially if your talks are likely to be covered or reviewed by trade or local press, *don't* include your jokes and anecdotes in press release copies. This will enable you to use your best material over and over again as you grow comfortable with it and as you find from experience that it works for you. This was an old trick of John F. Kennedy's, a master at using anecdotal material and one-liners. In place of the opening comments, your release copies should either carry the words *Introductory Remarks* (in the blank space where you deleted an opening story) or begin immediately with the first serious paragraph.

You will occasionally have people in the audience write to you for "a copy of that great fable you used at the end of your talk— which was not included in the script I wrote for, which you so graciously sent me. . . ." You can then decide whether you want to succumb to the flattery and send the writer your fable—or whether you want to tell him to get his *own* ghostwriter.

Finally, there are two indexes at the back of this book. They are more than just indexes, however. They are carefully designed to help you write and deliver a memorable speech. I urge you to read the comments that preface each of these listings. The explanations will suggest new ways to approach the talk you're preparing so that your final presentation will be varied, witty, and as enjoyable as those given by even the most gifted and sought-after platform personalities.

OPENERS

---◆•◦•◆---

Off to a Good Start

It is very comforting and reassuring to get some form of response from the audience shortly after you have uttered your first words. Whether that response is laughter, applause, or even an invited groan, at least you know the sea of faces out there is not some hostile force waiting for the first opportunity to snicker, sleep, or—heaven forbid!—snore. Only one thing can be worse than that: telling an opening story and having it lay an egg. The silence can be deafening.

Thus, the toughest job a speaker has is breaking the ice and developing some sort of rapport with the audience. Once that's done, most speakers will relax a bit. With relaxation comes better delivery and heightened audience attention. I do not advocate, however, that a speaker merely tell any old funny joke in order to unwind or to hear the welcome sound of laughter.

Openers should track directly into the talk—by acknowledging the introduction about you that the chairperson or moderator has just delivered, by explaining your presence on the program, by saying something about the audience or subject matter, or by letting the audience in on some aspect of your personality or state of mind. You will see how this works as you go through the openers.

I have also included some material dealing with the matter of writing and delivering speeches. Some of these lines, which can be inserted in a talk at the beginning or the end, are no more than attempts to woo the audience. Interestingly enough, audiences do not resent this. On the contrary, they set you up as being human or modest or maybe just one of them. Anyone in your audience who has ever dealt with the problem of preparing a talk or who would like to give one but feels inadequate to the task will identify with you if you share your own trepidations.

How do you know whether your opener is going to work? There is no guarantee. But there are a few things you can do to increase the odds in your favor. Every one of the openers given here *has* worked—for someone else. What you need to do is pick the one or two openers with which you will feel comfortable. Close the door and say them out loud several times. If your choice gives you a chuckle and you're not ill at ease with the concept, consider using it. Then consider your audience. Break it down in your own mind. Who will be out front? Have you met any of them? Do they have the intellectual capacity to grasp the tag line? Are they likely to have enough humor and self-confidence to appreciate a story that kids them a bit? Are they your peers? If so, will they allow that the story includes you, along with them, in the kidding?

When you've selected your opening, grow familiar with it. *This is very important.* Read it out loud ten times. Change the words you stumble over, and substitute words of your own choosing. Don't feel hemmed in by the particular phraseology given here. However, don't change any word or phrase essential to having the audience understand the punch line. You probably shouldn't change the punch line either.

Try out the story, if it *is* a story, on someone in your family or at the office. Possibly they won't like it. Don't be discouraged. Remember that your speech will be given in a big room to a large number of people waiting to hear something clever or astute or informative. The listener's mind-set will be quite different from that of the audience of one on whom you're practicing your material. The true purpose of such practice is for you to become accustomed to telling the story or saying the line so that your eyes will not be glued to the script page when you eventually deliver it from the platform.

Use your practice situation to learn where you might improve audience understanding by placing greater emphasis or by pausing at given points. While I do not recommend memorizing your talk, it will increase your self-confidence if you know your opening lines by heart.

And now, how about these for openers . . .

*

Before I begin, I'd like to tell you the name of that main course you just had for lunch—in case they ask you when you get to the hospital.

*

Thank you for that very complimentary introduction. Of course, I am not unaware that flattery is 90-percent soap. And soap is 90-percent lye.

*

I deeply appreciate your very generous introduction. Even if I believed only 50 percent of it, I would be flattered. I don't really think that flattery can hurt a person—unless she *inhales*.

*

I have considerable respect for your tolerance in inviting me to address you—and for my courage in accepting.

*

This is an appropriate story to tell when you've been called upon to give an impromptu talk. It can also be used for a prepared talk if a particularly large burst of applause greets the speaker:

Some years ago, the British House of Commons was interrupted by the news that the cable to Africa had been completed.

After the huzzahs and hat tossing had died down, Winston Churchill rose to say, "Excellent, excellent. Now, what shall we *tell* the Africans?"

*

The following is a fine story with which to open your talk if you are the last speaker on the program:

I cannot help thinking about the minister who gave the invocation at a church conference. "O Lord," he said, "give the first speaker the power to provide inspiration here today. And Lord, help the second speaker to convey the seriousness of his message to all assembled in this room. And Lord, have mercy on the last speaker."

*

On the way in, I noticed an announcement on the bulletin board that some of you may have missed. It said that the meeting of the local Clairvoyance Society had been canceled—due to unforeseen circumstances.

Follow this up with a comment such as:

I do not consider myself clairvoyant, but I've accepted your challenge to discuss the future, and so. . .

*

Being in this fine company will certainly add to my image. I hope it doesn't detract too much from yours.

*

In introducing another speaker with an impressive list of accomplishments and memberships, tick off his various associations and memberships, such as "member of the board of _____ ," etc., then use this line:

He is, in fact, so busy he couldn't make it here tonight. [Then bring on the speaker.]

*

This is an appropriate opening when you are substituting for someone who had been scheduled to speak but was unable to make it:

Mr. [name of scheduled speaker] sends his regrets and me . . . I mean, he regrets to send me . . . I mean, he sends me with his regrets.

*

Once upon a time, in the days of the Roman Empire, a mob was gathered in the Colosseum to watch as a Christian was thrown to a hungry lion. The spectators cheered as the wild beast went after its prey. But the Christian quickly whispered something in the lion's ear, and the beast backed away with obvious terror on his face. No amount of calling and foot stomping by the audience could get the lion to approach the Christian again. Fearlessly, the Christian walked from the arena.

The emperor was so amazed at what had happened that he sent for the Christian and offered him his freedom if he would say what he had done to make the ferocious beast cower in fear. The Christian bowed before the emperor and said, "I merely whispered in the lion's ear, 'After dinner, you'll be required to say a few words.'"

*

It can happen to anybody. You tell a funny story, and it fails to get a laugh. Don't let it upset you. Just say:

Well, everyone doesn't have to be funny all the time—and I've just proved it.

*

Asked by a reporter what she had thought of Mary Martin's performance on the opening night of *South Pacific*, Ethel Merman is reputed to have said, "Oh, she's all right, if you like talent."

If you're introducing some person of considerable talent, that story might be followed by your own comment that the next speaker "is all right if you like talent."

*

I'm not going to say that [name of speaker you are introducing; possibly the guest of honor at a roast] is self-centered. I'll just tell you that one day he was talking to someone on his staff and I heard him say, "Enough about me! Let's talk about you. What do you think of me?"

*

If you are speaking to people in your own company and don't want to take credit for recent successes, you might open with this line:

If I have all the attributes that have just been credited to me, I will tell you that I owe it all to the genius of a few and the dedication of many, all of whom are right here in this room.

*

If you are called upon to introduce another speaker, you might end your introduction by saying:

The relationship of the toastmaster to the speaker should be the same as that of the fan to the fan dancer. It should call attention to the subject—but not make any particular effort to cover it. Ladies and gentlemen, I give you [name of speaker].

*

This comment can be used by a speaker who is called upon to give a talk at breakfast or at any early hour of the morning:

I hope I can manage to keep myself awake during this talk. Frankly, I'm unaccustomed to getting up so early in the morning. Until I got the invitation to appear in this spot, I didn't even know there were two eight o'clocks in the same day.

*

I am, of course, pleased and flattered by your kind introduction. But then, I suspected all along that someday somebody would kick over the basket and unbushel my shining light.

*

I feel a little like the son of an Arabian sheik who was having a birthday. His father didn't quite know what to give a boy who had everything, but he finally hit on the idea of giving him a harem. After presenting the gift, the sheik left his son alone.

Some time later, passing by, he noticed the boy standing befuddled outside the harem door. "What's the matter, Son?" asked the sheik. "Don't you know what to do with it?"

"It's not quite that, Father," replied the son. "It's just that I don't know where to start!"

You might then bridge into your talk by saying that your

*subject is such a broad one or has so many ramifications
that you almost "don't know where to start."*

*

*This is a throwaway line that can be used as you adjust
the microphone to the proper height and direction:*

I'm always a little intimidated by a microphone. Of course, a microphone never made a fool of anybody. It only shows 'em up!

*

In fact, our luncheon speaker is so fabulous that if she didn't exist, we'd have to invent her.

*

I am not going to cover everything I believe on this subject. First, it would take more time than I have allotted to me. Second, I am ever mindful of something that Joseph Addison wrote in the year 1711.

"If the minds of men were laid open," wrote Mr. Addison, "we should see but little difference between that of the wise man and that of the fool. The great difference is that the first knows how to pick and cull his thoughts for conversation by suppressing some and communicating others; whereas the other (the fool) lets them all indifferently fly out in words."

*

*If you wear glasses and have to put them on to read your
script and take them off to see the audience or if you wear
bifocals, this story acknowledges the glasses at the onset
so that you need not apologize later on for any "business"
of putting them on and taking them off:*

I'm just getting used to these bifocals, and I hope I can manage to read this small type in my script. I know that when I look over the top of them at some of our younger people in the office, they probably think, "That guy's a little bit eccentric." But I'd rather have them think *that* than fumble for a word because I was *not* wearing glasses and have them say, "That poor old son of a bitch is going blind!"

*

Let me assure you at the outset that I am not here to tell you how to run your business. There are far too many people meddling in your business already.

*

I hope I can remember the lines I am going to ad-lib.

> *This line works particularly well if you make a thing of placing your script on the podium in such a way that the audience can see it is quite substantial. Or if you really want to play it for a laugh, bring an extra copy of your talk to the podium with you. Drop it helter-skelter so that the audience can see the pages fall all over the platform. Wait for the audience to gasp in sympathy, then deliver the line and proceed from there by reading your duplicate paper.*

*

[Name of program chairperson] wrote me a very flattering letter in which he asked me to appear before you today. Much as I appreciated those flattering words, I would have preferred a message like the one Francis the First of France sent to Benvenuto Cellini: "Come. I will choke you with gold."

*

That was one of the lengthiest introductions ever given me. For a while there I was getting a bit worried about the clock. [Turning to person who did the introducing and addressing him by name] I thought you'd *never* get the *bull* rolling!

*

If the audience laughs at your opening remark:

I'm glad to hear you laugh. We have a crying need for laughter.

*

I would like to quote Salvador Dalí, who once said, "I shall be so brief that I have already finished."

*

Many of you may be wondering why I'm here. I'm wondering about that myself.

*

Thank you for those nice words of introduction. You all have my permission to repeat them at any time in any place.

*

For use in introducing a speaker:

I couldn't possibly tell you all the impressive things about him that could be told. In fact, his *Who's Who* is more than seven inches long.

*

If you are called on to speak after being given an award:

I don't know if this award is important. What *is* important is that all of you came out tonight to see me get it.

*

If you are introducing a speaker:

And so here is [name of speaker], said to be the most important thinker [or philosopher or editor or concept man, etc.] since Freud, Einstein, Darwin, and Pavlov. Let's listen. What he tells us may even be interesting.

*

Good lines with which to introduce an after-dinner speaker:

Now, this man I'm introducing to you here tonight has a problem. His problem is he's half Irish and half Scotch. One half of him wants to get drunk, and the other half doesn't want to pay for it.

*

P. T. Barnum, invited to be an after-dinner speaker, asked how long he would be expected to talk. If his remarks were to last five minutes, he said, he would need to have time to prepare his speech. If his remarks could go for half an hour or more, he explained, he wouldn't have to prepare them, because he could develop his theme as he went along. Unfortunately, I've been given only ten minutes tonight, so I'll be reading my prepared remarks.

*

If your speech is to cover a number of topics, here is an opening that might alert the audience to what they might expect:

Your program chairperson gave me a list of eight topics to choose from, and finding almost all of them provocative, I've picked one from Column A, one from Column B, and part of the family dinner.

[Then mention the subjects you will cover in your talk.]

*

I remember a speaker who was asked how his speech had gone over with the audience. He replied, "Well, they didn't get up and disappear like dew in the desert." I hope that at the conclusion of my talk, I will be able to say the same thing.

*

If you are a speaker—possibly a politician—who will talk about a controversial matter, recognition of the controversy up front is a good way to begin:

This matter [act, legislation, tax, etc.] has been touted and taunted, praised and panned, deplored and defended. In short, everything that *could* be said *has* been said. All the pluses have been added up and all the minuses subtracted. Or have they?

*

When we had our last energy crisis, the president asked us to conserve energy. I've been doing just that. I always prepare two versions of any talk I'm to deliver. Today I'm going to give you the short version.

*

It is always flattering to receive an invitation to address an audience such as this as the after-dinner speaker. It is also somewhat unnerving to arrive at the moment of truth and wonder whether you have enough to say to keep a well-fed audience awake for another half hour.

*

The subject you have asked me to address myself to reminds me of a letter that a club once wrote to Charles William Eliot when he was president of Harvard. "Dear Mr. Eliot," the members wrote. "Our club committee, having heard that you are the country's greatest thinker, would be greatly obliged if you would send us your seven greatest thoughts."

> *The bridge between this opener and the body of the talk might go something like this: "I'm not going to burden you with my seven greatest thoughts. But I do have five [or seven, or ten] points I want to make here today concerning [subject of talk]."*

*

A man took his mule to a mule trainer and said he was having a lot of difficulty with the animal. The trainer agreed to take him on, and they started work immediately.

The trainer picked up a heavy club and smacked the mule on the rear end, causing the mule to fall down. It staggered to its feet, only to have the trainer deliver another mighty blow with the club. As the beast toppled again, the owner said: "Wait up! Hold on! I didn't bring that animal here to be clobbered. I brought it here to be trained. What kind of training is that?"

To which the trainer replied: "Oh, that's not part of the training. That's just to get his attention so that I can *start* to train him."

I confess that that story is not part of my talk. It's designed to get your attention so that I can start to make my pronouncements.

*

That was a very gracious introduction, and I thank you for it. It reminds me of the time a toastmaster delivered an equally flattering introduction when he was called upon to present Adlai Stevenson.

He thought he had invoked virtually every compliment and bit of praise that he could without being fawning, so he was surprised when Mr. Stevenson got up and said, "Thank you very much, sir. That is probably the *second* most flattering introduction I have received."

This really bothered the toastmaster, because he felt he had gone about as far in his comments as anyone could have gone. But Mr. Stevenson, sensing his dismay, went on to say that there had once been an occasion when a toastmaster had been delayed and was unable to perform the introduction. Under those circumstances, Mr. Stevenson had had to introduce himself.

I have never had to introduce myself, so permit me to say that I have *never* had a more generous introduction.

*

I am delighted that everyone here is in some way connected with the field of [title of subject].

Occasionally I am called upon to address an audience that is as heterogeneous as a low-priced sausage. In those instances, finding the common denominator is not easy. Fortunately, I have no such problem today.

*

As I stand before you, I can't help thinking about the man who was killed in a recent flash flood.

He made his way to heaven, and at the Pearly Gates he was asked to give his case history—to tell the story of how he died in a flood and came to heaven. This he obligingly did. Saint Peter thought the story so interesting that he asked the new arrival if he would agree to give a talk to the other angels in heaven, telling them all about the flood and his demise.

The newly arrived resident of heaven was very flattered, and he immediately accepted the invitation. As he flew away, a kind young angel tugged at the sleeve of his robe and said, "Sir, I think I ought to tell you that *Noah* will be in the audience."

My point is that I'm somewhat abashed at being up here and talking on the subject of [fill in] when so many of you in the audience are experts in the field.

*

Well, as Lewis Carroll wrote in *Through the Looking Glass:*

> "The time has come," the Walrus said,
> "To talk of many things:
> Of shoes—and ships—and sealing-wax—
> Of cabbages—and kings."

I am not going to talk of shoes, ships, or sealing-wax, but I do have on my list a number of subjects that include [list topics to be covered].

*

That introduction credits me with just about every flattering thing in the book. About the only thing you left out was the Boy Scout oath—I don't believe you mentioned that I am "trustworthy, loyal, helpful, friendly, courteous, kind, obedient, cheerful, thrifty, brave, clean, and reverent."

Well, I want you to know I am all those things too, although they have little bearing upon the subject of my talk, which is—as you know from your program—[name of talk].

*

If you are introducing a very hard-working and successful person:

His idea of relaxing after a hard day's work is to go home, take off all his clothes, and roll around in a closetful of dollar bills.

*

I love being here, but I have to admit I don't like plane travel. In particular, I don't like the food on those planes. On my trip here they served dinner. The menu offered me two choices, take it, or leave it. I had both. I took it . . . and I left it.

*

Richard Strauss, when instructing young composers how to begin a musical work, advised, "You must start with a bang."

Would that I had a pair of cymbals. Lacking that, let me tell you a story I just heard, and I hope your applause will be deafening enough to satisfy even a Richard Strauss.

That opening must, of course, be followed by a story.

*

I feel like I felt on my wedding night. As I said to my wife at that time: "I'm very warm and very nervous. But I'm glad to be here."

*

This is an anecdote that can be helpful to a speaker who is faced with communicating a great deal of material in a short period of time:

I'm reminded of the lady who was sailing on the ill-fated *Titanic.* She saw a steward go rushing by and grabbed his sleeve, stopping him in his tracks. "Steward!" she cried. "I know I asked you to bring me some ice—but this is *ridiculous!*"

The story can then be followed by a comment to the effect that the time allotted permits you to give "only the tip of the iceberg."

*

The art of persuasion can be stated in five words: Believing something and convincing others. Unfortunately, my talk will require more than five words. I didn't have time to write a *short* speech. But I hope that when I have finished, I will have persuaded you to share my point of view on the subject of [title of subject].

*

William Makepeace Thackeray once said that the two most engaging things a writer must do are to make new things familiar—and familiar things new.

In writing this talk, I have concentrated on making some new things familiar to you. I hope that when I have finished, I not only have familiarized you with these things but convinced you of their merit.

*

This is a nice opening line if you have been introduced with some flattering words:

Thank you for those nice comments. We all like flattery, and some of us will go a long way to get it. Many of us appearing here today had to travel 3,000 miles just to hear a few kind words.

*

Thank you for that flattering—if somewhat overstated—introduction. Usually you have to die to have such words spoken about you. For the moment, I am not so disposed.

*

If you have just made the introductory remarks about the speaker of the day:

He is, in fact, a man of such generosity that he is willing to forgive his foes everything he ever did to them.

*

A Supreme Court justice, commenting on an obscenity case, grew exasperated with the matter under discussion and finally cried out, "I can't define obscenity, but I know it when I see it!"

The subject we're going to discuss tonight may not be easy to define, but we all know it when we see it.

*

If you are a speaker in a foreign country, you might open with the following comment, changing the name of the country to fit your situation:

Before coming to France I took a quick course in elementary French. Unfortunately, when I got here, I found that no one in France *speaks* elementary French.

*

Before beginning my talk, I would like to give you Adlai Stevenson's rule for speechwriting:

If you would make a speech or write one
Or get an artist to indite one,
Think not because 'tis understood
By men of sense, 'tis therefore good.

Make it so clear and simply planned
No blockhead can misunderstand.

I know there are no blockheads in our audience today, but in writing my talk, I have tried to keep things clear and simple. If in so doing I have oversimplified things, bear with me, for I have done so in the interest of clarity.

*

There is an old speechwriter's maxim that goes something like this:

First you tell 'em what you're going to tell 'em.
Then you *tell* 'em.
Then you tell 'em what you told 'em.

Time does not permit me to follow that outline. So without any preamble—nor do I intend to make any summary in my conclusion—let me get to the heart of what I want to tell you.

*

Johann Wolfgang Goethe, the German writer and poet, once made this statement regarding his own work: "The greatest genius will never be worth much if he pretends to draw exclusively from his own resources. What is genius but the faculty of seizing and turning to account everything that strikes us? Every one of my writings has been furnished me by a thousand different persons, a thousand different things."

In what I am about to say, I lay no claim to originality.

*

I appreciate that fine introduction, but I will try not to forget that a wise man once wrote, "He who rests on his laurels wears them on the wrong place."

*

Here's a quotation that works well when used after a straightforward bio type of introduction:

"Those events in a person's life with which biographers are concerned are never the same as those moments which he, himself,

knows to have been crucial ones. The inner life is undramatic."
[W. H. Auden]

*

Forgive me if I do not seem as alert as I should be. I didn't sleep
well last night. I had a nightmare in which the man who invented
Muzak invented something else.

*

Carl Sandburg inscribed on a photograph of himself, given to Ed
Murrow: "To Ed Murrow, reporter, historian, inquirer, actor, pon-
derer, seeker."

I will borrow his technique in introducing [name of speaker]
tonight. Permit me to introduce [name of speaker]: executive, inventor, photographer, organizer, parent, husband, and seeker after
truth.

Insert those talents or qualities that apply to the speaker.

*

Good morning. I was told that I have fifteen minutes on this program.
To say what I want to say in so short a period of time reminds me
of the young lady who was coming into the golf club as her friend
was leaving. The friend asked, "Charlotte, what are you doing here?"

And Charlotte said, "I'm going to learn to play golf."

The young woman who was leaving said, "Wonderful! I learned
yesterday!"

To talk to you in fifteen minutes on the subject of [name of
subject] is something like that story. Actually, I could talk to you
about it for hours, for days—but I promise you I won't.

*

Every successful speech has two parts. First, there must be a plan
or a dream about what you want to say; the second part is the
execution of that plan. Both parts are necessary in order to achieve
success on the public platform. The hard thing about this is getting
started on the execution.

Most people who have a good plan for a talk find themselves
in a situation similar to that of the golfer who was teeing off on a
short hole. He told his golf partner, "I should be able to make this

in one long drive and a putt." Then he got up and took a couple of practice swings before he let go at the ball. The ball rolled off the tee a distance of a mere twenty feet. The golf partner turned to the fellow who had such a splendid plan for his play on the hole and remarked dryly, "Now all you need is one helluva putt."

Well, when I accepted this invitation, I had a helluva fantasy about what I was going to tell you and how I was going to say it. I hope that the talk I'm about to deliver proves as interesting to you as the plan was to me.

*

This is a nice way to acknowledge an excellent talk that preceded yours and to warn the audience not to expect as much from you as from the previous speaker:

Mark Twain was a speaker at a meeting. He was, of course, brilliant and witty. Chauncey Depew was scheduled to speak next, but he was embarrassed to follow the great Twain. He got up and said, "I want to thank Mark Twain for having given my speech."

*

A visiting clergyman was to deliver a sermon at the campus church at Yale University. He announced that his sermon would be divided into four parts, each initialed, so to speak, by the four letters of the university's name. Starting out with Y, he talked about the God of the Jews, using His Hebraic name, Yahweh. Moving on to A, he talked about Amos—or maybe it was Aaron. In like manner he found inspiration in the letters L and E.

After the service, two students who had heard the visiting clergyman talk were discussing what they had heard. "Quite ingenious," said one, "building his sermon around Y, A, L, E."

"It sure was," said the other, "but I'm glad I didn't hear him preach at the Massachusetts Institute of Technology."

I shall try to be brief up here today. . . .

*

I speak in public so often that many people often ask me if I have a ghostwriter. The fact is, I don't. I wouldn't dare let anyone write my speeches for me. Not since I heard the story of a very busy corporation executive who hired a speechwriter.

The writer did an excellent job for many months and felt he was entitled to a raise. He approached his boss with his demands and was flatly turned down. No amount of persuading would get the tycoon to raise his salary.

Not long afterward, he was called upon to write another speech, and he went to work on it. His boss didn't have time to look over the script before his scheduled appearance in public. Shortly before he was due to go on, he rushed into the writer's office, grabbed the manuscript, and ran for a taxi. He arrived at the luncheon just as he was about to be introduced.

He opened his script and, after reading some introductory remarks, began to read a castigation of the audience for having failed to take positive action on an important industry issue.

"There is not one of you here in this room," he read, "who is to blame. *Everyone* here is to blame! Have you not sat back and suffered the status quo to continue? Have you not been content to rest on your profits while the industry atrophies from lack of intellectual nourishment? I tell you, we must take some constructive action. And I am going to suggest to you a ten-point program, without which this industry will never survive its foreign competition. Here are my ten points."

With that sentence, the speaker reached the end of the paragraph and turned the page. The next page of his script was completely blank except for one sentence in the middle of the sheet. It read, "Okay, you cheapskate, from here on in you're on your own!"

And so, without benefit of ghostwriter, here goes with my own deathless prose. . . .

*

I'm going to read my talk to you today rather than deliver it off the cuff. That's because I believe it's a good idea to have thought through my thoughts carefully before I say them publicly. The trouble is that the talk never sounds any better than if I had just blurted it out in the first place.

*

I will not pretend that the ideas I am about to set forth in this speech have all originated with me. I am a great borrower. I am, in fact, a little like Dale Carnegie, who wrote these words in his famous book entitled *How to Win Friends and Influence People*:

"The ideas I stand for are not mine. I borrowed some from

Socrates. I swiped some from Chesterfield. I stole some from Jesus. And I put them in a book. If you don't like *their* ideas, whose *would* you use?"

*

Another teasing comment for use in introducing a speaker:

Judging from the way he rose through his company, you might think that [name of speaker] is an opportunist. Well, I wouldn't say that about him. But you should know that during Richard Nixon's reign, he was introduced to the president at the time when Nixon opened diplomatic relations with China, and the first thing he asked the president was whether Nixon could help him get the McDonald's concession at the Great Wall.

*

An excellent comment to use when introducing a speaker who can take some ribbing:

It has been said that [name of speaker] is the number one man in the whole world of business. And here, folks, is the man who said it: [name of speaker].

Naturally, if the person you're introducing is not from the world of business, substitute the words that describe his or her field of endeavor, such as field of medicine, world of academe, and so on.

*

I noticed that a lot of you came early so that you could get a seat in the back.

*

Thank you for that warm applause—which I so richly deserve and seldom get.

*

This is a good line to use if, in introducing you, the

chairperson or moderator has brought forth laughter from the audience:

Will everyone please laugh together. If you laugh individually, we'll never get out of here.

*

Thank you for that very flattering introduction. I'm sorry my parents aren't here. My father would have enjoyed it; my mother would have believed it.

*

Good morning. You all remember the Watergate affair, don't you? Do you remember that President Nixon, at that time, had a secretary named Rosemary Woods? Well, I ran into her on my way here this morning. She accidentally stepped on my foot, and my whole speech disappeared!

*

This woman I'm about to present to you is so full of ideas that I have heard her described as a manic expressive.

*

If you are introducing your boss:

[Name of person being introduced] is the greatest boss. And that's not only *my* opinion. It's *his* too.

*

A comment that can be used to open a roast when you are one of many speakers who will be roasting the guest of honor:

First of all, let me tell you about the rules of this evening. The first and most important one is this: If you can't say anything nice about [name of roastee], let's hear it! Keep in mind that [name of roastee] can take it. After all, he wasn't the first person to be roasted. I think the first was Joan of Arc.

*

A comment to open a speech about a person who is retiring:

I don't know why he's retiring—he isn't so old. I wouldn't say someone is old just because his Social Security number is in Roman numerals or because Wolfgang Amadeus Mozart played at his senior prom.

*

I received the invitation to address you here today with mixed emotions. On the one hand, I was pleased and flattered that you thought to ask me. On the other hand, I was somewhat intimidated by the thought of speaking to an audience that represents the upper crust in your field. I decided to accept the invitation, however, because—upon second thought—I realized that the upper crust is usually just a bunch of crumbs held together by dough!

> *If you don't know your audience makeup very well and are dubious about calling them "a bunch of crumbs held together by dough," you might say that you were somewhat nervous about appearing before the upper crust "until the program chairperson reminded me that the upper crust is just . . ." and so on.*

*

When I left home this morning, my wife advised me to be brief when I got to the podium. "Remember," she told me, "that the Lord's Prayer has 71 words, the Gettysburg Address has 271, and the Ten Commandments have 297. She also reminded me that we have been married for more than twenty years, and it only took two words, *I do*, to get us to this point.

I shall, indeed, endeavor to be brief.

*

I suppose I ought to explain how I came to be invited to appear as your luncheon speaker here today. What happened is this. [Name of program chairperson] called me up and said: "Say! I want to ask you something. You believe in free speech, don't you?"

And I said, "Yes, naturally, of course I believe in free speech!"

So he said, "Great! Come on down and give one."

So here I am.

THE SIMMONS SYSTEM

Your Speech Will Almost Write Itself

In most instances, you will probably have accepted your invitation to speak many weeks before the actual date of the speaking engagement. But if you're like most people, you're going to wait until you're up against the deadline before you actually sit down and commit your planned comments to paper.

With the exception of a handful of politicians and business tycoons who have their own ghostwriters on staff, the actual writing of a talk—even for a professional writer—looms as a dreadful task. Many speakers face a blank sheet of paper wondering what (besides the flattery inherent in the invitation) ever induced them to accept a place on the program.

Take heart! Over the years, having experienced my own share of the syndrome known as writer's block and having watched many a speechwriting colleague agonize over a cold typewriter, I have developed a foolproof system for organizing my thoughts and getting them down on paper in script form. I have introduced dozens of people to my system, not only speakers but writers of articles and books and even high school and college students faced with term papers, book reports, and graduate theses. This system has yet to fail—provided the speaker or writer has anything at all to say.

For want of a better name, I'll call it the *Simmons System*. (For all I know, many other people may have independently come up with the same system, for it's a device born of need, perfected

through usage, and heaven made for anyone faced with an irre-
vocable deadline. There is no reason why this system should have
evolved for me alone.)

The *Simmons System* is based upon the conviction that one's
subconscious can be hard at work on a problem or an assignment
even when one's conscious mind is not thinking about it. Take a
typical situation: You agree to appear on a program some six weeks
hence. You figure that six weeks gives you time enough in which
to write a brilliant and applause-winning talk. But you're busy.
Other matters have greater priority or closer deadlines. So you
procrastinate about getting started on the speech.

Actually, you may not be procrastinating at all. During the days
and weeks when the project is set off on a back burner, thoughts
relevant to your talk keep popping into your mind. An idea occurs
to you. Sometimes it's only a phrase. Or you read something somewhere and think, Maybe I ought to quote that. Pertinent facts come
to you when you're in the shower, in a meeting, at dinner. Often
they come during a sleepless moment at night.

The basic trick, which might be called Step 1 of the *Simmons
System*, is to *write down every one of these thoughts or items* as
soon as possible after it comes to you. And for reasons that will
become clear later, each should be written or typed on the same
size paper or card, one item per card or sheet. I prefer to use 5-
by 8-inch index cards, because each card gives me enough room
for several paragraphs of copy, should I have that much to record
or to add on at another time. A cheaper but equally effective method
is to tear in half a pad of 8½- by 11-inch paper. This provides you
with a stack of sheets very close to the size of my favorite index
cards.

Now, once you get these items down in writing, some of them
may not look as good or as wise or as well phrased as when they
were in your mind. Save them anyway. Later on, you may find
these bits and pieces work well in conjunction with other thoughts
you'll be jotting down. There'll be plenty of time to discard excess
or inferior material when you put your first draft on paper.

Step 2 in the *Simmons System* begins when you get to the point
where you really have to devote some time to thinking about your
talk on a conscious level. Armed with your stack of index cards,
you're ready to concentrate on your topic. Perhaps the best way to
start is to do some reading on the subject—articles, speeches, even
books if you have the time—written by other people about, or close

to, the subject. Hopefully you have someone on your staff—an assistant, a researcher, a good secretary, or a willing spouse—who can save you many hours by going to the library for you (after thorough briefing) and finding source material for you to read or scan.

As you go through this material, you'll unquestionably find things others have said that you agree with or take exception to. Transcribe onto your cards anything that may have bearing on your speech topic (only one item per card), making certain to jot down the source and putting quotation marks around anything you've excerpted verbatim so that you can properly credit the author, should you choose to quote directly.

Another stimulus to your thinking will often be found in conversations or interviews with authorities on your speech subject, with smart friends whose opinions you respect, and occasionally with people who hold an opposing point of view. Both socially and in business, try to steer conversation toward the subject of your speech. As you explore your topic in this manner, you are likely to unearth new information, facts, and figures, plus thoughtful or emotional viewpoints that had not previously occurred to you. Take notes, and remember to add them to your growing file of material.

If you can't get to see and talk to all the people whose knowledge and opinions are of interest to you, write to them, and request that they send you letters describing their attitudes or telling you what they know on the subject. You will be amazed at how many people reply to your inquiries with stimulating material! Bear in mind that most people like to be asked their opinions, particularly if they are to be quoted by name. One caution: If you're writing for information or an opinion, be certain to mention the deadline for receiving a usable reply.

The longer the lead time between agreeing to make a speech and the actual date of your talk, the fatter will be your file of accumulated ideas, arguments, phrases, quotations, examples, and so forth. You are now approaching the moment of truth, the day when you really have to clear your desk and date book, unclutter your mind, and begin to write.

This brings you to Step 3 in the Simmons System. Go through your stack of index cards. In the upper right-hand corner of each card write in pencil (because it's erasable and therefore changeable) a key word or two that tells you what the card is about.

Let me give you an example. Say you're going to give a talk

on the subject of free trade versus protectionism. On one card, you might have written, "Protectionism penalizes consumers; enables U.S. manufacturers to raise prices without fear of being undercut." On another card: "Permits inefficient industries to prosper." In the upper right-hand corner of each of these cards, you might write: "Cost of Protectionism." Another card carries this argument: "Internationally, more efficient allocation of resources and higher level of well-being with free trade." That card, along with others related to it, might carry the words: "World Impact."

Another card has these words: "Our economic future hangs in the balance; time to press the alarm button." And yet another: "Exporting jobs increases unemployment at home." Still another says, "We are already in a trade war and are losing it." On each of these cards, the notation in the corner might say, "U.S. Economy."

Then you have a card that says: "Today the Japanese are our friends. Protectionism would damage our mutual interests." You would write on the card: "Japanese." Another card says, "Trade deficits with the 'little dragons' continues to grow." The key words on that card might be "Competition, Non-Japanese."

Several cards may contain figures and statistics. For example, you may have recorded this fact: "Every $1 billion in exported products creates 40,000 jobs here at home." You're not certain at this point where you will be able to use that information. Put a question mark in the corner of this card. All the other cards that do not fall easily into categories you can identify *at this time* should carry penciled question marks. As your script starts to take shape, you'll find appropriate places where these items fit best.

You will probably come across several cards that appear to contain provocative things to say at the outset of your talk. On each of these write "Intro" in the upper right-hand corner. Others might seem like things that should be held until the end. On those write the word "Conclusion."

In Step 4 of the *Simmons System*, you're going to shuffle the cards, arranging them so that all cards with the same key words are together. Clip or place a rubber band around each group.

Step 5: Lay out the card groupings on a clear area of your desk or table, and move groups around until you have a subject sequence that makes sense to you.

You have now created *a natural outline for your talk*. It is unnecessary for you to write an outline before you begin to write your speech—despite the fact that every textbook on writing will advise you to do so. You have combined and organized your material, thus preventing the possibility of a disjointed address in which your ideas ramble, giving the impression of a person who is ill prepared or has not quite thought through his subject matter.

In Step 6 you're going to beef up your material, flavor it, make it come alive. That's where this book comes in. Attack the first group of cards marked INTRO. Do you find in this batch anything that will provide you with your opening comment—any provocative quotation, interesting story, wisely phrased showstopper? Do you have anything here that will make your audience want to listen? Provoke their undivided attention? Arouse their emotions? Make them laugh? Relieve the tension? If not, read through the section called Openers, and see if you find a suitable item to launch your presentation. If you find several possibilities, copy each one onto a separate card, and add them to the INTRO group. At this point you need not decide exactly which of the items you'll eventually use. You're merely considering some possibilities.

Here's how it works. Sticking with the hypothetical subject of free trade versus protectionism, you might copy onto a card this story, which appears on page 15: "The subject you have asked me to address myself to reminds me of a letter that a club once wrote to Charles William Eliot when he was president of Harvard. 'Dear Mr. Eliot,' the members wrote. 'Our club committee, having heard that you are the country's greatest thinker, would be greatly obliged if you would send us your seven greatest thoughts.' " On the same card, immediately after this excerpt, you could add some copy that ties the story to your own platform appearance: "[Name of chairperson] didn't ask for my seven greatest thoughts, but he did suggest that I might come prepared to give you a dozen or so of the best arguments for and against protectionism."

On another card, perhaps you would copy this story, which appears on page 16: "As I stand before you, I can't help thinking about the man who was killed in a recent flash flood.

"He made his way to heaven, and at the Pearly Gates he was asked to give his case history—to tell the story of how he died in a flood and came to heaven. This he obligingly did. Saint Peter thought the story so interesting that he asked the new arrival if he would agree to give a talk to the other angels in heaven, telling them all about the flood and his demise. The newly arrived resident of heaven was very flattered, and he immediately accepted the invitation. As he flew away, a kind young angel tugged at the sleeve

of his robe and said, 'Sir, I think I ought to tell you that *Noah* will
be in the audience.'

"My point is that I'm somewhat abashed at being up here and
talking on the subject of free trade when so many of you in the
audience are experts in the field."

On still another card, you could jot down this comment, which
appears in the same section, Openers: "I'm going to read my talk
to you today rather than deliver it off the cuff. That's because I
believe it's a good idea to carefully think through my thoughts
before I say something publicly. The trouble is that the talk never
sounds any better than if I had just blurted it out in the first place."

Eventually, when you actually write your speech script, you
might determine that you don't need all the INTRO material you
have now accumulated, and you might decide to discard one of
these three items. At this stage, however, it is better to have too
much material than too little.

Just as you use this book to enliven and strengthen your group
of ideas for the introductory section of your talk, Step 6 of the
Simmons System calls for you to go through each group of cards in
your collection, and wherever you feel you could use more or better
material, skim the appropriate sections in this book for additional
content. Be sure to use the Subject Index at the back of the book.
On pages 311–312 you will find specific advice on how to make the
most of that valuable tool. When you have finished with this step,
you should have quite a bit more material than when you first put
your card-file items in sequential groups.

In Step 7 you're going to draw upon your opinions and convictions to supplement the considerable copy you now have in your
card file. Check each group of cards again. Under each subject
category, ask yourself if you have noted every thought, every belief,
every argument, every example you wish to convey to your audience. If you did Step 1 over a period of many weeks and if you
are talking on a subject about which you have strong convictions
and have jotted them down whenever they occurred to you, don't
be surprised if Step 7 finds you with little to add. On the other
hand, additional thoughts might well come to mind as you concentrate on the various subheadings that you have written in the corners
of the cards.

When you have exhausted your ideas, when the core of every
thought you wish to convey has been noted, you are ready to write
the first draft of your script.

Getting the first draft on paper is Step 8. But now you will find to your amazement that instead of looming as a monumental and dreadful chore, your talk is all but written! By using the *Simmons System* up to this point, your speech has almost written itself.

With your cards arranged in a sequence that makes sense to you, choose the best material in each group and start writing. Much of it you will be able to copy off the cards. Some of it will require amplification, cutting, or improved phrasing. Do this as you go along, adding, subtracting, rewording, inserting bridges from idea to idea.

When you have gone through all your cards—discarding those that don't seem to fit in, perhaps moving a few into more appropriate groups, using the best of your material, and working in the previously uncategorized cards (the ones with the question marks in the corners)—you will have your rough draft. And no matter how many changes you may choose to make in the last two steps, the worst is behind you. You have committed to paper all the things you want to tell your audience, and you have done it in an organized, logical sequence, adding enough material from this book to make the script come alive.

The last two steps are the easiest. And they should be the most fun, because you will be doing them with the knowledge that the basics are already down on paper. However, the last two steps, though easy, make the difference between an *ordinary* speech and a *great* one. It is this extra bit of work that separates the stars from the mediocrities.

In Step 9 you're going to study and mark your rough draft very critically and objectively, searching for weak transitions, dreary stretches, passages that lack forcefulness, and sections where witticisms, anecdotes, or philosophical punch lines might be added. Mark each such spot in your script. With each of those faulty areas in mind, riffle through the chapters in this book that are related in subject to the passages that need improvement.

Pick out one-liners, proverbs, anecdotes, quotations—any material that can serve to perk up a sagging section or paragraph. If you don't find all you need in the sections directly targeted to your subject, comb the pages of nonrelated sections, and select items that can be reworded or adapted to fit your needs. At this point, the Subject Index can once again be a tremendous help in suggesting new categories under which you might find appropriate material.

Let me give you some examples of how Step 9 works.

Staying with the theoretical subject of free trade versus pro-

tectionism, it would be logical for you to check the Business section
as well as the section beginning on page 136 called Away From
Home, because it contains some good material about the Japanese
and about business done overseas. In the Business section you might
think about using this item: "You will recall that in *Through the
Looking Glass*, Lewis Carroll said that the Red Queen had to run
at top speed just to stay in one place." And then you'd add: "I'm
afraid that with the trade deficit as big as it now is, international
competition forces us to run as fast as we can, and we'll consider
ourselves lucky if we do not fall farther behind."

In the section Away From Home, you will find this item, which
you might add to your cards: "The old saying that money talks still
applies. Only today it's speaking Japanese." Or the item on page 72
that says, "We drive home from work in a Japanese car, sit down
for dinner on a Danish chair, have a cocktail out of a glass made
in Portugal, eat off English china, go to a French movie, come home
and write to our kids with a ballpoint pen made in Korea, put on
pajamas made in Taiwan, and go to bed worrying about unemployment in this country."

Elsewhere, you will find these sentences: "It's like the man
who emerged from a meeting and announced, 'There is a feeling
of togetherness in there. Everyone is reasonably unhappy.'" This
bit would work well toward the conclusion of the theoretical talk
on free trade if you were to add a comment such as this: "The
same might be said of us. Whichever side of the free-trade issue
we may be on, I'm sure all of us are reasonably unhappy about the
current trade deficit. Well, polarized as we may be, at least that
gives a feeling of togetherness!" Still elsewhere, in the section called
The World of Advertising—which, again, is not directly related to
the free-trade speech—you will find this item: "Al Capp, the cartoonist, once said that 'the public is like a piano—you just have to
know what keys to poke.'" In our hypothetical speech, this line
could be followed by a comment such as this one: "However, when
it comes to protectionism, we've been poked and pounded from all
sides with so many differing points of view that most people don't
know what to think. The problem is that, unlike the piano, the
arguments pro and con are not always black and white."

So you can see that improvement for your talk's weak spots
might be found in almost every section of this book. Just keep
looking. It's here, somewhere in these pages. Be sure to check the
Subject Index.

And now for Step 10—the final editing of your speech. After incorporating into your rough draft the new material you added in the last step, read through your talk again. This time, *read it aloud.* Stop at awkward phrases. Edit them as you go along until you are comfortable saying every word. If something seems unclear, clarify it. If anything seems repetitious, eliminate it. If all your sentences seem to be the same length, cut some of them, and add to others. The variety in sentence length will help you avoid a monotonous delivery. If some of the words you used in writing the talk looked good on paper but sound phony or artificial when spoken, substitute synonyms. Keep in mind that your talk is meant to be *heard,* not read. It makes a difference.

When you have edited the talk for sound, read it aloud once more. Now time it. If you have written a speech that takes longer to read than the time allotted to you on the program, read it once again, and this time cut out any sentence or paragraph that does not strengthen your thesis or enliven the script. It is important to recognize that you cannot time a talk if you read it silently. *You must read it aloud.*

While you may continue to make word changes here and there each time you rehearse your talk (see the section entitled "Rehearsals"), your script is now finished—in ten simple steps, some of which took only a few minutes. And as the material was transferred from card file to manuscript paper, the first draft all but wrote itself!

POLITICS

Poking Fun at Public Figures or Issues

There was a time when the word *politics* referred only to the art or science of government; or more precisely, to the art or science of winning and holding control over a government or a portion of it. Today, we also use the word *politics* to describe competition between interest groups or individuals who want to obtain power or leadership.

And so we speak of politics in business, in universities, in fraternal clubs, even in social circles. The word *politics* always raises a red flag because people who play politics outside of acceptable government campaigns are usually considered to be using less-than-acceptable tactics. Call someone a politician, and he may well challenge you to choose between swords and pistols at sunup. Cry "Politics!" when you think someone has made a statement that leaves a credibility gap, and you have accused that person of having a forked tongue. There are no cool heads or calm tempers where politics is concerned.

So you cannot fail to arouse your audience—either to sympathetic agreement or to controlled anger—when you take issue with political figures or their ideas. Unless, that is, you choose to approach the issues through humor. Political humor offers a great way to vent pent-up emotions over political figures and the political process. By poking fun at a political subject, you can be assured of arousing the instant interest that politics engenders while still keeping the goodwill of your audience.

Whether or not the talk you are preparing is directly concerned with politics, go through the material in this section, and see if one or more of the items might not enliven some section of your presentation. You may even find that poking fun at *yourself* can ward off the possibility that some members of the audience will silently think you a politician. Still others may admire your frankness and grow more sympathetic to your thesis or beliefs.

*

"The office of the presidency," said Woodrow Wilson, "requires the constitution of an athlete, the patience of a mother, and the endurance of an early Christian."

*

Emanuel Celler, a former congressman from New York, once said, "To be a successful congressman, one must have the friendliness of a child, the enthusiasm of a teenager, the assurance of a college boy, the diplomacy of a wayward husband, the curiosity of a cat, and the good humor of an idiot."

*

I recall something that John W. Gardner once said. Though he did not refer particularly to politicians, the application is a good fit. Mr. Gardner said that "people who break the iron frame of custom are necessarily people of ardor and aggressiveness. They are capable of pursuing their objectives with fervor and singleness of purpose. If they were not, they would not succeed. And it is sad, but true, that in shaping themselves into bludgeons with which to assault the social structure, they often develop a diamond-hard rigidity of their own."

*

We are living in an age when astronauts walk on the moon and politicians walk on eggs.

*

Whenever you hear a politician scream, you know that someone has just told the truth.

*

Calvin Coolidge once told us: "Nothing is easier than spending the public money. It does not appear to belong to anybody. The temptation is overwhelming to bestow it on somebody."

*

"What you are stands over you the while and thunders so that I cannot hear what you say to the contrary." [Ralph Waldo Emerson]

*

Once, when Edmund Muskie was campaigning for office, he tried to explain why a small-town boy from Maine dared to take on the leadership of a country with so many big-city problems. To make his point, he told this story: There was a Texas rancher who was bragging to a Maine farmer about the size of his estate, pointing out that if he drove his car as fast as it would go from morning till night, he could just about make it from his house to the edge of his property. "Yup," said the farmer, "I know what you mean. I had a car like that myself once."

*

Many a man goes into politics with a fine future and comes out with a terrible past.

*

"No government is better than the men who compose it." [John F. Kennedy]

*

Someone once said that Harry Truman was proof that the presidency could confer greatness on ordinary men. The vice presidency is something else again. Many a great man has taken on that office only to come out a mediocrity.

*

I will not say that my opponent is a liar. I will merely tell you that he has such respect for the truth that he uses it sparingly.

*

After serving as press secretary in the Carter White House, Jody

Powell became a syndicated newspaper columnist. Another member of the Fourth Estate, in writing to congratulate Powell, said, "No more the trappings of power—now you've got the real thing."

*

"You cannot beat somebody with nobody." [Abraham Lincoln]

*

When Alfred E. Smith was governor of New York, he gave a speech that a heckler didn't seem to like. "Tell 'em all you know," said the heckler. "It won't take very long."

Smith, without a moment's hesitation, retorted: "I'll do better than that. I'll tell 'em all we *both* know. It won't take any longer!"

*

After losing his third try for the presidency, William Jennings Bryan told this story: "I am reminded," he said, "of the drunk who, when he had been thrown down the stairs of a club for the third time, gathered himself up and said 'I am on to those people. They don't want me in there.' "

*

During a particularly bitter campaign, a candidate was trying to demean his opponent, who was the incumbent. Commenting upon crime in the city, he said: "The best way to get rid of garbage in this town is to gift wrap it and put it in a parked car. It'll be gone in half an hour."

*

The trouble with political promises is that they go in one year and out the other.

*

There were so many firings and replacements in the last days of the Nixon administration that staff members never knew who would be in the office next to them when they arrived at work. One week the secretary of the interior was a Kelly Girl.

*

Many people see politics as a no-lose profession. If they succeed, they enjoy the fruits of their success. And if they fail, they can make lots of money writing a book about it.

*

He's a man who likes to speak his mind. Unfortunately, that limits his conversation.

*

Politics is the art of putting people under obligation to you.

*

A sacred principle of government is that any promising enterprise must be regulated . . . or it may succeed.

*

Writing in the French newspaper *Le Monde*, Edgar Faure, a cabinet minister under both de Gaulle and Pompidou, commented on the people Americans choose as their presidential candidates. "Carter," he wrote, "was a cretin. Nixon was a crook. Reagan was a second-rate actor. And Kennedy, having drowned his mistress, went to sleep for twelve hours."

*

When asked his opinion about a new concept on the economy, a politician replied: "There are two areas where new ideas are terribly dangerous—economics and sex. By and large, it's all been tried, and if it's new, it's probably illegal or dangerous or unhealthy."

*

"I was recently on a tour of Latin America and the only regret I have was that I didn't study Latin harder in school so I could converse with those people." [attributed by the press to Dan Quayle]

*

And then there's the politician who was described as being a middle-of-the-roader, somewhere between Ronald Reagan and Louis XIV.

*

One politician in our state is so uninformed about the issues that when the press asked him how he felt about the abortion bill, he said, "If we owe it, we should pay it."

*

Of course, sometimes my opponent's enemies do speak the truth. Like when they tell you that he never turns away a job seeker empty-handed. They're right about that. He always gives them a letter of introduction to me.

*

This is a comment you might make if you are called upon to introduce a politician who is, or will be, running for office:

In fact, an introduction seemed so superfluous that I asked [name of politician] what he wanted me to say. And he replied, "Tell them that if they live in this city, they should vote Column A in November."

*

"Politics is too serious a matter to be left to the politicians." [Charles de Gaulle]

*

Adlai Stevenson once described a political opponent as "the kind of politician who would cut down a redwood tree, then mount the stump for a speech on conservation."

*

"Politics is the most hazardous of all professions. There is not another in which a man can hope to do so much good to his fellow creatures; neither is there any in which by a mere loss of nerve he may do such widespread harm; nor is there another in which he may so easily lose his soul; nor is there another in which a positive and strict veracity is so difficult. But danger is the inseparable companion of honor. With all the temptations and degradations that beset it, politics is still the noblest career any man can choose." [Andrew Oliver]

*

Apropos of the demise of a politician whom Mark Twain did not like, he wrote, "I did not attend the funeral, but I wrote a nice letter approving it."

*

"Men are qualified for civil liberty in exact proportion to their disposition to put moral chains upon their own appetites. Society cannot exist unless a controlling power upon will and appetite be placed somewhere, and the less of it there is within, the more there is without. It is ordained in the eternal constitution of things that men of intemperate minds cannot be free. Their passions forge their fetters." [Edmund Burke]

*

W. P. Tolley once delivered the Sol Feinstone Centennial Lecture at Syracuse University, and his comment on the meaning of freedom should be background reading for all politicians.

"Words are like coins," said Tolley. "They can be rubbed so smooth that the superscriptions are no longer visible. They can be worn so thin that they are no longer of true weight. And when they are of questionable value, they should be reminted.

"Freedom is such a word. By constant use and misuse its meaning is no longer clear. It has become too smooth—slippery with too many meanings; debased by careless contradictions. It is now used as a synonym for license, the right to do as one pleases, and to be a slave of appetite and desire.

"To many it is the right to be above all laws, whether spiritual, moral, or political. To some it is even the right to subvert the freedom of others. It is a word used by rogues, rascals, nihilists, existentialists, rebels, revolutionaries, society's drop-outs, the narcotics peddlers, the pornographers, the old right, the New Left, the absolutists, the anti-Americans, the angry young, and the tyrants of tomorrow."

*

You know you're in the middle of a political campaign when everyone shoots from the lip.

*

Sloganeering is not consensus.

*

"Politicians are the same all over. They promise to build a bridge even where there is no river." [Nikita Khrushchev]

*

"Presidential ambition is a disease. Once it gets into your blood, nothing can remove it except embalming fluid." [Theodore Roosevelt]

*

"The difference between a politician and a statesman is this: the former is concerned with the next election, while the latter is concerned with the next generation." [Will Rogers]

*

"Nothing in the world can take the place of persistence. Talent will not; nothing is more common than unsuccessful men with talent. Genius will not; unrewarded genius is almost a proverb. Education will not; the world is full of educated derelicts. Persistence and determination alone are omnipotent." [Calvin Coolidge]

*

"Nations would be terrified if they knew by what small men they are ruled." [Talleyrand-Périgord]

*

"In politics, the worst insult is to be forgotten." [Abe Beame]

*

"I am not a politician, and my other habits are also good." [Artemus Ward]

*

"A U.S. President, above all, must be a leader, able to direct a large, complex organization, or federation of organizations, and to deal with competing, often conflicting constituencies. He (or she) must be able to recognize talent, recruit it, deploy it, inspire it, oversee it (and fire people when necessary). A president must be a man of vision who knows in what direction he wants to guide the nation, a persuasive individual who can explain his means and ends in ways that will move people to support him." [Time magazine, 1976]

*

Alben Barkley of Kentucky, Harry Truman's vice-president, is famous for his line about two brothers. "One," he said, "ran away to sea; the other was elected vice-president. Nothing was heard of either again."

*

A tourist asked a guide at the Capitol building in Washington, D.C., who the man with the collar was. "He's the chaplain of the Senate," the guide told him.

"Really? Does he pray for the Democrats or the Republicans?" the man inquired.

"Well," the guide explained, "he stands before the senators—and prays for the country."

*

And on the subject of the vice-presidency, Thomas Riley Marshall, vice-president under Woodrow Wilson, is reputed to have said, "It's like being in a cataleptic fit—you're conscious of everything that goes on, but you can't do anything about it."

*

After a particularly embattled presidential nominating convention, this saying went the rounds: "It's better to go to a nominating convention than never to use your Blue Cross at all."

*

"The nose of a mob is its imagination. By this, at any time, it can be quietly led." [Edgar Allan Poe]

*

Satirist Mort Sahl described a former president this way: "If you were drowning twenty feet offshore, he'd throw you an eleven-foot rope and point out he was meeting you more than halfway."

*

"Politics is like coaching football. You have to be smart enough to understand the game and dumb enough to think it's important." [Eugene McCarthy]

*

A Democratic opponent of George Bush's once said of the president, "He was born on third base and thinks he hit a triple."

*

A freshman congressman, who by his own admission had spent some of his earlier years engaging in hard drinking and rough living, called a press conference when he came to Washington and decided to face the rumors about his past head-on. "There was a time in my life," he said, "when I spent ninety percent of my money on booze and broads. And the rest of it I just wasted."

*

If wishes could kill, there'd be a lot of dead politicians. I heard about a congressman who disliked his opponent so much that when he went to bed each night, he prayed that the man would get his shoelaces caught in the down escalator at the mall.

*

It has been said that Ronald Reagan was not really lazy. He was just energy efficient.

*

When George McGovern was defeated for the presidency, he commented, "I wanted to run for president in the worst way—and I did."

*

Talking about George Bush, Democrat Ann Richards said, "He was born with a silver foot in his mouth."

*

A good politician knows that it isn't essential to fool all of the people all of the time—only during the campaign.

*

"Become a candidate. No matter how much of an idiot you are, there will always be a sufficient number of greater idiots who think you are not." [Millor Fernandes]

*

"The men with the muck rake are often indispensable to the well-being of society, but only if they know when to stop raking the muck." [Theodore Roosevelt]

*

Johnny Carson once reported that the president had phoned the leader of every country in the world that supported the United States. "He ran up a phone bill," continued Carson, "that came to thirty-five cents."

*

One of the young men in my office said to me the other day, "You know, I have half a mind to go into politics."

"Well," I told him, "that's as good as most."

*

And then there was another young man who wanted to go into politics, and when he was asked what he could do, replied, "Nothing."

"Great!" said the politician to whom he was talking. "Then we don't have to break you in!"

*

The mention of politics calls to mind an argument among several professional men, each of whom claimed to be a member of the "oldest profession."

A lawyer spoke up and said: "Mine is obviously the oldest profession. It dates back to before the Garden of Eden. Surely you can recognize in the serpent the voice of an attorney."

A doctor quickly disputed him: "Before that, you remember, the Lord had to form a woman—Eve—out of Adam's rib. That surely took medical knowledge."

An engineer took up the challenge: "If you remember, before Adam and Eve, the Lord God said, 'Let there be light.' Surely that was a sign of engineering capability."

Then a politician spoke up: "I'm afraid that all of you gentlemen are not completely aware of our antecedents. The politician, I am certain, was clearly the first. You may remember the first words of the Bible: 'In the beginning, there was chaos.' And who else but a politician could have created *that?*"

*

As Prime Minister Macmillan once said, "I have never found from long experience in politics that criticism is ever inhibited by ignorance."

*

"Politics is as exciting as war—and quite as dangerous. In war, you can only be killed once, but in politics, many times." [Winston Churchill]

*

"That which unites us as American citizens is far greater than that which divides us as political parties." [Adlai Stevenson]

*

A politician complained during his campaign that his opponent was telling lies about him. "His stories," he said, "are not copyrighted. They're *patented* . . . because they're all invented!"

*

The three presidential comments that probably received the longest-lasting press coverage were these: "I have lusted after women in my heart." [Jimmy Carter]; "I am not a crook." [Richard Nixon]; "I have just taken a urinalysis test and I am not on dope." [Ronald Reagan].

*

President Warren G. Harding is reputed to have said, "Don't drop anchor until you're out of the woods."

*

During the Carter administration, people all over the world seemed amazed that a peanut farmer could rise to the presidency of this country. One TV comedian said everything about the Carters was unbelievable. "If I went to a television producer," he said, "and told him I had a terrific idea for a TV series about a peanut farmer who is a president, with a ten-year-old daughter who lives in a tree house and advises him on nuclear policy, and he has a brother who drinks a case of beer a day, and a sister who rides motorcycles, and another who is an evangelist, and a mother who joins the Peace Corps when she's in her seventies, the producer would tell me to get lost."

*

"Those who would beguile the voters by lies or half-truths, or corrupt them by fear and falsehood, are committing spiritual treason against our institutions. They are doing the work of our enemies." [Adlai Stevenson]

*

It was also Adlai Stevenson who once suggested that a proposal be made to the Republican party. "If they will stop telling lies about the Democrats," he said, "I will stop telling the truth about them."

*

If you are a speaker talking to an audience about the future of your political party, you might quote Winston Churchill, who said, "A great tradition can be inherited, but greatness itself must be won."

*

And then there's the politician who said, "Let me be known as the man who put *candid* in candidate."

*

A government that is big enough to give you everything you want is big enough to take everything you've got.

*

I'm very much like the little old lady who was encountered near a polling place on Election Day. "Who did you vote for?" asked a reporter.

"I never vote," the old lady snapped. "It only encourages 'em!"

YOUTH AND AGE

Bridging the Generation Gap

If you are in a different age group from your audience or if your audience is made up of people from both the over-thirty and under-thirty segments, a witty line or an incisive story about youth—particularly concerning its relationship to older people—is a good way to bridge the generation gap and win over your audience.

Your speech need not be specifically on the subject of youth for you to employ the stories and opinions in this section. For example, if you are talking about the problems of business, you might want to refer to the way young people see the business world. If you are discussing politics, perhaps you will talk about the fact that eighteen-year-olds now have the vote—but in most states they have to be 21 to drink—and this will give you opportunity for a tangential comment on the young.

You should also use the Subject Index at the back of the book to locate items about youth in sections other than this one. For example, as you glance through the index you'll see the words *knowledge (learning)*. Since knowledge and learning are often discussed in terms of the young, it would be worthwhile to check over the references suggested there. Not all of them will be applicable to youth, but you will find some references to material in Proverbs and One-liners that could easily be applied to young people.

Or perhaps your eye will spot the word *generations*. Under this listing you will be referred to items in the sections entitled "Doctors, Lawyers, Industry Chiefs," "Spellbinders," and "Facts, Figures, and

Research." Each of these references will provide you with an item applicable to youth and, possibly, to your speech subject.

Keep in mind that if you're talking to educators, doctors, parents, women's groups, or students, you have an audience involved with youth and quick to respond—on either side—to controversial and humorous remarks about young people. I'm not suggesting that you take the script of a talk on "Reversible Left-Ventricular Failure in Angina Pectoris" and try to work in a humorous story or philosophical statement about teenagers. On the other hand, there are many talks given that suffer for lack of liveliness. Don't let your speech be one of them. Go through this section. See if any of the material is particularly appealing to you. Then with this selected material in mind, reread your talk, and see if there is some place it might be fitted in.

If you yourself are young in either age or attitude, you will find that most of the material in this section can be converted to serve your own point of view. For example, this inscription was found on a six-thousand-year-old Egyptian tomb:

> We live in a decadent age. Young people no longer respect
> their parents. They are rude and impatient. They inhabit
> taverns and have no self-control.

Taking off from that tombstone inscription, you might then go on to point out that things obviously haven't changed much. If young people don't respect their parents today and didn't six thousand years ago either, the chances are reasonably good that the same thing applied to all the generations in between—in which case today's parents may be suffering from selective memory, thereby forgetting some details of their own youth.

Some of the material in this section can also be used in talking about man-woman relationships, education, logic, and motherhood.

*

An old French proverb tells us: "Ask the young. They know everything."

*

The whole subject of youth and today's mores puts me in great conflict. I'm not sure where I stand. I feel like the man who caught his teenage daughter coming home from a date at 3:00 A.M. with a Gideon Bible under her arm.

*

There is no freedom-loving man or woman who is not in favor of dissent. But we should keep in mind what Norman Thomas once said: "The value of dissent and dissenters is to make us reappraise our values with supreme concern for the truth. But rebellion per se is not a virtue. If it were, we would have some heroes on very low levels."

*

A high school class was taken to visit an elderly painter in his studio. He had just finished a painting, and it was drying on the wall. "How long," asked one of the students, "did it take you to produce that painting?"

"Two hours to put on the paints," replied the old man, "and forty years to learn how."

*

Youth has been very critical of the world handed to it by the previous generation. In answer to this, I would like to quote W. F. Rockwell, Jr., who wrote this in *The Forces of Change:*

"You (the young) are inheriting some 3,600,000 miles of paved roads and highways, along with all the bridges, cloverleafs, and tunnels pertaining thereto. You won't have to build those. You may have to pay for them, but you won't have to build them. You are inheriting almost one-third of the world's railroad mileage and almost one-half of the world's capacity to produce electric power. You are inheriting some 2,200 colleges and universities, 7,127 hospitals, about 4,000 industrial research laboratories, 9,566 airports, 194 major art galleries and museums, 14,295 banks, 2,890 merchant ships, and 305,838 places of worship. These are part of your national inheritance. You can hand them down, with what you add yourself, to your children and grandchildren."

*

Not all the motives of the young are what they may appear to be on the surface. Take the very nice little boy in his Boy Scout uniform who helped a nun across the street. He was very solicitous, guiding her carefully through traffic and giving her a smart Boy Scout salute when they got to the other side.

"Thank you very much, young man," the nun said.

"Oh, that's all right," said the scout. "Any friend of Batman's is a friend of mine!"

*

Knowledge can be passed along, person to person, generation to generation, but wisdom can never be communicated. It has to be experienced.

*

"The attempt to make boys moral by the teaching of moral textbooks is a vanity and a delusion precisely because the heart is not the mind and to instruct the mind does not necessarily improve the heart." [Aurobindo Ghose]

*

One way parents can get cooperation from their teenagers is to pull a few wires: telephone, TV, ignition.

*

Most vacations with children are anticipated with great joy and remembered with great nostalgia—but experienced with great difficulty.

*

Adolescence is that time in life when kids apologize to their friends for having old-fashioned parents.

*

At a party celebrating Gloria Steinem's fiftieth birthday, a guest said to Ms. Steinem, "You look fabulous for fifty!" To which Ms. Steinem replied, "That's what fifty looks like today!"

*

In this high-tech age, the old joke about the devoted mother chastising her grown son goes like this: "What kind of a son are you? You never call, you never write, you never fax. . . ."

*

"I would make (the young) all learn English, and then I would let the clever ones learn Latin as an honor, and Greek as a treat. But the only thing I would whip them for would be for not knowing English. I would whip them hard for that." [Winston Churchill]

*

A youngster was asked to explain why he liked a particular TV show that he always watched. "I like it," he said, "because as soon as it's over, 'Sesame Street' comes on."

*

"It is the task of every generation to build a road for the next generation." [John F. Kennedy]

*

"He hath eaten me out of house and home." [William Shakespeare, *Henry IV*]

*

A young boy came home from school with a black eye and torn clothes. His mother asked him what had happened. "It started," he said, "when the other guy hit me back."

I think we are in a similar situation: We don't quite know who is doing what to whom.

*

"I am always ready to learn, although I do not always like being taught." [Winston Churchill]

*

Through the ages, men of wisdom and learning have been preoccupied with the subject of youth. In 322 B.C., Aristotle, it is said, praised the young by stating "Youth loves honor and victory more than money." Cicero, in his day, committed himself to the belief that "the desires of youth show the future virtues of the man." Goethe made the remark that "even if the world progresses generally, youth will always begin at the beginning." And Longfellow, in his poetry, said, "How beautiful is youth . . . with its illusions, aspirations, and dreams!"

*

I have concluded that there is definitely a generation gap. Jim is a local high school boy who comes over every week to mow our lawn. One day, Jim and I were sitting on the back steps eating our lunch when I remarked that I had just finished reading quite a good book about the Old West and Billy the Kid. I told him that, according to this book, Billy the Kid had killed twenty-one men before he was twenty-one years of age.

"No foolin'!" said Jim, wide-eyed. "What kind of a car did he drive?"

*

If you want to recapture your youth, cut off his allowance.

*

"A professor of classics at a major eastern university told me recently that, in a discussion with his students of the heroes of Greek legend, he tried to elicit their concept of the hero without success, and resorted to asking if anyone could name a hero. Only one student, a girl, raised her hand, and replied, 'Dustin Hoffman.' " [Barbara W. Tuchman]

*

"Children are the world's most valuable resource and its best hope for the future." [John F. Kennedy]

*

"I don't believe in age. Age is relative to one's appetite for life, a curiosity about everything around. It's the way you look at things, as though you were looking at them always for the first time." [Martha Graham]

*

Hans Neumann, M.D., the international public health physician, told this story. "Just the other day," he said, "I was in consultation with a patient, a man who had been in the army during World War II. He told me that when he was overseas, the army put saltpeter in the GI food to cut down on the sex drive of the soldiers who were in combat areas.

"Well," continued the patient, "they kept putting this saltpeter in the food, and they kept putting it in, and the stuff never worked on me. *Now*, after forty years, it's *finally* starting to work!"

*

It's better to wear out than to rust out.

*

Young boys and girls in school are said to know it all; and as a parent and a person with some experience in life, I am inclined to believe that this observation is more or less true. One of the things youth does *not* know, however, is that what counts most in life is what you learn *after* you know it all.

*

Youth may seem to be very different today, but I really don't think young people have changed so much. At least, not according to a story told by General Mark Clark about a time during World War II.

His son Bill was a cadet at West Point during those fighting years, and, as with most sons, he seldom wrote to his parents. As General Clark tells it: "Of course, I wanted to know what he thought about the fighting in Italy, because it was tough going at times, as you know. Finally, when we captured Rome, I thought to myself, 'Certainly he'll break down and write to his old man.' And sure enough, he did. His letter read something like this:

" 'Dear Dad: It is now June in West Point.' (That was enlightening, because it was June in Italy, too.) 'I am now a first classman, anxious to get going. I am a cadet sergeant. Yesterday we beat the Navy at baseball. Last night I took a very good-looking blonde from New York to a cadet dance. I'm sorry I cannot write any more. So long. I love you.' It was signed, 'Bill.'

"But down at the bottom of the letter, there was a little post-script. It said: 'By the way, I see you're doing all right, too.' "

*

It was Voltaire who told us that ideas are like beards. Men do not have them until they grow up.

*

I am often amazed by the language of today's young people. It is not so much shock at the preoccupation with four-letter words or the frequent use of hyphenated words that begin with the endearment "mother." Listening to some of the popular rock music, I miss the sound of lyric poetry. Recently, for example, I heard a recording of a song that contained this bit of deathless prose: "You didn't do nothin'. You just let her walk by!"

Perhaps the new language confuses even some of the young people themselves. I heard my daughter discussing with her girl-friend their dates of the previous evening, two high school seniors. "My date was very interesting," my daughter's friend remarked, "but I couldn't quite get used to his strange dialect." To which my daughter, a bit older and more experienced, answered, "That wasn't his dialect, silly, that was his vocabulary."

*

Most young people are also convinced of the generation gap, although a few feel they have something in common with their parents. Like the twelve-year-old boy who told his friend, "I had a long talk with my father last night about girls. He doesn't know anything about them either."

*

A young person can consider himself educated, not when he receives a diploma for completing school, but when he arrives at that point in life where he stops answering questions and begins questioning the answers.

*

The life of a young person today is tough and confusing. Most of his early years are spent listening to someone tell him to get lost. When he begins to grow up, everybody puts pressure on him to start finding himself.

*

J. B. Priestley, the English novelist, reported that an acquaintance asked him, "How are you, Mr. Priestley?" and he replied, "Old and fat."

"You said that the last time I asked you," declared the friend.

"Well, there you are," said Priestley. "Now I'm old, fat, and repetitive."

*

It's hard to say when one generation ends and the next begins— but it's somewhere around 9 or 10 at night.

*

The better part of maturity is knowing your goals.

*

Children see things from a quite different perspective from grown-ups. For example, I took my young daughter to see *Swan Lake*. It was the first time she had ever attended a ballet. After several minutes of watching the dancers on their toes, she leaned over and whispered, "Mom, why don't they just get taller ladies?"

*

The trouble with aging is that by the time you finally know your way around, you don't feel like going.

*

This is a very serviceable piece of copy that need not be reserved for speeches dealing with the generation gap. It can easily be adapted for use in any speech talking about changing times:

A septuagenarian was telling his grandchildren what life was like when he was their age. "When I was young," he told them, "closets were for clothes, not for 'coming out of.' Fast food was what we ate during Lent. There was no such thing as computer dating, house husbands, dual careers, commuter marriages, or support groups. There were no tape decks, CDs, artificial hearts, or word processors. And to us, letters grouped together like *DDT, VCR, DNA,* and *IUD* would have meant lovers' initials carved on a tree."

*

"Psychological maturity entails finding greater satisfaction in giving than in receiving (the reversal of the infantile state); having a capacity to form satisfying and permanent loyalties; being primarily a creative person; having learned to profit from experience; having a freedom from fear (anxiety) with a resulting true serenity and not a pseudo absence of tension; and accepting and making the most of unchangeable reality when it confronts one." [William W. Menninger]

＊

You're only young once, but you can be immature forever.

＊

It has been said that anyone who was not a liberal when he was young had no heart and that he who is not a conservative when middle-aged has no brains.

＊

An old-timer is a person who remembers when charity was a virtue, not an organization.

＊

One of our employees brought his little boy into the office, and as the two of them walked past the office of the company president, the big man happened to come out of his lair. The father proceeded to introduce the two by saying, "Son, this man is the president." To which the youngster responded, "The president of what?"

＊

Despite all we hear about admissions to college, there are still a number of institutions of higher learning that are tough to get into. They tell the story of the dean of one of our fine Ivy League schools who seemed very upset one morning. When his wife asked him what the trouble was, he replied that he hadn't slept very well. "I had the most frightening nightmare last night," he said. "I dreamed that the trustees required me to pass the freshman examination for admission."

＊

Young people beginning their careers nowadays are anxious to move very fast and get in on the decision-making process early in the game. One young man went into his father's business, and maybe because he was the owner's son he thought that he knew everything about this business. He wasn't there very long before he was telling everybody what to do and how to do it. Finally, one of the older men, who had been with the firm for a long time and who held quite a responsible position, took the young man aside and said: "Son, you will have to show more patience with us. After all, we're not young enough to know everything."

*

Perhaps we all worry too much about our youngsters being exposed to too much sex on television and in literature and movies. I really believe that if a child has never encountered a particular sex reference, he won't understand it when he hears it; and if he has heard it before, then hearing it again won't do him any harm.

I remember a story about a little boy who was in his first year in school. Walking home at night he took a shortcut. On this particular route, he passed a place with a board fence and couldn't resist peeking through a hole. He saw some people playing badminton. Oddly enough, they had no clothes on, because it was a nudist colony. The little boy told his mother about this when he got home, and she merely asked him—wanting to appear interested but not overwhelmed by the story—"Were they men or women?" To which the boy, in his complete innocence, replied: "I couldn't tell. You see, none of them had any clothes on."

*

I am reminded of the educator who was asked by an anxious mother, "When should a child's education begin?" To which the educator replied, "About two hundred years before he's born."

*

I'm pretty far removed in age from the now generation. Why, I can remember when the air was clean and sex was dirty.

*

Understanding the workings of the teenage mind is not always easy.

A friend of mine who has a sixteen-year-old daughter told me this story. The girl, who had recently had a sweet-sixteen party, had a date with a young man whose family had just moved into their suburban town. They were all sitting around in the living room during those awkward moments just before the youngsters took off for whatever it is that youngsters do today on dates. The girl's mother, making conversation, asked the young man where his family had lived before they moved to this town.

He said they had lived in New England. The girl's mother commented that she and her husband had lived in New England eighteen years ago, right after they were married. The two young people seemed to be startled by this remark, but they said nothing.

The next morning, the girl came down to breakfast and said with disgust, "Mother, you really stuck your foot in it last night. You told him that you lived in New England when you were married eighteen years ago. And I had told him I was eighteen years old. So then, of course, I had no choice; I *had* to tell him I was *illegitimate*."

*

You all know the saying, "Old generals never die—they just fade away." We have also begun to find out that old university presidents never die—they just lose their faculties.

*

"The Pepsi generation drinks, smokes, overeats on junk food, sits on its seatbelts, and is obsessed with sex. It swaps spirochetes and other crawling things, acquiring chancres in sites formerly afflicted only with tonsillitis or hemorrhoids, and cheerfully makes fetuses, expendable, en passant." [Naomi Bluestone, M.D.]

*

A man who went to his thirty-fifth college reunion returned home and reported, "My classmates have all gotten so fat and bald they didn't even recognize me."

*

Many young people today have little respect for the classics. One high school student said to his English teacher when they were studying *Hamlet*: "What's so great about it? It's just a lot of quotations."

*

"To be busy with material affairs is the best preservative against reflection, fears, doubts—all those things which stand in the way of achievement. I suppose a fellow proposing to cut his throat would experience a sort of relief while occupied in stropping his razor carefully." [Joseph Conrad]

*

The teenage girl was shopping for a dress and found one she decided to buy. "I love it!" she told the salesperson. "It's beautiful! I adore it!" Then, as it was being wrapped, she grew thoughtful and asked the salesperson, "Just in case my mother likes it, can I bring it back?"

*

"Youths have exalted notions because they have not yet been humbled by life or learned its necessary limitations." [Aristotle]

*

Many people, as they age, do not like to think of themselves as old. Take, for example, the elderly woman who was robbed on the street. "Your money or your life," said her attacker. "Take my life," she told him. "I'm saving my money for my old age."

*

And then there's the comedienne who was asked her age. She refused to give it. "All I will say," she told the inquirer, "is that I was born in New York, and my birth certificate is written in Dutch."

*

When I was a kid you paid twenty-five cents to get into the movies, and you could see two movies in any movie house. Nowadays, it costs $500 for a television set, and what do you get? The same two pictures.

*

"Forty is the old age of youth; fifty is the youth of old age." [Victor Hugo]

*

No one grows old by living—only by losing interest in living.

*

Today's youth has, perhaps, put its finger on an age-old truth: namely, that there is a difference between success and happiness. And with maturity youth will learn how to define the difference: Success is getting what you want, and happiness is wanting what you get.

*

"Youth is a circumstance you can't do anything about. The trick is to grow up without getting old. It is a spirit, and if it's there after they put you in the box, that's immortality." [Frank Lloyd Wright]

*

Man is not born to happiness. He has to achieve it.

*

Oftentimes, youth's hostility to its parents is poorly concealed. An old man, very ill in a hospital, told his son that he had made out his will and that all his wealth—his money, stocks, property, and so on—would be the boy's when the end came. The son grew very emotional and wept at these words. "I am so grateful to you, Dad," he said, "I hardly feel worthy enough to be your beneficiary. Tell me, is there anything I can do for you? Anything at all?"

And very feebly the old man answered him. "Yes, Son," he said, "I'd appreciate it very much if you were to take your foot off the oxygen hose."

*

Here is an excellent message to deliver to the staff of a company or an institution. It was given to a freshman class by A. Bartlett Giamatti when he was president of Yale University:

"Female and male, Christian and Jew, black, white, brown, and yellow, you must find, as we all must, what binds us together, in common hope and need, not what divides us. You may or may not come all to love one another, but to be part of the best of this place you must have the moral courage to respect one another."

*

There is nothing so easy but that it becomes difficult when you do it with reluctance.

*

Lord Melbourne is reputed to have said of Macaulay, "I wish I was as cocksure about anything as Macaulay is about everything." Which is more or less how I feel about my teenage kids.

*

And then there's the story of the mother who passed her teenager's room one night and overheard the girl's bedtime prayer. "Oh God," said the teenager, "make me good. But not yet!"

*

It is important for everyone, especially for young people, to have the right aim in life. However, it is just as important to know when to pull the trigger.

*

A concerned mother in a toy department asked the clerk, "Isn't this toy rather complicated for a small child?"

To which the sympathetic clerk replied: "It is, madam, an educational toy. It's designed to prepare your child to live in the world of today. No matter how he puts it together, it's wrong."

*

"Age cannot wither her, nor custom stale her infinite variety." [Marc Antony speaking of Cleopatra]

*

You know you've reached middle age when you'd rather not have a good time than recover from it.

*

Sometimes I think we have a tendency to put a halo around those young people who are fortunate enough to make it into some highly respected college or university.

Recently, I was visiting a friend in Cambridge, Massachusetts, home of several well-known institutions of higher learning. I accompanied my friend to the supermarket on Saturday, and while we were on line, I saw a young college student wheel a heavily laden cart up to the cash register that was clearly marked THIS LINE FOR PEOPLE WITH ONE TO SIX ITEMS ONLY.

The young girl at the cash register looked at the loaded cart, turned to the boy who was helping her bag the groceries, and said, "That guy either goes to Harvard and can't count—or to M.I.T. and can't read!"

*

Some aspiring young actors and actresses were taken by their teacher to meet George Burns. They asked him for some career advice. "Acting," he told them, "is simple. All you have to do is tell the truth. And if you can fake that, you've got it made."

*

"The older I get the more I believe that nothing in the world equals friendship—that marvelous assurance that everything will always be true and good between two beings and that this state is unchangeable." [Iphigene Sulzberger]

*

If addressing an audience of young people, perhaps as a commencement speaker, the following might prove useful, either as a direct quotation or paraphrased:

"Those who elect exclusively the pragmatic approach to life's challenges you may well one day visit in jail. And those who opt for the other extreme, who embrace total idealism and ignore practicality altogether, risk measuring their frustrations in psychiatrists' fees." [Mary E. Cunningham]

*

"American youngsters tend to live as if adolescence were a last fling at life, rather than a preparation for it." [Arnold Toynbee]

*

"The great catastrophe of our society is that it does not welcome a great number of temperaments. My father used to say that people think more of their children's feet than of their brains, since they pick their shoes according to the size of their feet but send them all to the same school." [Daniel Bovet]

*

Middle age is a time when people would do anything in the world to cure what ails them—except give up what's causing it.

*

Apropos of the communication gap between generations, I want to tell you about an incident I recently witnessed. A teenager stood in front of me in the line at the ticket window of the railroad station, and I overheard the conversation she was having with the ticket clerk.

"I'd like a round-trip ticket," the teenager said.

"To where?" asked the clerk.

The teenager gave him a condescending look. "To *here*, of course," she answered.

*

J. B. Priestley put it all together when he said, "One of the delights known to age, and beyond the grasp of youth, is that of *not going*."

*

Sometimes, all that youth wants is to be left alone—a point well made in the old story about Alexander the Great visiting Diogenes. Standing before him, Alexander asked, "Is there anything at all I can do for you?"

"There is," said Diogenes. "Stand out of my light."

The literal translation is "Stand from between me and the sun," but usage has altered it to "Stand out of my light."

*

"Whatever you can do, or dream you can do, begin it." [John F. Kennedy]

*

Age doesn't matter unless you're a cheese.

BUSINESS

---◆◼◆---

Raising Your Listeners' Blood Pressure

Ralph Waldo Emerson, of all people, once said, "The philosopher and lover of man have much harm to say about trade. But the historian will see that trade was the principal of liberty . . . trade planted America and destroyed feudalism . . . and trade makes peace and keeps peace!"

Trade, or business, does not exactly make peace nowadays. Business has become the whipping boy for consumerists and for those legislators who feel they can woo their constituents by taking up the cudgel against the money-makers. Despite the fact that the profit motive has led to innovation, greater efficiency, and the largest gross national product in the world, modern business is frequently under attack—for real or imagined reasons—by ecologists, anti-materialists, scientists, entertainers, and large segments of the youth population.

Talking about business and businesspeople on the platform is almost certain to provoke your audience. If in reviewing the rough draft of your talk you find any opening where a comment about business seems appropriate, don't hesitate to insert one. In addition to this section, read the one entitled "Doctors, Lawyers, Industry Chiefs." It contains many pertinent comments and stories about the upper echelons of business.

Properly delivered, a good line, witticism, or anecdote about the business community is like administering a dose of Benzedrine to the members of your audience. Whichever side they're on, it's bound to raise their blood pressure!

*

One of our executives was showing some VIPs through the company offices, and I happened to overhear one of the visitors ask the question, "How many people work here?" To which her guide replied, "About half."

*

What John Ruskin told us in the nineteenth century applies as much today as it did then. Said Ruskin: "It's unwise to pay too much . . . but it's worse to pay too little. When you pay too much, you lose a little money—that is all. When you pay too little, you might lose everything, because the thing you bought was incapable of doing the thing it was bought to do. The common law of business balance prohibits paying a little and getting a lot. It can't be done."

*

Unless the cash register rings, the factory whistle can't blow. Nothing happens in our economy until something is sold.

*

A woman on a plane found herself seated next to a priest. They went through some very rough weather, and the woman, who was obviously very nervous, turned to the priest and asked, "Father, isn't there anything you can do about this?" To which the priest replied, "I'm very sorry, but I'm in sales, not management."

I am in *management*, not sales. But if my telling you how to manage your company better does not affect your sales, I will be very surprised.

*

A free enterprise system is a system of voluntary contract. Neither fraud nor coercion is within the ethics of the market system. Indeed, there is no coercion in a free enterprise system, because the competition of rivals provides alternatives to every buyer or seller.

*

Perhaps our motto for too long has been Don't Just Do Something— Stand There!"

*

A corporation was about to hire a new department head, and the board of directors was sitting in session trying to decide what sort of person was needed for the job. The board chairman opened the meeting by saying, "Let's remember that we want someone who is not too conservative and not too radical. In other words, we want somebody just mediocre."

*

How do you evaluate a business idea? I will give you my criterion. If an idea is communicated but if that idea is not important enough, not pointed enough, not dramatic enough—if it didn't influence someone, if it was a small idea, if it didn't really make any difference to a lot of people—then it wasn't a good enough idea.

*

"A good leader is best when people barely know that he leads. A good leader talks little; but when his work is done, his aim fulfilled, all others will say, 'We did this ourselves.' " [Lao-tse]

*

"If you can't write your idea on the back of my calling card, you don't have a clear idea." [David Belasco]

*

A Russian comic recently said, "A wonderful future lies behind us." I hope that will never be said of our industry.

*

Someone has referred to the eighties, to the days of corporate takeovers, as the decade when The Raiders of the Lost Art of Industry Development abandoned the economic good of the country to push up stock prices and make themselves a bundle of money.

*

"People find their way back to the things they like. If a product satisfies, you can count on repeat purchases, whether it's a can of Drano or an episode of 'Dallas.' If the quality is missing, you've lost them after the first time around." [Lee Rich]

*

A television panelist who had been an economic adviser to a couple of presidents was asked what he saw ahead for the economy. He replied, "Anything can happen—and it probably will."

*

Despite the fact that the feminist movement has opened new doors for women, the old saying about women in the business world still seems to apply: Too often if you're a woman, you have two chances to make it to the very top: slim and fat.

*

"An institution may hold itself to the highest standards and yet already be entombed in the complacency that will eventually spell its decline." [John Gardner]

*

As we move into a service economy, you may have occasion to address an audience of people who are already in a service industry (such as insurance, investments, nursing, teaching, repairs, consulting, and so on). If you wish to encourage them about the future need for their industry's services, say something such as this:

You are not selling sneakers, whose limited use may be for jogging. You are not selling food, which is consumed and must be repurchased next week. You are not selling an appliance or a car that will eventually have to be fixed or replaced. Nor are you selling blue smoke, thin air, or pie in the sky. You are selling a service that will be needed over and over for years to come.

*

"When it is not necessary to change, it is necessary *not* to change." [Lucius Cary Falkland]

You might follow up this quotation by adding, "Put another way, if it ain't broke, don't fix it."

*

"In the short space of twenty years, we have bred a whole generation of working Americans who take it for granted that they will never go a single year without a salary increase." [K. K. Duvall]

*

The best speech a salesperson can deliver is one that says all that *should* be but not all that *could* be said.

*

The business executive who can smile when something's gone wrong has probably just thought of someone he can blame it on.

*

I refuse to believe that someone who is careless in small things is careful in large ones because that person has the sort of mind that doesn't waste itself on unimportant matters. On the contrary, I think that a person who cannot copy a sentence correctly is not likely to be a dependable reporter.

*

When your boss tells you to be sure to "go through channels," what he really means is that you should leave a trail of interoffice memos.

*

When you call someone and are told by his secretary that he's in conference, it could mean he's chatting with a guy who stuck his head in just to comment on last night's basketball score; it could mean he's gone to the gent's; or it could mean that he is actually in a conference room with a group of people who, like him, prefer to substitute conversation for the dreariness of labor and the loneliness of thought.

*

I saw a wonderful bumper sticker the other day. It said, "Love America! Support America! Keep America strong!" It was on the bumper of a Toyota.

*

Successfully completing a job is the ultimate turn-on.

*

In the business world, as in the army, when someone asks for a clarification, what she usually gets is a background of so many details that the matter in the foreground goes underground.

*

Whatever women do, they have to do twice as well as men to be thought half as good. Fortunately, this is not difficult.

*

It has always been my policy in business that no fence should be taken down until I know why it was put up.

*

Many groups—consumerists, feminists, legislators—are agitating for greater protection for women in the marketplace. It is my contention that the smartest purchasing agent in America is the American housewife.

*

Watch out for the guy who sends you a memo and asks you to "note and initial it." What he's really telling you is that he wants to spread the responsibility for the subject under discussion.

*

"Those who attain to any excellence," said Samuel Johnson, "commonly spend life in some one single pursuit, for excellence is not often gained upon easier terms."

*

On the subject of an achievement-oriented society, David Rockefeller once said, "The ultimate dedication to our way of life will be won, not on the basis of economic achievements alone, but on the basis of those precious yet intangible elements which enable the individual to live a fuller, wiser, more satisfying existence."

*

Business is like sex. When it's good, it's very, very good; when it's not so good, it's still good.

*

On the subject of retirement, I can promise you that you will probably keep busy if your pattern in life is to be a doer. A man

I know retired, and when his friends asked him why he seemed
so busy, he said, "All I can tell you is that when I wake up in the
morning, I have absolutely nothing to do, and when I go to bed at
night, I have only half finished." ·

*

Some years ago a book called *View From the 40th Floor* made the
best-seller list. It told the story of the desperate attempts of a man
to save two magazines from folding. With truly heroic effort, this
man had drawn on every resource to save his magazines. Ultimately
he found himself in consultation with his lawyer, a wise and patient
man. The two were trying to find solutions to the publications'
problems when suddenly the lawyer posed an interesting question.

He said to his client, "If you succeed in saving these magazines,
what do you want to *say* with them?" The question was greeted
with a loud silence.

And then the lawyer made this statement: "Remember," he
said, "*first* the dream, *then* the dollars."

> *As a speaker, you can then go on to spell out your own
> or your company's dream and how profits will follow the
> successful achievement of that dream.*

*

A recession is a period in which you tighten your belt. In a depression, you have no belt to tighten. When you have no pants to hold
up, that's a *panic.*

*

Take your average American. We drive home from work in a
Japanese car, sit down for dinner on a Danish chair, have a cocktail
out of a glass made in Portugal, eat off English china, go to a French
movie, come home and write to our kids with a ballpoint pen made
in Korea, put on pajamas made in Taiwan, and go to bed worrying
about unemployment in this country.

*

I owe my success to the genius of a few and the dedication of
many.

*

During the last recession, an unemployed executive was overheard to remark that at least if you have a trade you can always tell what kind of work you're out of.

*

It is usually the case that people who worry about themselves aren't helping the business, but people who worry about the business are helping themselves.

*

And then, of course, there is the story of the fellow who shares his marketing knowledge with a bartender. This guy has just ordered a beer. When the bartender gives it to him, he says, "Hey, how many kegs do you sell a week?"

"Four," replies the bartender.

"How would you like to make it five?" asks the customer.

"I'd love it," says the bartender.

"Just fill up the damn glasses," says the patron.

*

"Every job has some components which are unrewarding, unfulfilling, and often tedious. But there is no utopian job, no job made up only of the things we love to do. Much of the world's work is unpleasant—no one wants to pick up garbage." [Leo-Arthur Kelmenson]

*

Too many committee decisions are based upon inadequate information and defective knowledge about a specific problem.

We seem to have reached a time when the concept of committee rule implies an infinite wisdom greater than any one person or even one homogeneous group might enjoy. It even implies that the majority possesses a certain infallibility. Because a deliberating body has been joined together with a committee name, it does not necessarily mean that its conclusions are always right. Sometimes these conclusions are hastily reached without sufficient study and deliberation and without the advice of specialists. Sometimes all these factors act less in the interest of finding truth and truthful solutions than as stumbling blocks to progress.

*

When in charge, ponder.
When in trouble, delegate.
When in doubt, mumble.

*

"If you elect an executive because he is agreeable, charismatic, and folksy, you can't complain if incidentally he turns out to be inefficient." [Robert Moses]

*

"Committees cannot create; they can only criticize. I came across a poem the other day and it's only two lines:
    'Search all the parks in all your cities
    You'll find no statues of committees.' " [David Ogilvy]

*

Filmmakers, television producers, and publishers are all known to be afraid to take chances—although rarely afraid to be imitative. It's said that in those industries, everyone wants to be first to be second.

*

"Power is all perception. Its nonuse is its most powerful use. The trick is to use the least amount of power to create the maximum amount of change." [Peter Guber]

*

Mortgage and interest rates on loans are so high today that if John Dillinger, the master criminal of the 1930s were alive, he wouldn't rob a bank—he'd open one.

*

If you want a job done poorly, turn it over to a committee. Performance, the rule goes, will be inversely proportionate to committee size.

*

Being successful in business is still more difficult today for a woman than for a man. She's expected to look like a lady, act like a man, and work like a dog.

*

You will recall that in *Through the Looking Glass*, Lewis Carroll said that the Red Queen had to run at top speed just to stay in one place. I'm afraid that in the tough months ahead, we, too, may find this necessary.

*

"Large meetings are often used to share the blame." [Paul Foley]

*

An IBM executive, in addressing members of his staff, is said to have remarked that "you can take people out of IBM, but you can't take IBM out of the people."

> *This remark can be adapted to many situations. If talking to your own employees, substitute the name of your company. Or: "You can take a student out of Harvard, but you can't take Harvard out of the student."*

*

"There is hardly anything in the world that some man cannot make a little worse and sell a little cheaper, and the people who consider price only are this man's lawful prey." [John Ruskin]

*

I heard that the doormen's union is planning to go on strike. That doesn't really worry me. What are they going to do? Go on strike and stand in front of the building?

*

"A 'whistle blower,' " says Ralph Nader, the consumer advocate, "is anyone in any organization who has drawn a line in his own mind where responsibility to society transcends responsibility to the organization."

*

Many people in the work force today insist upon having what they call security. Regarding this demand, I refer you to a remark made by that great woman, Eleanor Roosevelt. Said Mrs. Roosevelt: "No one, from the beginning of time, has ever had security. When you leave your house, you do not know what will happen on the other side of the door. Anything is possible. But we do not stay home on that account."

*

The safest way to double your money is to fold it over once and put it in your pocket.

*

Some people work to live; others live to work. It's my hope that most of us here strike some sort of happy balance. It is not enough to work to live—if that's all your job does for you, then perhaps you should be doing something else. Nor do I believe that living just for your work gives one the nourishment, the revitalization, that we all need.

*

Barbara W. Tuchman had this to say about the decline of quality: "Although I know we have already grown accustomed to less beauty, less elegance, less excellence, yet perversely I have confidence in the opposite of egalitarianism: in the competence and excellence of the best among us. The urge for the best is an element of humankind as inherent as the heartbeat. It may be crushed temporarily but it cannot be eliminated. If incompetence does not kill us first, we will win. We will always have pride in accomplishment, the charm of fine things—and we will win horse races. As long as people exist, some will always strive for the best. And some will attain it."

*

Do not be fooled by a business associate who maintains his silence. Behind the quiet facade he might know everything that's going on. Keep in mind the story about the girl at the high school dance who sat in a corner all night. Everybody thought she didn't know how to dance. The problem was that nobody asked her.

*

There is no such thing as a free lunch. In the end, you pay for everything.

*

Mel Brooks told this story: "I went to the local delicatessen to buy a six-pack of beer and noticed that all the shelves, top to bottom, were filled with boxes of salt—thousands of boxes of salt.

I asked the grocer, "Do you really sell so much salt?"

"No," he said. "I sell maybe two boxes a month, if that. To tell you the truth, I'm not a good salt seller. But the guy who sells *me* salt—*he's* a good salt seller!"

*

"It must be remembered that there is nothing more difficult to plan, more uncertain of success, nor more dangerous to manage, than the creation of a new order of things." [Niccolò Machiavelli]

*

Admiral Nelson, who sank Napoléon's fleet, followed four simple rules that have direct application to business:

1. Sail in when least expected.
2. Concentrate your fire.
3. Sustain the attack until the enemy line breaks.
4. Pursue!

*

"The initiator has the enmity of all who would profit by the preservation of the *old* institutions." [Niccolò Machiavelli]

*

Many famous people have equated their success with hard work and the ability to immerse themselves in the project of the moment. For example, Michelangelo said, "If people knew how hard I work to get my mastery, it wouldn't seem too wonderful after all."

And this from Thomas Carlyle: "Genius is the capacity for taking infinite pains."

Alexander Hamilton: "All the genius I may have is merely the fruit of thought and labor."

Thomas Edison: "Genius is one percent inspiration and ninety-nine percent perspiration."

*

"Both tears and sweat are wet and salty, but they render a different

result. Tears will get you sympathy, but sweat will get you change."
[Jesse Jackson]

*

"In order that people may be happy in their work, these three things are needed: They must be fit for it. They must not do too much of it. And they must have a sense of success in it." [John Ruskin]

*

Innovation is not likely to come from calm and contented people or companies. It usually takes a near disaster or a challenging and driving leader to stimulate and inspire change.

*

During the recession of the early nineties, when many a Yuppie of the eighties had to retrench, an economist remarked, "We've gone from an era of swashbuckling to one of belt buckling."

*

George Bernard Shaw told us that "the reasonable man adapts himself to the world. The unreasonable one persists in trying to adapt the world to himself. Therefore, all progress depends on the unreasonable man."

I hope that in this company we have among us some unreasonable men and women.

*

We have had a lot of changes take place in our business. Change for most people is hard to accept. Some see change as progress; others see it as the end of something good. In 1829, Martin Van Buren, then the governor of New York, wrote this to the president:

"The canal system of this country is being threatened by the spread of a new form of transportation known as 'railroads.' The Federal government must preserve the canals for these reasons: If canal boats are supplanted by railroads, serious unemployment will result. Captains, cooks, drivers, hostlers, repairmen, and lock tenders will be left without means of livelihood. Canal boats are absolutely essential to the defense of the U.S. In the event of expected trouble with England, the Erie Canal could be the only means by which we could ever move the supplies so vital to waging modern war.

"As you may well know, railroad carriages are pulled at the

enormous speed of 15 miles per hour by *engines*, which in addition to endangering life and limb of passengers, roar and snort their way through the countryside. The Almighty certainly never intended that people should travel at such breakneck speed."

I would remind you that changes are always initially hard to accept.

*

If you and your company are celebrating a good piece of news or a new piece of business, you might quote Winston Churchill, who said:

"Everyone has his day, and some days last longer than others."

You would then add: "This is our day. Let us celebrate it together."

*

"We had an unlimited budget and we exceeded it." [Jay Chiat]

*

We in business are every bit as much in favor of consumerism as the consumerists are. The difference is that they want it, and we have to figure out how to pay for it.

*

A friend of mine who recently retired from business remained active in a number of civic and social projects. One of his acquaintances had difficulty getting him on the phone. When he finally reached my friend, he said, "I thought now that you had retired from your hectic business you'd be sitting around the house all the time."

"Hell, no!" answered my energetic friend. "I may have retired from business, but I haven't retired from life!"

*

It's like the man who emerged from a meeting between management and the union and announced: "There is a feeling of togetherness in there. Everyone is reasonably unhappy."

*

Let's not be so quick to criticize business. I really think the business community is making progress. Why, just the other day a friend of mine dialed a phone number and got the operator. "Why did I get you?" he asked. "I am sorry, sir," she replied, "but all our recorded messages are busy!"

*

I remember something that Franklin D. Roosevelt once said on the subject of introducing new ideas into government, and I think it applies equally to business. "New ideas," said FDR, "cannot be administered successfully by men with old ideas, for the first essential of doing a job well is the wish to see the job done at all."

*

"Only first-class business, and that in a first-class way." [J. P. Morgan]

*

On the subject of businesspeople who find it difficult to make decisions, I am reminded of something that John Gardner wrote. "We cannot evade the necessity to make judgments," said Gardner. "I was discussing these matters with a young man recently, and he said, 'I don't mind making judgments that involve myself alone, but I object to making judgments that affect other people.'

"I had to tell him," continued Gardner, "that would make it impossible for him to be a second-grade teacher, a corporation president, a husband, a politician, a parent, a traffic policeman, a chef, a doctor, or a horse-race handicapper—in fact, it would force him to live a hermit's life."

*

In the city of Baghdad lived Hakeem, "the Wise One." Many people went to him for counsel, which he gave freely to all, asking nothing in return. There came to him a young man, who had spent much but received little, and he said: "Tell me, Wise One, what shall I do to get the most for that which I spend?"

Hakeem answered, "A thing that is bought or sold has no value unless it contains that which cannot be bought or sold. Look for the Priceless Ingredient."

"But what is this Priceless Ingredient?" asked the young man.
The Wise One answered him, "My son, the Priceless Ingredient

of every product in the marketplace is the honor and integrity of he who makes it. Consider his name before you buy."

＊

In these days of mergers and acquisitions, an executive told her secretary, "When I get in tomorrow, remind me to find out who I'm working for." With the trend toward conglomerates and holding companies, we can alter that story. The woman in business tells her production manager, "When we get into the meeting tomorrow, be sure to tell me what we're making."

＊

In most large corporations, one has to be something of a translator. For example, when you call someone to inquire about a matter and you're told, "It's under active consideration," you know that what they really mean is: "We're looking for it in the files."

＊

The three biggest lies in business are these: "The check is in the mail," "Of course I'll respect you in the morning when we get to work," and "I'm from the federal government, and I'm here to help you."

＊

Business operates in a glass house . . . so it had better keep its windows clean.

＊

A businessman received a questionnaire from Washington that contained this request for information: "State the names and addresses of all employees broken down by sex."

To which the businessman responded: "None—our principal problem is alcoholism."

＊

"A corporation—or any business for that matter—must first do well before it can do good." [Richard C. Gerstenberg]

＊

"Corporate culture is a compound of many things—tradition, my-

thology, ritual, customs, habits, heroes, peculiarities, and values."
[David Ogilvy]

*

When Mark Twain was asked what he thought of Richard Wagner's
music, he said that "it's not as bad as it sounds."

> As a speaker about to present bad news to your audience—
> perhaps at a stockholders' meeting—you might then follow
> the Mark Twain line by saying, "However, regarding the
> subject at hand, I'm afraid that things are as bad as they
> sound."

*

"A bottle is just a bottle until you put something in it. You put
milk in it—it becomes a milk bottle. You put whiskey in it—it
becomes a whiskey bottle. People buy the contents. No matter what
kind of entertainment technology is developed in this high-tech age,
sales will depend on the software. The programs you put into your
VCRs will determine how well the VCRs sell." [Lee Rich]

*

Business has always been affected by change. What is different now
is the pace of change and the prospect that it will come faster and
faster, affecting every part of life, including personal values, morality,
and religion—things that are most remote from technology.

*

"Profit is today a fighting word. Profits are the lifeblood of the
economic system, the magic elixir upon which progress and all good
things ultimately depend. But one man's lifeblood is another man's
cancer." [Paul A. Samuelson]

*

"Never make business an excuse to decline the offices of humanity."
[Marcus Aurelius]

*

The last dying gasp of an organization is usually the issuance of
an even larger procedures manual.

*

The corporation that doesn't give, doesn't get.

*

This is a story about four people:
Everybody, Somebody, Anybody, and Nobody.
There was an important job to be done and
Everybody was asked to do it.
Everybody was sure Somebody would do it.
Anybody could have done it, but Nobody did it.
Somebody got angry about that because it was
Everybody's job.
Everybody thought Anybody could do it, but
Nobody realized that
Everybody wouldn't do it. It ended up that
Everybody blamed Somebody when actually
Nobody asked Anybody.

If you use this in a speech and want some action on the part of the audience members, you might wait for laughter or applause and then say, "I'm asking each of you. . . ."

FACTS, FIGURES, AND RESEARCH

Shoring Up Credibility, or Kidding the Statisticians

If you are an absolute and recognized authority on the subject you are talking about, there is no real need to prove or substantiate any of the points you make. The mere fact of your saying it makes it so. But if you choose to make a point that your audience may not immediately believe or if your audience is likely to include some skeptics or if you merely want to give emphasis to your point by dramatizing it, then there is no better way to convince than with a piece of statistical information. Actual numbers carry much more weight than generalized statements.

Let me give you an example. You might in a talk make a statement such as this: "Americans are really a very cultured people." Depending upon the makeup of your audience, chances are that between 5 and 99 percent of the people listening to you might not be convinced. However, you could then go on to substantiate your point by adding comments such as these: "Seven million young Americans are studying full time in colleges and universities. Thirty-seven million Americans either play, or are learning to play, some musical instrument. And last year, although the sound of rock was very much in the air, twenty million *classical* records were sold in the United States."

At other times, you may be using research figures in such a

way that you want to admit to your listeners that even numbers sometimes leave room for doubt. In these instances, you can present your statistical data together with a comment or two, given in a half-joking manner, indicating your awareness of the fallibility of statistics and statisticians. Often, if you must use a large number of statistical charts and slides, you may feel the need to break the monotony by offering your listeners some pleasantry that kids even an obviously accurate set of figures.

The material in this section is but a small part of the statistical bank from which you can draw information. Obviously, the readers of this book will be writing speeches on thousands of different topics, and even a giant computer would be hard-pressed to print out samples for use in such a variety of scripts. What you find here are examples to spark your imagination and to suggest ways in which a few lines of factual copy can make a point of view more believable.

Specialized books in your field will turn up more research and data than you can probably use. A particularly good source of inspiration is your world almanac.

*

You have to be careful how you interpret statistics, or you'll make the mistake of the researcher who read: "Most auto accidents happen within eight miles of your own home." So he moved.

*

The science, or perhaps the art, of statistics was born in France in 1654 when a nobleman, the Chevalier de Mère, asked a famous mathematician, Blaise Pascal, to help him solve a gambling problem.

Today, ironically, statistics are used in business and politics to take the element of risk—or the gamble—as far as possible *out* of decision making.

*

"Statistics," said Mark Twain, "are like ladies of the night. Once you get them down, you can do anything with them."

*

Of course, you all know the definition of a researcher. She's the one who sends one of her kids to Sunday school and keeps the other one at home as her experiment control.

*

I realize, of course, that it is often possible for facts to get in the way of real truth.

*

There are ninety-eight member countries of the United Nations who have a smaller population than the metropolitan area of New York City.

*

"Information, its communication and use, is the web of society; the basis for all human understanding, organization, and effort." [John Diebold]

*

Even with birth control, a baby is born every 8.45 seconds in the United States. Ten years ago, a baby was born every 12 seconds.

*

In a single *week*, close to 300 million customers pass through the checkout lines of supermarkets in the United States. That's equal to the combined populations of Spain, Mexico, Argentina, France, Italy, Sweden, Switzerland, Belgium, and what was formerly West Germany.

*

In the United States 47 million persons own shares in American corporations, and the value of these shares—though the figure fluctuates—is close to a *trillion* dollars.

*

Since the end of World War II, Americans have won, or shared, 179 Nobel prizes.

*

Although the United States accounts for only 4.59 percent of the population of all the nations in the free world, for which figures are available, our people enjoy as much as 25 percent of the free world's income.

*

The vegetarians in this audience will be interested in this bit of information. According to the U.S. Department of Agriculture, meat consumption in Japan per person is only one-tenth of meat consumption in the United States. The combined consumption of beef, veal, pork, and lamb in this country approaches two hundred pounds annually per capita, while the Japanese consume an average of only twenty pounds. However, there are some countries—notably New Zealand, Australia, and Argentina—where meat consumption is even higher than it is here.

*

In 1976, there were about fifty thousand VCRs in the United States. At the end of the eighties, there were more than forty-five million— one in every two homes that have television sets.

*

Charles Darwin used to say that a man cannot make good systematic observations unless he is looking for something.

*

Nature provides each of us with a twelve-billion-cell computer. It often makes mistakes, but most of the time it can be counted on.

*

"There are two kinds of people in the world: those who divide people into two kinds, and those who don't." [William James]

*

Never forget that when you mine for gold, you have to shift three tons of rubbish for each ounce of gold extracted.

*

One of the most striking aspects of television is that it caught on so fast, reached its heyday so rapidly. It took eighty years for the telephone to be installed in thirty-four million American homes. It took sixty-two years for electric wiring, forty-nine years for the automobile, and forty-seven years for the electric washing machine to arrive in that same number of homes. Television reached that saturation point in a mere twelve years.

*

"The scope of change today is so great that the world alters even as we walk in it. The years of a man's life measure not some small growth or rearrangement or moderation of what he learned in childhood, but a great upheaval." [J. Robert Oppenheimer]

*

There are some researchers who take nothing for granted without proof, not even facts that appear obvious to everyone else. I remember traveling on a train with a friend who was in research. The train passed a field where a large number of sheep were grazing. "Look!" I cried. "Those sheep have all been sheared!" To which my friend replied, "On one side, only on one side."

*

Of course, even figures can be misleading. We all know about the man who drowned walking across a lake with an average depth of three feet.

*

More than 350,000 babies are born into the world every day—two-thirds of them into families that are poor, hungry, ignorant, or sick.

*

The problem of overpopulation is not only one of available space but also of food production. The New York Times, reporting on a government study, tells us these painful facts: Almost ten thousand persons die every day from malnutrition and starvation, and with the population increasing, the world will soon be hard put to feed itself.

About 70 percent of the children in less developed countries are undernourished or malnourished. About 50 percent of all children up to six years old and about 30 percent of the age group from seven to fourteen are labeled seriously malnourished, and it has been reported that half the children in the less developed Latin American countries never reach their sixth birthday. In much of Africa, half die before their fifth birthday.

*

If current trends continue, by the time we enter the next decade there will be 6.127 billion Africans, Asians, and Latin Americans, and they will make up 81 percent of the world's population.

*

Statistics nowadays, whether we're talking about a population explosion or the gross national product, run to such huge figures that
a major problem for any speaker is to bring the numbers down to
something less galactic.

*

"Women, though not necessarily the gentler sex, are far less inclined
to pick up a .38 than men are. They're seldom quick to reach for
a knife. And they're much more apt to wring their hands than other
people's necks. For as long as anyone's been keeping tabs on such
matters, women have accounted for no more than 10 to 15 percent
of all murders." [from "Femme Fatale," the New York Times editorial
page, February 2, 1991]

*

The middle-aged in the United States form a sizable group—both
politically and economically. Look at it this way: There are 46.9
million people in this country between the ages of 45 and 64. That
is *almost double* the population of Canada, which at last count had
a population of just over 26 million.

*

In a single year, the New York Times consumes 273,000 tons of
newsprint and 3,866 tons of ink. The average Sunday edition of the
Times contains twelve to fifteen sections, between five hundred and
seven hundred pages, and weighs between five and seven pounds.
Were it not for the support of its advertisers, the Sunday edition
would cost each of us approximately fifteen dollars per copy, while
the daily edition would have to be priced at four dollars.

*

Fifty percent of the people of middle age in the middle class who
acquire venereal disease do so while traveling or at a convention.

*

In recent years, Americans have tended to flee both the city and
the country, converging on suburbia. Three quarters of the nation's
population now live in urban areas, but more than 42 percent live

not *within* the cities themselves but in the nearby suburban areas surrounding them.

＊

Little more than a decade ago, in 1980, only 14 percent of U.S. homes had microwave ovens. By 1990, 80 percent of homes had them.

＊

When the population of the United States went past the two-hundred-million point in 1968, that was twenty million people more than we had in this country in 1960. This meant that in a period of eight years, we had added the equivalent of the combined populations of Alaska, Arizona, Arkansas, Colorado, Delaware, Hawaii, Idaho, Maine, Montana, Nebraska, Nevada, New Hampshire, New Mexico, North Dakota, Oregon, Rhode Island, South Dakota, Utah, Vermont, West Virginia, and Wyoming.

As this book goes to press, our population, based on the 1990 census, has reached 226,545,805.

＊

It took the United States 350 years to get to a population of 100 million. It took us only fifty-two years to add another 100 million. And we will be at the 300-million mark in a mere thirty years. I do not think that the term *population explosion* is inaccurate or alarmist.

＊

Although we are only on the threshold of the space age, there are already more than seven thousand man-made objects flying through space.

＊

On the subject of the population explosion, a Yale sociologist said: "The population explosion is making our overgrown cities uninhabitable; and the mounting frustrations of urban life manifest themselves in such symptoms as a chronic restlessness and discontent, the breakup of families, the growth of drug addiction, obscenity, freak cults, and violent forms of protest and defiance. Industrial pollutants are beginning to spread over land, sea, and air. Clamor, dust, fumes, congestion, and violence, as well as visual destruction in the form of graffiti and vandalism, are the predominant features in our urban areas. And most of us are mere spectators to what is going on around us, manipulated creatures, whose psyches are choked and smothered and filled with explosive tensions."

*

"Accumulating knowledge is a form of avarice. It lends itself to another version of the Midas story, this time of a man so avid for knowledge that everything he touches turns to facts. His faith becomes theology, his love becomes lechery, his wisdom becomes science; pursuing meaning, he ignores truth." [Malcolm Muggeridge]

*

Perhaps the single most striking characteristic of our times is the *speed* with which change occurs. And we have not yet reached the maximum point of acceleration. It is not unusual to read about supersonic transports traveling three times the speed of sound; automobiles that can go 150 miles an hour; transports that can carry 600 people and their luggage at sonic speed; or even a rocket liner that can carry 170 passengers at 17,000 miles per hour, connecting any point on the globe with any other in a mere forty-five minutes.

*

In the past twenty years, we have seen more technological change than in all recorded history. Tex Thornton, formerly of Litton Industries, put together some stunning facts to prove this point. "It took 112 years," he tells us, "for photography to go from discovery to commercial product; 56 years for the telephone; 35 years for radio, 15 for radar; 12 for television; but only 6 for the atomic bomb to become an operational reality. And only 5 for transistors to find their way from the laboratory to the market." Nowadays, a product can be invented, produced, packaged, marketed, and obsolesced in the course of a year.

*

The computer arrived just in time. The amount of technical information available to our researchers and scientists and social scientists doubles every ten years. Throughout the world, about 120,000 journals are published in more than sixty languages, and it is expected that that number will double in fifteen years.

*

Dr. Daniel Bovet, the Nobel prize-winning biochemist, once reported
that he had overheard a particular mouse in his laboratory talking
to another mouse. "I've got that lab assistant perfectly trained," said
the mouse. "Every time I run through the maze, he feeds me."
   So much for the results of research.

*

On the subject of the proliferation of information, there is the story
of a natural scientist in the Cayman Islands who had spent something
like eighteen years studying turtles. To keep up with all the new
information in his field, he would have had to subscribe to fifty
different journals. Imagine, then, the amount of information pouring
into the knowledge vats of the world in *our* field!

*

Researchers come in many forms and varieties, and you find them
in any number of fields. I remember hearing about the unemployed
actor who wanted to play the role of Abraham Lincoln in a new
play that was being produced. He was determined to get that job,
and he researched the role to the hilt. He read almost everything
that had ever been written about Lincoln. Then he grew a beard
and practiced in front of a mirror, moving and talking like Lincoln.
He bought a stovepipe hat and a cape and a shawl, and when he
left his home—all dressed up like Lincoln—you couldn't have told
him from the original. He was a cinch for the part. But he didn't
get it. He was assassinated on the way to the theater.

*

I have burdened you with so many facts and figures in the last half
hour that I hope you will bear with me while I give you just a few
more—on the lighter side.
   I want you to know that it has been rumored by usually reliable
sources that 196 million people in the United States will *not* be
arrested this year, 89 million will *not* file for divorce, 49 million
students will *not* petition for anything, and 84 million people will
not go on diets.

*

Though no one questions the need for research, we often have occasion to question the researcher's interpretation of his findings. Take, for example, the case of the researcher who spent his life studying the household fly. Using the technique of the Pavlovian response, he had taught a fly to jump on command. Once the fly could do this unerringly, he removed one of the fly's wings and commanded him to jump—which the fly did, if a bit lopsidedly. He then removed the other wing, but according to the researcher's notes, the fly still jumped at the given command. He then removed one of the fly's legs and recorded the fact that at the "Jump!" command, the fly did so but toppled immediately to the ground. One by one, he removed the second, third, fourth, and fifth legs. Each time, the fly responded to the cry of "Jump!" by jumping, but each time he landed with less stability. Finally, the researcher removed the fly's last leg and ordered him to jump. The fly remained motionless. At which point the researcher wrote in his journal, "It is strange that when all six of the fly's legs are removed, the fly becomes deaf."

*

I can hardly believe that our country is made up of people who are ill informed about national, local, and worldwide events. Every night, Monday through Friday, fifty-two weeks of the year, a total of some fourteen million people watch an average of thirty minutes of national and international news on TV.

*

If New York state were a separate country, its gross national product of $362.7 billion would make it rank ninth of all the countries in the world.

*

When a newly elected American president delivers his inaugural address, he speaks to some eighteen thousand persons seated outdoors at the Capitol Plaza. But it is estimated that more than *forty million* persons watch him give that address on their television sets. This is not so much a tribute to the new president as it is an example of the pulling power of television.

*

On the subject of polls, let me tell you something Mark Twain said about the manner in which men and women form their opinions.

He quoted a former slave on this subject: "You tell me whar a man gits his corn pone, en I'll tell you what his 'pinions is."

*

"When a man sits with a pretty girl for an hour, it seems like a minute. But let him sit on a hot stove for a minute and it's longer than any hour. That's relativity." [Albert Einstein]

*

I'm a great one for sticking to the facts. I remember hearing the story of a man who made a million dollars in oil. The story would have been correct, except that it wasn't the man, it was his brother; it wasn't oil, it was gas; it wasn't a million dollars, it was a hundred thousand; and he didn't make it, he lost it.

*

Too many people use research the way a drunk uses a lamppost: to lean on rather than to shed light.

*

"The so-called science of poll-taking is not a science at all but mere necromancy. People are unpredictable by nature, and although you can take a nation's pulse, you can't be sure that the nation hasn't just run up a flight of stairs, and although you can take a nation's blood pressure, you can't be sure that if you come back in twenty minutes you'd get the same reading." [E. B. White]

*

No researcher is in sole possession of truth.

ONE-LINERS

Establishing Yourself as a Sage, Wit, Philosopher

After you've written a rough draft of your speech, it's a good idea to read it through with this special question in mind: Are there any passages where the insertion of a meaningful one-liner will help me to clinch a point, get a laugh, bridge two topics, relieve seriousness with a light touch, or reemphasize a point without repeating it?

The right one-liners can do precisely these things for your talk and, perhaps less frequently, these things as well: They can show that you have a philosophical bent; that you are well-read and have culled important ideas from your reading; that you are familiar with the ideas of sages, poets, historians, and statesmen; that you have a broader outlook about life and the world than the limits of your speech topic might indicate.

Many of the one-liners in this section might also make good closing lines for a talk. If you find a line you particularly like or agree with and it fits in with your thesis, you might find that you can edit your last paragraph or two so that they lead into the one-liner with which you'd like to end.

In some cases, the one-liner you choose for an ending will serve you best if you use it as the next-to-the-last line. For example, in this section you will find the line: "Fewer sleeping pills would be sold if more people went to bed at night content with what they are doing to others." If you want to use that line as your concluding idea, you might then follow it with a line of your own, one that says something such as this: "Let's hope that all of us sleep well tonight." Or perhaps: "If we follow the programs talked about at these meetings, I have a feeling that all of us will be able to sleep a little bit better."

Don't hesitate to change a word or two in any of these one-liners if such a change brings the statement more in line with your style. However, should you change a direct quotation, don't say, "As Abraham Lincoln said. . . ." Instead say, "Abraham Lincoln, if I recall correctly, said something like this. . . ."

After each draft of your talk has been written, check through it again with an eye toward including additional one-liners. Like a bit of salt in a salad, they can heighten the flavor of otherwise unexciting, but necessary, ingredients.

*

Sam Goldwyn once said about a chronic critic, "Don't pay any attention to him; don't even ignore him."

*

A former secretary of state, John Foster Dulles, was fond of saying that he was making progress if today's problems were different from yesterday's.

*

As Mark Twain said about something or other: It's like the difference between lightning and a lightning bug.

*

Consciousness once raised cannot be lowered.

*

"Progress may have been good at one time, but it's gone too far." [Ogden Nash]

*

"An idealist is one who, on noticing that a rose smells better than a cabbage, concludes that it will also make better soup." [H. L. Mencken]

*

"Responsibility is the price every man must pay for freedom." [Edith Hamilton]

*

We all learn from the mistakes of others. That's because we haven't got the time to make them all ourselves.

*

A diplomat has been defined as a person who makes you feel at home—even when he wishes *you were.*

*

Someone else has defined a diplomat as a person who thinks twice before saying nothing.

*

Put yet another way, a diplomat is someone who, when asked what her favorite color is, says, "Plaid."

*

And then there's the definition of a diplomat as someone who can tell you to go to hell with such tact that you look forward to the trip.

*

"The assumption that men were created equal, with an equal ability to make an effort and win an earthly reward, although denied every day by experience, is maintained every day by our folklore and our daydreams." [Margaret Mead]

*

When F. Scott Fitzgerald once told Ernest Hemingway that "the rich are very different from you and me," Hemingway replied, "Yes, they are, they have more money."

*

Someone suggested that the times we live in should be marked "Subject to Change Without Notice."

*

There was a time when a fool and his money were soon parted, but now it happens to everybody.

*

"We all have within us a center of stillness surrounded by silence." [Dag Hammarskjöld]

*

"Freedom of the press belongs to the man who owns one." [A. J. Liebling]

*

"For every complex problem there's a simple answer, and it's wrong." [H. L. Mencken]

*

"A tradition is something you did last year and would like to do again." [Ralph Turner]

*

And so the time has come for us to unquo the status.

*

"As scarce as truth is, the supply is greater than the demand." [John Billings]

*

"An appeaser is one who feeds a crocodile hoping it will eat him last." [Winston Churchill]

*

"All the good meetings are taken." [Woody Allen]

*

"Writing is essentially about going into a room by yourself and doing it." [William Goldman]

*

"What can be added to the happiness of a man who is in good health, out of debt, and has a clear conscience?" [Adam Smith]

*

Money is no guarantee of happiness. The man with ten million dollars is no happier than the one with nine million.

*

"Moderation is languor and idleness of the soul, ambition is its activity and energy." [La Rochefoucauld]

*

A problem becomes a pleasure when you come up with the solution.

*

"Language has created the word *loneliness* to express the pain of being alone and the word *solitude* to express the glory of being alone." [Paul Tillich]

*

No matter what you do, no one is ever going to thank you.

*

"Minds are like parachutes . . . they only function when they are open." [Thomas Dewar]

*

While the little man grabs for credit, the big man gives it away.

*

"The world belongs to the articulate." [Edwin H. Land]

*

"Idealism increases in direct proportion to one's distance from the problem." [John Galsworthy]

*

"It is better to ask some of the questions than to know all the answers." [James Thurber]

*

"A man is seldom better than his conversation." [old German proverb]

*

"Always look at those whom you are talking to, never at those you are talking of." [C. C. Colton]

*

America's best buy for a few cents is a telephone call to the right person.

*

"Show me a thoroughly satisfied man and I will show you a failure." [Thomas A. Edison]

*

"The greatest happiness is to know the source of your unhappiness." [Fyodor Dostoyevski]

*

Income tax is the most equitable of all taxes—it gives everyone an equal chance at poverty.

*

There is no subject however complex, which, if studied with patience and intelligence, will not become more complex.

*

"We are always more anxious to be distinguished for a talent we do not possess than to be praised for the fifteen we do possess." [Mark Twain]

*

Prosperity is buying things we don't want with money we don't have to impress people we don't like.

*

"There is one thing stronger than all the armies in the world, and that is an idea whose time has come." [Victor Hugo]

> Often quoted this way: "No army can withstand the strength of an idea whose time has come."

*

"A hero must be a minority of one, an ethical model who breaks the mold of conformity." [Ralph Waldo Emerson]

*

"To be conscious that you are ignorant of the facts is a great step to knowledge." [Benjamin Disraeli]

*

"The characteristics of genius are these: inspiration, spontaneity, periodicity (the phenomenon by which geniuses seem to produce their work in regular cycles), originality, honesty, a sense of significance, concentration, a degree of skepticism, and credulity." [Ernest Jones]

*

You do not control the press by silencing it any more than you control a man you have silenced.

*

"We suffer primarily not from our vices or our weaknesses, but from our illusions." [Daniel Boorstin]

*

"Life is a bus ride to the place of execution: all our squabbling and vying are about seats in the bus, and the ride is over before we know it." [Eric Hoffer]

*

A man who thinks he is more intelligent than his wife has a very smart wife.

*

"A man is eloquent who is drunk with his own belief." [Ralph Waldo Emerson]

*

Not only is it more blessed to give than to receive, but it's also more deductible.

*

"Work expands to fill the time available for its completion." [Parkinson's Law]

*

"It is better to understand a little than to misunderstand a lot." [Anatole France]

*

A businesswoman who uses a different last name from her husband's was asked how come. "I let him keep his own name," she replied.

*

"Things do not happen; they are made to happen." [John F. Kennedy]

*

Hindsight is always twenty-twenty.

*

"A fanatic is one who can't change his mind and won't change the subject." [Winston Churchill]

*

"Man does not live by words alone, despite the fact that sometimes he has to eat them." [Adlai Stevenson]

*

In discussing our country's budget for the military, there are some who say America cannot afford to be strong, while others say that America cannot afford to be weak.

*

When you hunker down for the marbles, be sure you don't kick sand in someone else's face.

*

Nowadays too many journalists define the public interest as "anything that interests the public."

*

"If a thing is worth doing, it's worth doing badly." [G. K. Chesterton]

*

"In the spring, a young man's fancy . . . but a young woman's fancier." [Richard Armour]

*

"We work to become, not to acquire." [Elbert Hubbard]

*

A critic of our country's contemporary housing once said that the great advantage of suburban tract housing is the fact that it's junk, and we can throw it away without losing anything.

*

"Fewer sleeping pills would be sold if more people went to bed at night content with what they are doing to others." [John W. Gardner]

*

The head of a company that I once worked for used to say, "If I should ever die. . . ."

*

Golfers lie so much about their scores that a golfer who makes a hole in one will often report that he made it in nothing.

*

"If quality is your goal, then persistence must be your battle cry." [Lee Rich]

*

"God grant me the serenity to accept the things I cannot change, the courage to change the things I can, and the wisdom to know the difference." [Alcoholics Anonymous serenity prayer]

*

"Give me somewhere to stand and I will move the earth." [Archimedes]

*

"The only people who gain importance are those who crave it." [Napoléon Bonaparte]

*

There are old pilots, and there are bold pilots, but there are no old, bold pilots.

*

"If you want to tell people the truth, you had better make them laugh—or they'll kill you." [George Bernard Shaw]

*

"Human time is the fundamental scarce resource." [F. Thomas Juster and Frank Stafford writing in the *Journal of Economic Literature*]

*

The artist creates. The artisan reproduces.

*

"The age of the common man is rapidly becoming the age of the common denominator." [Joseph Wood Krutch]

*

"I don't even like money; it just quiets my nerves." [Bob Hope]

*

"Egotism is the anesthetic that dulls the pain of stupidity." [Frank Leahy]

*

Of all our human resources, the most precious is the desire to improve.

*

To define a problem is to begin to solve it.

*

Opportunities carry with them obligations.

*

Though the words are sometimes angry, the blows are scarcely mortal.

*

"Life and opulence are not compatible inasmuch as life is a quest while opulence is a status." [Paolo Soleri]

*

"There are two classes of travel: first class and with children." [Robert Benchley]

*

Beating around the bush not only raises the pollen count—it also bores your listener.

*

"Those who cannot remember the past are condemned to repeat it." [George Santayana]

*

Asked why he robbed banks, Willie Sutton, the master bank robber, replied, "Because that's where the money is."

*

"Absolute power corrupts absolutely." [Lord Acton]

*

When you're up to your ass in alligators, it's difficult to remember that your initial objective was to drain the swamp.

*

"Be not merely good; be good for something." [Henry David Thoreau]

*

"We live in an age of haste: some people look at an egg and expect it to crow." [Orison Swett Marden]

*

"Confidence contributes more than wit to conversation." [La Rochefoucauld]

*

An old Roman maxim tells us that it matters not what you are thought to be but what you are.

*

"A great many people are perfectly willing to sit on a porcupine if you first exhibit it at the Museum of Modern Art and say that it is a chair." [Randall Jarrell]

*

"It is better to have loafed and lost than never to have loafed at all." [James Thurber]

*

"A man has made at least a start on discovering the meaning of human life when he plants shade trees under which he knows full well he will never sit." [Elton Trueblood]

*

Conversation is an art in which a person has all mankind for competitors.

*

"You're talking through your hat and your hat is full of holes." [Theodore Pratt]

*

"A free society is one where it is safe to be unpopular." [Adlai Stevenson]

*

An optimist is a guy who hasn't had much experience.

*

"I've been rich and I've been poor; but believe me, rich is better." [attributed to both Texas Guinan and Sophie Tucker]

*

"Everyone goes to the forest; some go for a walk to be inspired, and others go to cut down the trees." [Vladimir Horowitz]

*

The trouble with staying home from work is that you have to drink coffee on your own time.

*

Inflation is a time when you never had so much and parted with it so fast.

*

"If you can talk about it and do it, then, buddy, you ain't braggin'!" [Dizzy Dean]

*

André Malraux, when asked what the secret of success was, replied that he didn't know but that he could state what the secret of failure was: "Trying to please everyone."

*

"Half of America does nothing but prepare propaganda for the other half to read." [Will Rogers]

*

When told by a headwaiter that there would be a long wait for a table, Yogi Berra is reported to have said: "No wonder no one comes here anymore. The place is always too crowded."

*

"I disapprove of what you say, but I will defend to the death your right to say it." [Voltaire]

*

"I shall not seek, and I will not accept, the nomination of my party for another term as your president." [Lyndon B. Johnson]

*

A bird in the hand is an awful nuisance.

*

Money can't buy love, but it can put you in a strong bargaining position.

*

"People rise to a level of importance just one step beneath that which makes them feel secure." [Harry S. Truman]

*

No pain, no gain.

*

"He's the kind of actor John Wayne would have been if he'd been an actor." [Pauline Kael]

*

If you want to talk about firsts, creating Eve was the first splitting of the Adam, and Atlas was the first holdup man.

*

The first casualty of war is truth.

*

"What sane man would let another man's words, rather than his deeds, prove who was at peace and who was at war with him?" [Demosthenes]

*

"I would rather be a poor man in a garret with plenty of books than a king who did not love reading." [Thomas Macauley]

*

Grief is a solo trip, and you must plot your own course through it.

*

"The reason why so few people are agreeable in conversation is that each is thinking more about what he intends to say than about what others are saying, and we never listen when we are eager to speak." [La Rochefoucauld]

*

Howard Gossage, a famous adman, once remarked that he had waited twenty years for someone to say to him, "You have to fight fire with fire," so that he could reply: "That's funny—I always use water."

*

If fortune has handed you a lemon, squeeze it and make lemonade.

＊

"I never met a rich man who was happy, but I have only very occasionally met a poor man who did not want to become a rich man." [Malcolm Muggeridge]

＊

Peter De Vries once wrote that "a suburban mother's role is to deliver children: obstetrically once, and by car forever after."

＊

The work of the wise is to repair the work of the well-intentioned.

＊

We are living in a world where *sell* is a four-letter word, and "profits," spelled *P, R, O, F, I, T, S,* are without honor.

＊

April is the month when the green returns to the lawn, the trees, and the Internal Revenue Service.

＊

"Trust everybody—but cut the cards." [Finley Peter Dunne]

＊

"One of the reasons mature people stop learning is that they become less and less willing to risk failure." [John W. Gardner]

＊

"I am a great believer in luck, and I find the harder I work, the more I have of it." [Stephen Leacock]

＊

Imagination was given a man to compensate him for what he is *not.* A sense of humor was provided to console him for what he *is.*

＊

There is nothing more disappointing than failing to accomplish a thing—unless it is to see somebody else accomplish it.

＊

After attending a performance of *Parsifal*, Mark Twain is reputed to have said, "Wagner's music isn't as bad as it sounds."

*

"The most stubborn protector of his own vested interest is the man who has lost the capacity for self-renewal." [John W. Gardner]

*

"Every woman should marry, and no man." [Benjamin Disraeli]

*

The only thing that most people understand about money matters is that it does.

*

Sam Goldwyn has been credited with saying, "If people don't want to see a show, nothing can stop them!"

> You might use this Goldwynism as a proverb in modern dress or as a conclusion; or you can make it serve as a warning to manufacturers that they had best start improving their products. It can also be used with groups of parents during discussions on such things as why students drop out or with faculty members when talking about ways in which a curriculum needs to be improved.

*

"A free society is a critical society." [John F. Kennedy]

*

It has been said that, with reasonable care, the human body will last a lifetime.

*

"Truth may often be eclipsed, but never extinguished." [Livy]

*

"You have never converted a man because you have silenced him." [Viscount John Morley]

*

"Give me six lines written by an honest man and I will find something in it with which to hang him." [Cardinal Richelieu]

*

The best way to kindle a fire is to rub together two opposing opinions.

*

"Stupidity is always amazing, no matter how used to it you become." [Jean Cocteau]

*

No good deed goes unpunished.

*

"To be ruthless, a man must be Attila the Hun; a woman just has to put you on 'hold.' " [Marlo Thomas]

*

"We are of different opinions at different hours, but we always may be said to be at heart on the side of truth." [Ralph Waldo Emerson]

*

As Tom Seaver once told the Mets baseball team on the opening day of the Series, "There are only two places in this league: first place and no place."

*

There is no pleasure in having nothing to do. The fun is in having lots to do and not doing it.

*

He who laughs last didn't get the point.

*

"Creativity is the sudden cessation of stupidity." [Edwin H. Land]

*

"The idea is there, locked inside; all you have to do is remove the excess stone." [Michelangelo]

FABLES, TALES, AND ALLEGORIES

Making Your Point Without Sermonizing

In literature, the fable is an imaginative tale, sometimes true but mostly fictitious, which is designed to present a moral lesson entertainingly. The moral is indispensable to the fable. In a speech, you may want to make a point, not necessarily moralistic, but one that has some element of preaching or sermonizing to it. In order to make such a point without running the risk of offending the audience by lecturing them, you can use an old fable or a modern tale that you have read or even made up.

A good source for fables is the children's section of your local library. You'll find the oldest and most enduring fables to be the Oriental ones; but the Greek and Latin writers were also prolific in this category, with Aesop and Phaedrus the best known in those two groups. Later on, from the fourteenth to seventeenth centuries, the Germans, French, and English all contributed heavily to the fables of their lands. Of course, there are also many modern fables in English and American literature and quite a few translated from the Russian.

An allegory uses symbolic fictional figures to point up some generalization about human conduct. Thus the characters or words in allegorical tales signify something besides their literal meanings. To a speaker, the allegory offers a memorable way to make a point, for an interesting tale is more likely to be remembered than an injunction or a command.

It goes without saying that any tale so used in your speech should be interesting in and of itself. There is no quicker way to lose an audience than to inject a long, rambling, and dreary story into your talk. On the other hand, a speaker who selects such stories with an eye to their applicability and to their built-in suspense qualities can be spellbinding.

*

There is an old story—a very durable and useful one—about the man who comes across a construction project, and he goes up to this one fellow and says, "What are you doing?" And the man says, "Oh, I'm taking some mud and making some bricks."

So he goes to the second man and says, "What are you doing, friend?" And the second man replies, "I'm earning some money cutting these logs and making boards out of them."

The man sees a third fellow with a hod on his back, loaded up with bricks, and he says, "What are *you* doing, friend?" The man says, "Me? I'm building a magnificent cathedral."

*

When a music critic disparaged Margaret Truman's singing, President Truman sent him this note: "I have read your lousy review in the back pages. You sound like a frustrated old man who never made a success, an eight-ulcer man on a four-ulcer job."

*

This story is told about Jerome Robbins, the choreographer and Broadway director. Mr. Robbins went to dinner with several other theater personalities, and when asked by the waitress for his beverage order, replied, "I'd like some hot tea. Bring it to me in a glass."

The waitress replied that the restaurant didn't serve hot tea in glasses. Robbins implored her and suggested she take it up with the manager before turning down his request.

Finally, one of Robbins' dinner companions, growing embarrassed, suggested that the waitress bring a pot of hot tea along with a glass and a spoon in it. Then Robbins could pour his own tea in his own Russian style.

The waitress said okay and asked the man who had solved the problem what *he* would have to drink.

"I'll have iced coffee," he said, "in a cup."

*

Sam Levenson, the teacher and comic, once reported that after spending a week at a resort hotel, he was standing next to his car watching a bellboy load his luggage into the trunk. Suddenly the doorman rushed over. "Mr. Levenson," he said breathlessly, "you're not going to forget me, are you?"

"I should say not," replied Levenson. "I'll write you every week."

*

The famed writer-wit Dorothy Parker was on her way to lunch at the Algonquin Hotel with Beatrice Lillie, the brilliant British musical comedy star. Ms. Parker waved Ms. Lillie through the hotel entrance with the words, "Age before beauty," to which Ms. Lillie quickly retorted as she floated through the entrance, "Rather, pearls before swine."

*

On the subject of protocol, there is the story concerning a former British secretary of state for foreign affairs who was a respected gentleman, except that he appeared to have a low tolerance for alcohol.

Having arrived in a foreign country on a government mission, it was determined that an official reception should be held at the British consulate, with a suitable retinue of foreign office brass in attendance. The secretary of state for foreign affairs proceeded to get plastered, in spite of much fussing by his staff. Propped up on each side by devoted assistants, the minister reached the salon where the reception was being held and immediately the band struck up a tune.

Sniffing the air like a gundog, the minister said: "Ah, a waltz. My favorite tune. And who is that gorgeous creature over there in red? I'm going to dance with her."

His aides tried to discourage him, but undeterred, he made his way across the floor to the beautiful creature. "Let me introduce myself," he said, and then proceeded to do so. "I should very much like to dance with you. A waltz is my favorite tune."

The gorgeous creature turned and said in impeccable English, "Sir, I am unable to dance with you for three reasons. First, I regret to say that you are very drunk. Next, this is not a waltz but the national anthem of this country. And, finally, I am the Papal Nuncio."

*

Any speech in which you touch on the subject of tact can use this story:

After a preview of a disastrous theatrical production, the producer stood in the lobby and asked his friends what they thought of the play. Not wishing to offend the producer, one friend blurted out: "I'm speechless! I can't even talk to you about it!" while his wife managed to say: "Wow! I never saw anything like it!"

*

All the angels in heaven were concerned because they noticed that God had been walking around with a long face and seemed to be depressed. Gabriel convinced God that he should have a long talk with Sigmund Freud. So God took to the couch, and after several fifty-minute sessions, Freud reported to the angels. "Indeed," he told them, "God is deeply depressed, and his problem is serious. He is suffering from delusions of grandeur. He thinks he's Donald Trump."

For your own purposes, you can substitute the name of any businessperson or public figure known to be arrogant; or for that matter, the name of anyone in your company or group—or even your audience—known for conceit or overconfidence.

*

Noah Webster, the lexicographer, was embracing his chambermaid when his wife unexpectedly burst into the bedroom.

"Noah, I'm surprised!" Mrs. Webster exclaimed. Whereupon the great definer calmly replied: "No, my dear. You are amazed. It is *we* who are surprised."

*

In a recent novel, when asked what she wanted out of life, a housewife replied, "I want to die thin."

"To few among us is such clarity of purpose given." [Joseph Epstein]

*

When Elizabeth Taylor made her Broadway debut in *The Little Foxes*, tickets were sold out for the run of the play. I happened to be at the theater one night when I noticed an empty seat in front of me. I leaned over and spoke to the woman in the seat beside it. "Pardon me," I said, "but do you know why this seat is empty?"

"Yes," she said, "I wrote for tickets many months ago for my husband and myself. Unfortunately, he died."

"I'm sorry to hear that," I replied, "but don't you have any friends who might have liked to use the ticket?"

"Yes," she whispered, "but they're all at the funeral."

*

There's a wonderful contemporary tale about a traveler who was passing through a small town in the South. As he entered town he saw a big billboard. On the white portion someone had drawn a target, and right through the middle of the target was a bull's-eye. He went down the road a bit, and there was a big, wide magnolia tree with a white target on it, and right through the middle, a bull's-eye. All over town, bull's-eyes.

And he thought to himself, Somewhere in this town there's one heckuva marksman, and I'm going to find him. By asking a lot of people he finally did. The marksman turned out to be the village idiot. The traveler said, "Young man, you certainly have a great gift. No matter what they say about you, you have developed a unique skill. Tell me," he said, "how did you get to be such a champion marksman?"

The boy answered, "There's nothing to it. First you shoot, and then you draw the target!"

> This story can be used to illustrate many points. For example, if you're at a sales meeting or community council meeting you might follow the tale with a sentence such as this: "As a group, we're going to set up our targets first— and then test our marksmanship!"

*

This tale is a commentary on our times. Seems like a man held up a bank but was unable to make his getaway because the teller had pressed an alarm button, and the police arrived in seconds. Thinking quickly, the thief took the money to another window, opened a new account, and as he walked out the manager gave him a television set.

*

Some Talmudic students were discussing with their professor the infinite capabilities of God. The teacher gave them the example of the woodcutter who one morning found that someone had left an infant child on his doorstep. He was penniless and distraught about where he would find food for the child. That night he prayed to God, and in the morning, awoke to find that he had grown a breast.

When the teacher had cited the example, one of the Talmudic students raised the question as to whether it would not have been wiser for God to have provided the poor woodcutter with money so that he could have gone to the town and hired a wet nurse for the infant.

"What!" said the teacher. "God should spend money when he can make a miracle?"

*

Jimmy Carter told this anecdote when he was still in office:

"Every Sunday morning at our church a large number of people come now to visit—I started to say 'worship'—with us. Some of them apparently haven't been in church very often, but we always make room for them there. A couple of Sundays ago, there were two tourists from Miami. After the service one of them turned to the other and said, 'How did I do in the service?' And the other fellow said, 'Well, you did okay, but the word is *hallelujah* and not *Hialeah*.'"

*

A wise man of ancient China was noted for his wisdom and ability to solve problems. One day a merchant came to him seeking advice. It seems that the merchant had a problem in his accounting department.

"I have six men and six abacuses (abaci, if you are a purist), but my needs have expanded to the point where I need a 20 percent increase in output. I cannot afford the capital investment of another man and another abacus; and even if I could, one man would not be enough, and two men would be too much."

The wise man pondered the problem for several days and finally summoned the merchant.

"The solution to your problem," he told him, "is simple. Each of your present accounting staff must grow another finger on each hand. This will increase your abacus output exactly 20 percent and will solve your problem."

The merchant smiled. His problem was solved. He started to leave, paused a moment, and looked at the wise old man. "Oh, Wise One," he said, "you have truly given me the solution to my problem. But . . ." and he paused, "how do I get my people to grow extra fingers?"

The wise man puffed on his pipe. "That is a good question," he said. "But alas, I only make policy recommendations. The details of execution are up to you."

*

Victor Borge tells this tale. "My wife and I checked into a hotel. There was a sign in the bathroom that said, PLEASE PLACE THE CURTAINS INSIDE THE TUB.

"Being good guests, we decided to oblige, although with all of their staff, we couldn't see why they couldn't do it themselves. However, we decided to help them out. It took my wife and me twenty minutes to get that curtain off all those little hooks. Then we weren't sure whether they meant *all* the curtains in the suite—or just the one. To be on the safe side, we did them all."

*

There were two young men who thought they knew all the answers. They had been able to outsmart all the people in town and make a great deal of money, by fair means or foul. But there was one man, a wise old man who lived up on a hill, whom they simply could not outfox. One day one of the men said to the other: "We're going to show that old man that he doesn't know everything, that he doesn't have all the answers. We'll go up on the hill, and we'll catch us a bird. We'll ask the old man what we have in our hands, and he'll answer, 'It's a bird.' Then we will say, 'If you are so wise, old man, if you know everything, tell us, is the bird alive or is it dead?' And if he answers, 'The bird is alive,' we'll crush it in our hands and kill it. And if the old man answers, 'The bird is dead,' we'll open our hands, and the bird will fly away."

So the two know-it-alls went up on the hill and got a bird and knocked on the old man's door. "Tell me, old man, if you know everything," one of them said, "if you are so wise, what's this I have in my hands?" The old man said, "Why, it's a bird, my son." And the smart aleck said, "Then tell me, wise old man, is the bird alive or is it dead?" The old man hesitated, and then, looking deep into the young man's eyes, he replied, "Its destiny, my son, is in your hands."

*

There is an old tale about a man celebrating his hundredth birthday who was interviewed by a newspaper reporter. "To what do you attribute your longevity?" asked the interviewer.

The birthday boy's reply came quickly, considering his age. "I never smoked," he said, "and I never drank hard liquor. I watched what I ate, and I got plenty of exercise."

The interviewer then said: "Very interesting. But I knew a man who did all those things, and he only lived to be eighty. How would you explain that?"

"Easy," said the centenarian. "He didn't keep it up long enough."

*

Gorbachev, Bush, and Yitzhak Shamir met with God, and each was given the opportunity to ask Him a single question. "God," asked Gorbachev, "do you think that Russia and the United States will ever be more than temporary allies?" "Yes," replied God, "but not in your lifetime."

Then Bush asked, "God, do you think we will ever see friendship between the blacks and the whites?" And God answered, "Yes, but not in your lifetime."

Shamir then asked, "God, do you think there will ever be peace between the Jews and the Arabs?" "Yes," said God, "but not in my lifetime."

*

This is a true tale. At the memorial service for Mary Martin, Helen Hayes recalled a trip with Miss Martin to Paris many years ago. "Ms. Martin took along grand clothes," Ms. Hayes recalled. "As we walked through the city, suddenly, overhead there was a swoosh of birds, one of whom took perfect aim on Mary." Ms. Hayes reported that Ms. Martin looked at her with a half smile and said, "For some people, they sing."

*

One of the most disliked movie producers in Hollywood died, and a large number of people showed up at his funeral. One of the mourners expressed surprise to a friend about how many people had come. "Yeah," said the friend, "goes to prove that if you give the public what they want, they'll come."

*

The truth is not always easy to come by.

To make my point, I will tell you the tale of a woman who worked for a foundation and was in charge of giving away its money in the form of grants to museums and other centers of art.

Several years in a row, she had made grants to a well-known Chicago museum. Then one year their committee came to her with a request for a large sum of money that they needed in order to improve their collection of sculpture.

The foundation woman asked what had happened to the charts they were to have submitted to her, showing figures on museum attendance.

One of the museum men was quite miffed at this request. "Good grief," he replied, "we're talking about aesthetics! Charts and figures have nothing to do with that!"

But the dispenser of foundation funds was persistent. "Last year," she went on, "you told me you needed more money because your attendance had gone up. And I gave it to you. Now I want to see the figures you promised me."

Finally, after great difficulty, she extracted the truth. The committee told her that the city had built a public lavatory three blocks away, and museum attendance had *dropped* by 5 percent.

*

An American hunter was in search of big game in West Africa. He was getting close to his prey when his hard-running native guides suddenly sat down to rest. The American protested to their leader. He threatened, implored, cajoled, offered bribes—but the natives wouldn't budge.

"But why," he asked the leader, "why must they stop now?"

The leader replied: "The men say they have hurried too fast. Their bodies have run off and left their souls behind. They must wait now for their souls to catch up."

Perhaps that may be one of our problems today. Our technology may be outrunning our souls.

*

A young man went to a psychiatrist's office, and by coincidence the doctor had just had a cancellation and agreed to see him. As the young man entered he walked directly to the doctor's desk, refused to sit down, and stood very stiffly beside the desk. He informed the doctor that he was there against his will and had only come to please his family.

The doctor asked the young man why his family wanted him to see a psychiatrist. "Well, you see, doctor," he said, "I'm dead."

The doctor had had them all, he thought, but this was a new one. "Really?" he asked. "How do you know you're dead?"

"How do you know you're alive?" shot back the young man. The psychiatrist decided this tack wouldn't get him anywhere, so he tried another. "You're intelligent looking," said the doctor. "I'm sure you'll agree that dead people don't bleed." The young man agreed that this was true.

The doctor reached quickly into the drawer of his desk, asked the young man to roll up his sleeve, and jabbed a small needle into his arm. A spot of blood appeared, and the doctor pressed a glass slide against the blood, then held it up for the patient to see. "There!" he said triumphantly. "It's blood!"

"My God!" said the young man. "Dead people *do* bleed, don't they?"

*

An actor gave a less-than-laudatory performance as Hamlet, which brought forth from the audience a mixture of boos and hisses. At soliloquy time, his performance was met with a barrage of tomatoes.

Stepping to the front of the stage, he abandoned Shakespeare's lines and spoke directly to the audience. "Listen," he said, "don't blame me. I'm just an actor. I didn't write this garbage."

*

This story may be apocryphal, but it's an excellent laugh

*getter and can be used if you're talking about modesty,
education, the theater, a teenager, a political campaign,
and so on:*

Toots Shor, the famous saloon keeper of the fifties, did not have
much formal education. He was taken by friends to see a Broadway
production of *Hamlet*. During the intermission, he commented to
his friends, "I bet I'm the only guy here who don't know how the
thing comes out."

*

You may remember Charles Lamb's "Dissertation on Roast Pig."
The hero discovered roast pork—and how delicious it is—when his
house burned down with a pig inside it.

Being shrewd, he put two and two together. Thereafter, every
time he wanted roast pork he burned the house down.

*This story might then be followed by a comment to the
effect that "it really isn't necessary to have a disaster every
time you want a good dinner—or its equivalent."*

*

The driver of a pickup truck rapped at the door of the farmhouse
and asked the farmer, "How much is that old bull out there on the
road worth to you?"

The farmer replied with a question of his own. "It depends,"
he replied. "Are you the tax assessor, do you want to buy him, or
did you run him down with your truck?"

THE WORLD OF ADVERTISING

Getting Your Audience All Worked Up

Some people are indifferent to advertisements. A man or woman might see or hear an ad and remain untouched by it. But few thinking people today are indifferent to the *subject* of advertising, the *business* of advertising. Not only aren't they indifferent—most people are capable of becoming very heated on the subject, whether they are for or against it. Those whose business and livelihood depend upon advertising can cite chapter and verse to prove its necessity; others, particularly those on campuses or in intellectually oriented careers, have feelings about advertising that range from acid scorn to an almost homicidal urge to destroy the perpetrators.

Consequently, an appropriate reference to advertising in a speech can almost always be counted on to involve, or even excite, the audience. Your selection of material will depend, naturally, upon which side of the quarrel you favor. This section contains material to support either side of the debate.

*

Advertising is primarily concerned with communicating ideas on a commercial basis—with a frankly commercial aim. This distinguishes it from Billy Graham's sermons, which also communicate ideas hoping to make a sale—but *not* on a commercial basis.

*

Lee Iacocca, after engineering the successful turnaround of the
Chrysler Corporation, was asked what he thought was the most
important marketing fundamental. "Create a quality product," he
said, "deliver it to the marketplace, and make sure you let everyone
know about it."

*

Making a good product and trying to sell it without advertising is
like winking at a pretty girl in the dark. You know what you're
doing, but nobody else does.

*

When British advertising agencies began buying up American ones
in the 1980s, someone on Madison Avenue said that British advertising—which tends to employ understatement, subtle humor, and
only indirect reference to the product—is easier to export because
the attitudes and emotions it tries to exploit are more universal.
"The British are convinced," said this American adman, "that advertising is a commodity they can send around the world just as
they once exported spices and tea."

*

I would like to explain the difference between a scientist, a philosopher, and an advertising man.
    The scientist is like a man who's blindfolded and goes into an
utterly black room seeking a black cat. The philosopher is like a
man who's blindfolded and goes into a black room seeking a black
cat that isn't there.
    And the advertising man is like a blindfolded man seeking a
black cat in a black room who shouts: "I've got it! I've got it!"

*

Advertising is not a twentieth-century phenomenon. There's nothing
new about it. In the early days of our country, merchants whose
wagons cleared the plains ran through town shouting what there
was for purchase—or they put out a bulletin.

*

A man gave a speech at a Rotary club on the subject of advertising and advertising people. It is one of the tenets of the Rotarians that they may not use swear words. But the speaker—not being a Rotarian himself—didn't know this, and in his talk he used a curse word he shouldn't have used in that particular hall to that particular audience.

At the end of the meeting, a local minister in the audience approached the speaker and dressed him down for having used the language he did. The speaker apologized profusely, and the minister went on about how the Rotarians, to say nothing of the church, strongly disapprove of bad language. He then walked away.

He got about ten feet down the corridor, then turned around and approached the speaker again. "Off the record," he said, "and just between us, any time you want to call an advertising man a sonovabitch, it's okay with me."

*

A terrible thing happened to me once. A commercial came on, and I didn't have to go to the bathroom.

*

The difference between an advertising man and a publicity man might best be explained through a sexual analogy. The man who sits at the edge of his girlfriend's bed and tells her how great it was is a publicity man. The man who sits there and tells her how great it's going to be is in advertising.

*

We don't argue that technology is a failure just because the production lines occasionally turn out a dud. We might blame the manufacturer but not technology. Why do we blame all of advertising if a few practitioners turn out a product that insults or offends?

*

"Fame is the spur, but to achieve it a writer must shun delights and seek laborious days." [John Milton]

*

Famous men throughout history, including presidents and prime ministers, have thought highly of advertising. Here, to quote but a few, are some opinions:

CALVIN COOLIDGE: "The preeminence of America in industry, which has constantly brought about a reduction of costs, has come largely through mass production. Mass production is only possible where there is demand. Mass demand has been created only through the development of advertising."

THOMAS JEFFERSON: "I read only one newspaper, and that more for its advertisements than its news. Advertisements contain the only truths to be relied upon in a newspaper!"

WINSTON CHURCHILL: "Advertising nurses the consuming power of man. It creates wants for a better standard of living. It sets before man the goal of a better home, better clothing, better food for himself and his family. It spurs individual exertion and greater production."

FRANKLIN D. ROOSEVELT: "If I were starting my life all over again, I am inclined to think that I would go into the advertising business in preference to almost any other. This is because advertising has come to cover the whole range of human needs and also combines real imagination and a deep study of human psychology. Because it brings to the greatest number of people actual knowledge of useful things, it is an essential form of education. The general raising of the standards of modern civilization among all groups of people during the past half century would have been impossible without the spreading of the knowledge of higher standards by means of advertising."

SAMUEL JOHNSON: "Every man has the right to utter what he thinks truth, and every other man has the right to knock him down for it!"

*

Al Capp, the cartoonist, once said that "the public is like a piano—you just have to know what keys to poke." Every advertising practitioner knows this to be true.

*

"Originality is the ability to present facts and ideas as nobody has before, even though the facts and ideas are not in themselves new." [Ernest Jones]

*

When you write an advertisement, you have to assume that the person to whom it's directed may have a record playing in her head that is different from your own. It's important, therefore, to focus her attention in the appropriate channel.

For example, there is the story of a husband and wife on animal safari in East Africa. They were walking in the bush when a lion leapt from its hiding place and grabbed the woman in his claws.

"Shoot, Harry!" she yelled to her husband. "Shoot!"

"I can't!" he yelled back. "I can't! I've run out of film!"

*

"The right to fail is the catalyst of creativity. Give dedicated people the right to fail and their enthusiasm will spark ideas that may seem fantastic and far out at first examination." [Oscar Dystel]

*

Creativity involves a search for new knowledge; or techniques for using old knowledge in new ways.

*

Advertising practitioners, particularly those in the creative end of the business, are often accused of vanity. They sometimes counter with the explanation that what may appear to be vanity is merely pride in their work. On the difference between pride and vanity, let me quote Arthur Schopenhauer:

"Pride is an established conviction of one's own paramount worth in some particular respect, while vanity is the desire of rousing such a conviction in others. Pride works from within; it is the direct appreciation of oneself. Vanity is the desire to arrive at this appreciation indirectly, from without."

*

"It is impossible to build up a backlog of goodwill; ill will, yes— but goodwill starts from scratch at nine o'clock every morning." [Paul Foley]

*

"The truly creative man is not an outlaw but a lawmaker. Every great creative performance since the initial one has been in some measure a bringing of order out of chaos. It brings about a new relatedness, connects things that did not previously seem connected, sketches a more embracing framework, moves toward larger and more inclusive understandings." [John W. Gardner]

*

Osborn Elliott, former dean of the Columbia Graduate School of Journalism and former editor of *Newsweek*, cites five things as "the writer's basic tools." They are these:

1. An open mind, a willingness to learn, and the knowledge that things are not always what they seem to be.
2. Belief in the dignity of man and compassion for those upon whom the world too often heaps indignities.
3. High regard for the riches of the English language and an eagerness to learn its proper use.
4. An appreciation for the conflicts and complexities of modern life, and an understanding that they often cannot be reconciled.
5. An awareness that even the best-motivated persons make mistakes, and a willingness to admit your own.

*

"We all like to believe that we don't have to be 'sold'—that if someone builds a better mousetrap (or anything else) the world will beat a path to his door. But it simply is not true. Almost literally, nothing has ever been 'sold' in this way. Not religion, or democracy, or automobiles, or anything else. Someone must tell us about the 'better mousetrap' and why it is better, and convince us of its value and importance to us.

"Advertising and selling perform this function of information and persuasion that is essential to the operation of a dynamic economic society." [reprinted from *Advertising Age*]

*

If we lie to people in our ads to get their money, that's fraud. But if politicians lie to them to get their votes, that's politics.

*

There is no denying that advertising men are often arrogant. If I were to pass one in the office corridor some morning and say, "Beautiful morning!" he would probably say, "Thank you!"

*

Being creative does not mean that one is given to sudden flashes of inspiration that provide solutions to difficult problems. Einstein did not have a sudden flash of intuition about his theory of relativity. He labored seven years on the problem before a surge of intuition revealed the theory. He was then able to put it into finished form in only five weeks.

*

A writer without values is nothing but a stenographer.

*

A good television or radio announcer understands that the meaning of what is said depends upon the *emphasis* given to words more than on the words themselves. Take the couple that had eleven children. The man explained that this was because his wife was hard-of-hearing. Every night when they went to bed, the husband would ask, "Do you want to go to sleep or what?" "What?" his wife answered.

*

The person who has something unusual to offer will always play second fiddle to the person who has nothing to offer but the art of offering it.

*

Advertising has often been criticized because it sells a benefit rather than a product. Well, I can only tell you that, in my experience, people don't want fertilizer, they want green lawns. No one really wants stock certificates, they want capital gains.

*

Bertrand Russell has told us that television is chewing gum for the eyes.

*

Because so many TV commercials show men of warm friendship having a great time drinking beer together, beautifully clad women, radiant because of their shampoo, enraptured couples walking along heavenly Caribbean beaches, and elderly people deliriously happy in the company of their adoring grandchildren, we should think of

TV commercials as our modern fairy tales, where everyone lives happily ever after.

*

"Writing is to persuasion what breathing is to health." [Paul Foley]

*

"To be persuasive, we must be believable; to be believable, we must be credible; to be credible, we must be truthful." [Edward R. Murrow]

*

On the subject of what advertising *cannot* do, Russell Johnston, in his book *Marion Harper, An Unauthorized Biography*, reports on something Mr. Harper, the advertising genius of the fifties, said to the staff of the McCann-Erickson Agency at a company seminar.

"Advertising cannot produce a desirable product. It cannot establish an optimum price. It cannot acquire the best retail outlet. It cannot provide a convenient, salable package. It cannot put the product in the best shelf position. It cannot maintain inventory. It cannot train a sales force. It cannot report on the product or on its own performance in the market. Advertising can *affect* some of these activities, but it cannot cancel their influence as roadblocks to sales."

*

"Advertising is a substitute for a salesperson, so it should be likable. You wouldn't buy from a salesperson who's rude, arrogant, insulting, would you?" [William Backer]

*

"No man but a blockhead ever wrote except for money." [Samuel Johnson]

*

It doesn't speak too well for the power of television advertising when you stop to think that headaches have somehow managed to keep pace with all of those new pain relievers.

*

In a meeting, an advertising copywriter made a point of telling the assembled group how important he considered the work of the writer to be in the creation of a campaign, to which an art director commented, "In response, let me quote Mae West. She once said that 'being important is like being a lady. If you have to tell people you are, you ain't.' "

*

"Our society is not threatened by the man in the gray flannel suit; it is threatened by the man with the gray flannel mind." [Ellison L. Hazard]

*

Britain's John Hobson defends advertising this way: "We shall always be open to criticism unless we can bring home to our critics that advertising is like the electric cables that stretch across the countryside—sometimes unsightly, always expensive to maintain, but necessary—so that someone, somewhere, can turn on the cooker, whenever she wants to."

*

What is a great advertisement? I like what Raymond Rubicam, one of the founders of the Young & Rubicam advertising agency, once said. "There are many successful ads," said Mr. Rubicam, "but few great ones. The great ad, by virtue of the very adjective applied to it, must not be merely successful, but phenomenally so.

"Yet phenomenal results alone—whether in number of readers, or inquiries, or even sales—do not make people feel that an ad is great unless its message is made memorable by originality, wit, insight, conviction, or some other notable quality of mind or spirit.

"And even those qualities do not make it great if its claims are dishonest, if it impairs the goodwill of the customers toward the advertiser, either before or after the sale, or if it impairs the goodwill of the public toward advertising."

*

Ever since the days of *The Man in the Gray Flannel Suit*, the rumor has persisted that advertising men are heavy drinkers. The president of an advertising agency circulated this memo among his account executives: "If you people are determined to go out and drink martinis at lunch, will you please order your martinis made with gin rather than with vodka, which is odorless? When our clients see you in the afternoon, I'd much rather you gave off an odor of booze. At least then they'd know you were drunk rather than stupid."

*

Advertising is, of course, a form of communication. If the communication is faulty, the advertisement may amuse or entertain—but it won't sell. Let me explain what I mean by faulty communication by telling you a story about Sir Thomas Beecham.

Sir Thomas was conducting the orchestra in a piece that called for an offstage trumpet to sound a long call. Beecham got to the point where the trumpet was to sound—but no trumpet. He paused, then had the orchestra repeat the section leading up to the trumpet call. Once again, no trumpet. He threw down his baton and strode into the wings to see what had happened. There was his trumpeter in a tussle with the backstage guard, who was insisting, "You can't play that darn fool trumpet in here—there's a concert going on!"

Obviously, a crucial piece of information had not been communicated to the guard.

*

When I was a child, my grandfather saw an advertisement for a book called *How to Grow Tomatoes*. Grandpa sent for the book, but he found it very confusing, and what was even worse, his tomato crop failed. I remember Grandpa complaining, "The person who wrote the ad should have writ the book."

Of course, that advertiser never intended to sell more than one book to a customer. However, the person selling repeat products will soon find that there is no better way to kill off a poor product than with a good advertisement. The ad will bring in the customers—lots of them—who will find out after a single trial that they don't ever again want to buy that particular product.

*

Did you hear about the media executive who got married last week and traded reach for frequency?

*

Advertising has always been something of a cutthroat business. Two Madison Avenue advertising men were chatting over lunch. It seems that an acquaintance of theirs had just gone to the Great Big Agency in the Sky.

"Did you hear about Jack Mueller?" asked one of the admen. "He died last night."

"Good Lord," said the other, "what did he have?"

"Nothing much," replied the first adman, "just a small toothpaste account and a local car dealer—nothing worth going after."

∗

It has been said that advertising, because of its constant deadlines, is one of the most stressful occupations of our times. Let me tell you what Dr. Hans Selye wrote about stress.

"Total absence of stress," he said, "would be death. The important thing is not to avoid stress as much as learning how to deal with the stressful moments of life. Every person has a different level of stress—every person must find his own way. You cannot force a turtle to run like a racehorse. You will kill a racehorse if you force him to slow down like a turtle."

∗

You might like to know the difference between sales promotion, advertising, and public relations. Well, if when a boy meets a girl he tells her how lovely she looks, how much she means to him, and how much he loves her, that's sales promotion.

If, instead, he impresses on her how wonderful *he* is, that's advertising.

But if the girl agrees to go out with him because she's heard from *others* how great he is, that's public relations.

∗

A former editor of the *New Yorker* magazine, William Knapp, once made this comment in talking to some writers: "The more brilliant a person is in his or her field, the less vocal self-advertisement he or she indulges in."

∗

In advertising, it is not uncommon for the client to always want to see an idea rendered in yet another way. I recall one morning I was walking a client through our offices when we passed an art director. "Good morning," said the A.D. To which the client replied: "That's great, John. Let me see it made up four ways."

∗

"The consumer is not a moron. She is your wife. Don't insult her intelligence." [David Ogilvy]

*

Today's young generation, being brought up on television, thinks mostly in terms of that medium. Like the little girl who went to her first church service, and as she left the church the minister asked her what she thought of it. "The music was nice," she told him, "but the commercial was too long."

*

"I warn you against believing that advertising is a science. It is intuition and artistry, not science, that develops effective advertising." [William Bernbach]

*

"Many ideas grow better when transplanted into another mind than in the one where they spring up." [Oliver Wendell Holmes]

*

I don't know why I put such faith in the advertising I see on my television screen. I've been using turtle oil for ten years—despite the fact that I've never seen a really good-looking turtle.

*

A good idea doesn't care who has it.

*

It's a strange thing about advertising people. If you put three of them in a barrel and rolled them down a hill, one would be on top all the way.

*

Advertising people are continuously looking for new media, new places, and new ways to display their ads. In recent years, companies have taken to placing advertisements on the sides of their trucks, which seems to be an excellent medium, provided the message is provocative.

I say this because I witnessed quite a large crowd gathered around a Consolidated Edison repair truck that was parked on a

New York City street. On the side of the truck was a large painted sign that read, "Ask me how you can save on your electric bills."

Underneath the sign someone had scrawled, *"I don't talk to no truck."*

*

Some degree of ego is justifiable in a good creative person. After all, you know the old saying: What's the good of a sundial in the shade?

*

On the subject of what is legal and what is right, John E. O'Toole, the former CEO of the advertising agency Foote, Cone & Belding, had this to say: "It is legal to fill prime-time hours of network programming with smashed, burning cars and broken, bloody bodies. It is legal to present the viewer with depictions of sadism, rape, homicide and even more esoteric varieties of brutality. But it is not *right.*"

*

Creativity is nothing more than common sense developed to a fine art.

AWAY FROM HOME

Out of Town or
Out of the Country:
Make It Work for You

As every ball club can tell you, the game calls for something extra when you're playing away from home. Though the program chairperson is proud to have nabbed you as a speaker, the audience, eager as it may be to hear what you have to say (after all, they probably paid to attend the meeting or luncheon), is also a bit wary. Will you be patronizing? Assume the audience's knowledge of your subject is less than it actually is? Sometimes a speaker can almost sense an undercurrent of feeling that makes an unspoken challenge: We have our own smart people here. Let's hear what *you* have to say that we don't already know.

I was at the Waldorf-Astoria Hotel in New York when Lee Iacocca, at the height of his fame, addressed an audience of business executives. He had just performed a miracle in turning around the Chrysler Corporation, his first book was on the best-seller list, and people were saying he should run for president. When he entered the Grand Ballroom, the audience actually got to its feet and applauded. And yet as he approached the microphone I could feel in the silent room the electricity of anticipation as well as some small degree of skepticism. "Okay, big man," the audience seemed to say, "tell us how great you are." Iacocca is known, after all, as a man not given to modesty. In seconds he broke down any audience resistance that might have existed. After acknowledging a generous introduction, he added, "But I do not walk on water!" The audience laughed, everyone relaxed, and he began his talk.

Wooing an audience when you're out of town or out of the country is not difficult to do, although it's harder in a country where you are not wholly familiar with the culture. First, some open recognition of the fact that you're a stranger come to town is almost a must. Speakers who launch right into their prepared remarks without first paying homage to the specialness of this audience make a mistake and lose a fine opportunity to build rapport with their listeners. It doesn't take much. A few gracious lines about enjoying their city, their country if you're abroad, something flattering about a pleasant experience you had at your hotel, or even something that jests kindly about a publicized local problem (crime in one of the bigger cities; poor airline connections to a small town; local taxi drivers who get lost or talk too much; a politician who made a gaffe or is about to go to jail; and so on) not only makes you seem human but shows you're knowledgeable about this particular part of the world. An audience response to this sort of material also serves to relax you.

In some instances you might find it appropriate to bring your audience closer by first referring to a common ethos or to television's being the great common denominator or to the speed of communications in our high-tech age in which the fax machine and the conference call provide instant exchanges of information. You then want to segue quickly into your local comments.

One of the things I always do when writing a speech to be given away from home base is obtain copies of the daily newspapers in the host city. I scan these for human interest stories or local goings-on. Then I get on the horn and call every contact I have in that city: the program chairperson of the sponsoring group, the public relations person or office head in the branch office of the speaker's own company, even the newspaper reporter who wrote a story that might provide grist for the mill. I pick their brains. I tell them what I'm looking for and ask for their input. But before I make the calls, I prepare a few specific questions—just to get them started. You'd be amazed how eager people are to give you behind-the-scenes information or just plain local gossip. I've mined pure gold in some of these conversations. You will too.

If your talk is to be given in the United States, there are two books you can find in most libraries that offer background information on cities where you are likely to be speaking. One is called

The Book of States, and the other is *Places to Live in the U.S.* Between the two, you can learn everything from the names of government dignitaries to the color of the dome on the state capitol building.

Getting information for an offshore talk is a bit more difficult but only because you need more lead time. The fax machine is, of course, a godsend. The best time to start digging for usable material is the day after you've accepted the invitation to speak. Contact people in the overseas host city with a list of questions you'd like answered. Ask the person who issued the invitation for detailed information on the number and makeup of the audience (e.g., level of achievement), who the other speakers will be, what subjects they will cover, what the sponsoring group considers to be their three major concerns of the moment. Obtain copies of the city's leading newspapers (and hope you can find someone to translate the headlines for you); get copies of the *International Herald Tribune* for the country where you'll be speaking and scan them for local interpretations of events; and if *Time* magazine has a foreign edition in that country, get copies. Wherever it's published, *Time* is in English.

Of course, so many American companies have gone global that you may have a branch office or subsidiary in the country where you will speak. Don't be shy about asking the people in that office to help you with local color and with a review of your text to guarantee it's not offensive in any detail. They are probably proud to have you visit and pleased that you will get local publicity for them as a result of your talk. They will be more than happy to contribute to your success.

It is absolutely essential that you arrive in the foreign country a minimum of two days, preferably three, before you're scheduled to speak. I once wrote a speech for a corporate executive who was to be a featured speaker in Singapore. He left the States with what he thought was enough time to make his platform date. Unfortunately, he forgot that he would cross the international dateline and was asleep in a Tokyo hotel room when he should have been on the platform in Singapore. He arrived in that city a day after the program chairman had told a disappointed audience that the guest speaker from America had failed to show!

Everyone suffers from jet lag except those people who lie about it. Jet lag is not a character flaw, it is a fact of nature, and there's nothing wrong in telling your company or colleagues that you plan to leave early on this trip, not to go sight-seeing but because you need to rest when you get there. Such a request does not mean you're old, "the weaker sex," or an inexperienced traveler. It just means you have common sense. After recovering from some or all of your jet lag, you will want to spend time with a local person or persons (from your company or the sponsoring organization) to review your speech and make certain that you have nothing in the text that could offend the audience or turn you into the ugly American. This is more important than you might imagine. Many a speaker has received minimal applause because of a single remark that would have been okay at home but proved offensive to an international audience.

Finally, your chances of delivering a successful talk out of town or out of the country improve immeasurably if you have a useful repository of humor and stories that you can tap—often more than once, in more than one city, in the States or abroad. Here are fifty-six bits from which to choose. Although I have separated them into "Out of Town" and "Out of the Country," many of them can be adapted for use anywhere. So read both sections as you consider where in your speech an item can enliven your script and change your talk from merely interesting to absolutely unforgettable.

Out of Town

Some of the following speech bits refer to specific cities, such as New York or Washington, D.C. However, most of these can be easily adapted to fit other cities where you may be a speaker. For example, several items refer to crime in New York City. You can easily substitute Chicago, Atlanta, Washington, D.C., Miami, or other high-crime cities:

Whoever said we are a nation indivisible was dead wrong. There are more regional differences in the United States than one could catalog.

*

A Washington aphorism: Friends come and go, but enemies accumulate.

*

I like New York. I love it here. I like it a lot. You just have to be careful. Don't go out. Ever.

*

New Yorkers believe that they were born three hours before us, and we are spending the rest of our lives catching up.

*

In *The Culture of Narcissism*, Robert Sinai is quoted on the subject of big cities: "The population explosion is making our overgrown cities uninhabitable," he says, "and the mounting frustrations of urban life manifest themselves in such symptoms as a chronic restlessness and discontent, the breakup of families, the growth of drug addiction, obscenity, freak cults, and violent forms of protest and defiance. Clamour, dust, fumes, congestion, and violence as well as visual destruction in the form of graffiti and vandalism, are the predominant features in our urban areas. And most of us are mere spectators to what is going on around us, manipulated creatures whose psyches are choked and smothered and filled with explosive tensions."

*

This story can be used to fit any middle-size, middle-America city:

I remember being at a dinner in Iowa City. The man on my right, eager to show that he was as knowledgeable and sophisticated as any big-city guy, had this to say: "I've done a lot of traveling," he told us. "I've been around a lot. I've been to Dubuque. I've been to Cedar Rapids. I've been to Waterloo and to Fort Dodge. And you know what? People are the same everywhere!"

*

New York is a city that people love and hate at the same time. It has the best of things and the worst of things. It's literally heaven on earth. Every time a gun goes off, an angel gets its wings.

*

New York City is a strange place. I was walking along Fifty-second

Street when I stopped a man and asked, "Do you know where Fifth Avenue is?" "Yes," he answered, and walked away.

*

In an interview, the brilliant actress Meryl Streep said she liked the hurly-burly of New York and its people. "I admire those people," she said. "They keep their pores open to experience. They're hungry all the time for experience. They *devour* both people and events."

*

When John Lindsay was mayor of New York City, he once commented that "New Yorkers don't trust any air they can't see."

*

Lots of people criticize New York City taxicab drivers. But I'm not going to criticize them. After all, maybe the best way to get to Macy's *is* by way of Canada.

*

For use in a city known for its high crime rate:

I like this city. I spent a couple of months here last year on business. Twenty-five days after getting here, my car was broken into. A local friend apologized to me this way: "You see, they have a lot of cars here to break into, and they break into them as fast as they can. That's why it took twenty-five days."

*

Here's another line for use in high-crime cities:

I always carry twenty-five dollars in my wallet for the muggers in case I'm held up. I consider the money to be street rent.

*

During one of the frequent periods when New York City was having fiscal troubles, Bob Hope visited the Big Apple and was given the key to the city. "A week later," he said, "I was billed for it."

*

In addressing a meeting of journalists from up north, a down-home congressman joked: "You think I'm not sophisticated just because I'm from down in Georgia? Believe me, we're sophisticated down there. We had sushi before you did. We just used to call it bait."

＊

According to Russell Baker, "when everybody has fled to the suburbs and there are no more cities for suburbanites to refresh themselves in, it will be said of America, 'It's a restful place to visit, but I wouldn't want to live there.' "

＊

This is indeed a strange nation. Philadelphia cream cheese is made in Chicago, Palm Beach suits are made in Maine, and the old *Saturday Evening Post* always came out on Tuesday.

＊

An MC introducing a speaker in the Midwest said, "[Name of speaker] is the kind of guy who has all the qualities of St. Joseph, which we all know is a very dull town in northern Missouri."

＊

If you're talking in one of the states in the deep South and want to kid your locale, tell this story. It can be adapted to fit any small, southern town or city:

The pilot of a private plane stopped for refueling at an airport with one runway. When ready to take off again, he notified the control tower, which replied, "Okay for takeoff on runway one!" Almost immediately he heard the tower tell an approaching plane, "Okay for you to land now on runway one!" The departing pilot got on the intercom and shouted, "What did I just hear you say?" To which the tower responded, "You-all be careful now, ya hear?"

＊

I love Beverly Hills. The teenagers are always looking in their mirrors—except when they pull out of a parking spot.

＊

If you're a Californian speaking away from home, you

might inject this modest comment at the opening of your talk:

People think we folks in California are arrogant, that we make claims about being the place where all trends begin. I don't know . . . I hardly think we can lay claim to being in on the beginning of everything just because we lead the nation in purchases of guacamole, herbal tea, and alfalfa sprouts.

*

The fog is so thick in Los Angeles that if you smile, you're in danger of cracking a tooth.

*

How many Californians does it take to screw in a light bulb? Four: one to screw it in and three others in the group to share the experience.

*

After spending several years writing for the movies in L.A., the playwright Neil Simon returned to New York City. Asked in an interview how he felt about L.A. versus New York, he said that L.A. was all right. "When it's zero degrees in New York," he said, "it's seventy degrees in L.A. And when it's one hundred and ten degrees in New York, it's still seventy degrees in L.A. The only problem is that there are only seventy interesting people in L.A."

*

"California isn't a place; it's a way of life." [Ronald Reagan]

*

"Every year you live in California, you lose two points off your I.Q." [Truman Capote]

*

If you had to fly a very small, local airline in order to get to your meeting, you might open by saying what a nice flight you had:

"It's really a cute airline." You could then add: "Half an hour before flight time the passengers get together and elect a pilot."

Out of the Country

The old saying that "money talks" still applies. Only today it's speaking Japanese and Arabic.

*

An American was explaining our country's flag to a foreign visitor. "It has something to do with our taxes," said the American. "We see red when we talk about them, turn white when we calculate them, blue when we pay them, and we see stars when we're audited."

*

Since this audience is made up of people from many countries, it is possible that my remarks have struck each of you somewhat differently. For there is, certainly, a difference in the way people in various parts of the world see things. I once read a book called *The Rich Man's Guide to Europe* in which the author, one Charles Graves, explains such differences this way:

"The Danes are great jokers; they love a laugh. It was a Dane who invented the story of an International Congress of Zoologists who were requested to prepare a thesis on elephants. Most people remember that the American contribution was 'How to Raise Bigger and Better Elephants.' The British contributed 'On Safari Through Darkest Africa,' which was subtitled 'Preparation of Tea for Elephants.' The French contribution was 'Les Amours de l'Elephant,' while the Germans came up with 'A Cursory Introduction to the Biology of Elephants' (in fourteen volumes). The Scandinavian variants may be less well known. The Swedish version was 'What Title to Use in Addressing Elephants,' the Norwegian one was 'Norway and the Norwegians,' and the Danish, 'One Hundred Ways to Prepare Elephants for the Cold Table.' "

Despite the possibility of varying interpretations, let me make a few statements that we will probably all interpret the same way.

*

The inequality of the world can be seen in the fact that two thirds are starving and the other one third is dieting.

*

The Japanese are often said to be masters of understatement. For example, Emperor Hirohito, in 1945, observed in the imperial announcement of Japan's surrender, "The war situation has developed not necessarily to Japan's advantage."

*

And how about the boat built in Taiwan, owned by a Bermuda company, registered in Monrovia, flying a Liberian flag, with an Italian crew, chartered to an Australian billionaire? Naturally, when it went aground, it was in international waters.

*

The trouble with foreign aid is that it allows too many countries to live beyond our means.

*

I have been asked about global advertising, whether a good advertising message can cross borders. It is true that people everywhere have the same basic desires, that wherever you go there are similarities: Everyone wants good plumbing, a green lawn, and the best for their children. So an idea *can* cross a frontier successfully.

But the differences may be greater than the similarities. Attitudes toward children, sex, and toilet-bowl cleaners vary from country to country. So do moral standards and local customs.

For advertising to work, these differences must be recognized.

*

Foreign films can be very confusing when viewed outside their country of origin. In the English films, the lovers won't upset their spouses by asking for a divorce, so he goes off to Africa on an architectural assignment. In the French films, the lovers are married—but not to each other. In the Japanese, the lovers can't marry, so they kill themselves. In the Swedish films, they raise a family—four generations—and we're told in detail about all of them. In the Russian films, they're married until he runs away with an American spy. In the American version, the lovers fall out of love, divorce, marry each other's former spouse, and live happily ever after.

*

During the cold war with Russia, there were many Americans who felt we should quit the military arms race and hoped that Russia, too, would come to her senses. A politician, opposing such a nuclear freeze, had this to say: "When you make love to a gorilla, you don't quit when you're tired. You quit when the *gorilla* is tired!"

*

When an American became the first man to walk on the moon, a Russian official in the Russian space program reassured his colleagues. "Don't worry," he told them, "we will be the first nation to put a cosmonaut on the sun."

"But comrade," one cosmonaut said, "we will be burned alive!"

"Do you think I am ignorant?" replied the official. "You need have no fear. We will plan it so that you can complete your landing at night."

*

A woman who was new to this country went to the supermarket. She returned home and told her husband she would never learn to cope with our American system. "I had a list of thirty items," she told her husband. "And I had sixteen coupons, but ten had expired. I gave them a check written on our out-of-town account, and they said it would take seven days to clear. I put all the items back on the shelves. In this country, I'll die of hunger!"

*

Frequently, the subject comes up about whether the Japanese are better managers of their employees than we are here in the States.

Abraham Maslow, a famous psychologist, believed that there is a capacity in each of us for self-actualization. "Within us," he wrote, are "capacities clamoring to get out." It was his contention that the urge for accomplishment and esteem could be unleashed by tapping into an individual's inner resources. Perhaps the Japanese are, indeed, better business managers because they are adept at tapping such inner resources in their employees.

*

True Polish jokes are not the odious ethnic ones most of us frown on. They are ironic and subtle criticisms (usually originating in Poland) about the social system under which the Polish people have lived for so many years. Many of these jokes revolve around the relationship between Russia and the Polish people. There is, for example, a wonderful tale about a Polish man who is in Russia and wants to know the time. He sees a man carrying two heavy suitcases and asks him if he knows what time it is. The Russian puts down the bags, looks at his watch, and tells the Polish man, "It is 10:17 and 12 seconds, the date is April 22nd, and the atmospheric pressure is on the rise."

The Polish visitor is amazed and asks if the watch providing all this information was made in Japan. "No," says the Russian, "it's a product of Soviet technology." The Pole expresses his admiration and congratulates him. "Yes," says the Russian, straining to pick up the two suitcases, "but these batteries are still a little heavy."

*

A Polish joke book entitled *Kawal Polski* (A Piece of Poland) offers five rules of socialism:

1. Don't think.
2. If you do think, don't speak.
3. If you think and speak, don't write.
4. If you think, speak, and write, don't sign.
5. And if you think, speak, write, and sign, don't be surprised.

*

An American visiting Russia asked a Russian professor of law to explain the difference between the Russian constitution and the American one. "Under the Russian constitution," said the professor, "the citizens are guaranteed freedom of speech. But under the American one, they are guaranteed freedom *after* speech."

*

When Nikita Khrushchev was in power, he himself, it is said, told the story about the Russian who ran through the Kremlin shouting, "Khrushchev is a fool! Khrushchev is a fool!" He was sentenced, the premier said, to twenty-three years in prison: three for insulting the party secretary and twenty for revealing a state secret.

*

When John F. Kennedy was president, China still had a closed-door policy, and the United States had little contact with that country. Kennedy and Premier Khrushchev were having a discussion about the nuclear test ban, and Kennedy made a point by using the Chinese proverb, The journey of a thousand miles begins with one step.

"You seem to know the Chinese," said Khrushchev. To which Kennedy replied, "We may both get to know them better."

If you are in an industry with which the Japanese are just starting to provide competition, you can follow that story by saying, "As for the Japanese, we in our industry may soon be getting to know them better!"

*

"We have no eternal allies and we have no perpetual enemies." [Viscount Henry John Palmerston]

*

An American is boasting to a Russian visitor that the United States is so great, has such great freedom of speech, that she can stand in front of the White House and yell, "To hell with George Bush!" To which the Russian replies: "So what? I can stand in front of the Kremlin and yell, 'To hell with George Bush,' too."

*

In these days of shortages in the Soviet Republic, they tell the story of a Russian man who goes to the official agency in charge of automobiles and puts down his deposit on a car. He is told that he can take delivery of it in ten years. "Morning or afternoon?" the purchaser asks. "What difference does it make, ten years from now?" asks the clerk. "Well," says the car buyer, "the plumber's coming in the morning."

*

In talking to the international press corps, President Mikhail Gorbachev told a joke about himself, President François Mitterrand,

and President Bush. "They say that Mitterrand has a hundred lovers. One has AIDS, but he doesn't know which one," President Gorbachev said. "Bush has a hundred bodyguards. One is a terrorist, but he doesn't know which one.

"Gorbachev has a hundred economic advisers. One is smart, but he doesn't know which one."

*

Alberta Wright, American owner of the Paris branch of an American restaurant, is reported to have said of Paris, "This isn't a city, this is *art!*"

*

"Where justice is, there is my country." [Polish saying]

*

Advertising slogans, when translated into other languages, sometimes misfire, as when the Pepsi slogan, "Come alive with Pepsi!" was translated into German. In translation, the slogan said, "Come out of the grave with Pepsi!" Elsewhere, it was translated as "Pepsi brings your ancestors back from the grave!"

General Motors also had a problem when it prepared to market the Chevy Nova in Puerto Rico and had to change its whole marketing strategy because in Spanish *no va* means "won't go."

And then there's the U.S. airline that advertised its "rendezvous lounges" on flights to Brazil. They lost a lot of customers. In Portuguese, *rendezvous* means "a place to have sex."

*

A comedian in a dictator-run country dared to make this comment in talking to an American: "In a democracy like yours, you are all equal before the law. In a dictatorship like ours, we are all equal before the police."

*

When Ferdinand Marcos headed the Philippine government, it was no secret to the Filipinos that his wife, Imelda, was a big spender. In fact, the Marcoses were secretly referred to as The Mink Dynasty.

*

There are places in this world where my remarks might be misunderstood, not because others lack in understanding, but because our ways are not always the ways of others. Much of what we think and do would be puzzling in other lands. Americans don't always recognize this.

For example, the actor Donald Swann tells about an Indian man he sat next to on a flight from Fiji to Calcutta. The Indian was completely baffled by the breakfast served on their Pan Am jet. First, he poured his coffee into the cornflakes and ate them. Then he mixed the milk and the sugar and drank it. Next, he licked the butter from the small square of paper. And for a chaser, he drank the melted marmalade.

*

Replying to a reporter's question, Joan Rivers said: "Am I interested in foreign affairs? My idea of foreign affairs is a motel room with Julio Iglesias!"

DOCTORS, LAWYERS, INDUSTRY CHIEFS

Needling the Untouchables

Our feelings about successful professionals and businesspeople are often mixed. When we are in need of a doctor or lawyer, it's not uncommon for us to say, "I want the *best*." Such confidence and loyalty, while necessary and admirable, often carry with them the seeds of resentment: "Why does he charge so much? Doesn't he like me?" "How come he's so smart? If I had the time to study law, wouldn't I be just as smart?" "What makes him more successful than I am? Did he inherit it or get some of the breaks I never had?"

Because there is often some safely concealed hostility beneath the outward show of respect for doctors, lawyers, and industry heads, just about everyone enjoys a little public needling at the expense of these three groups of professionals—especially since it's so difficult to rib them individually when you may be at their mercy! Can you imagine saying to your surgeon—just after she has informed you that she will have to operate on your gallbladder—"I hope you leave me with enough gall, doc, to complain about your bill!" Or imagine telling the convalescing chairman of the board of the company you work for, "The board of directors voted to wish you a speedy recovery—by a vote of four to three!"

Obviously, anyone even marginally interested in survival is going to refrain from making such remarks on a person-to-person basis. But let a speaker say the same things from the platform, and laughter convulses the audience. After all, doc, the speaker's only making a little joke, right?

Audiences that are themselves made up of doctors, lawyers, or industry bigwigs are also quick to respond to humor aimed at them as a group. Although the same barb in a one-on-one conversation might offend, it will usually evoke good-natured laughter when used before a group. Because, of course, it's the *other* guy the speaker's talking about, isn't it?

A good deal of the material in this section is interchangeable among groups. For example, you will find under "Doctors" a comment about an admirable surgeon who "never operates unless he *really* [pause] needs the money." Talking to, or about, lawyers, a speaker can easily adapt that line by referring to a lawyer "who never suggests a lawsuit unless he *really* [pause] needs the fee."

So whether you're looking for suitable material concerning doctors, lawyers, or industry chiefs, read this entire section. If you don't find what you need under a specific category, chances are you'll find something referring to one of the other categories of "successfuls" that can be adapted for use in your talk.

Doctors

"The only solid piece of scientific truth about which I feel totally confident is that we are profoundly ignorant about nature. Indeed, I regard this as the major discovery of the past one hundred years of biology." [Lewis Thomas, M.D.]

*

If you are a physician speaking to a large group, try this line shortly after your opening comments:

I like talking to a captive audience. Two hundred sitting ducks listening to a quack.

*

"To lose one's health renders science null, art inglorious, strength unavailing, wealth useless, and eloquence powerless." [Herophilus]

*

There is an old saying that tells us God cures, and the doctor takes the fee.

*

Some people think of a dentist's office as a filling station.

*

Most doctors today specialize. My own doctor's specialty seems to be banking.

*

Of course, there are some doctors who don't charge very much. They're the ones who can bring illness within the reach of anyone.

*

We physicians have all had hypochondriacs as patients, but I recently had one that takes the cake. He told me he was certain he was dying of a fatal disease of the liver. I told him: "You have to be wrong. With that particular ailment there's no pain or discomfort of any kind." "Good God!" he cried. "My symptoms exactly!"

*

Dental bills are so high today that the American Dental Association is thinking of changing its motto to this: Put Your Money Where Your Mouth Is.

*

A man called a plumber to make a minor repair. The plumber fixed the trouble in about five minutes. When asked for his bill, the plumber said it was seventy-five dollars. The homeowner was aghast. "Good grief," he said, "we only pay our doctor fifty dollars for a house call, and he usually spends fifteen or twenty minutes here."

"Yes," said the plumber, "I know. That was what I used to get when I was a doctor."

*

An old French saying tells us: He is a fool who makes his physician his heir.

*

Three surgeons—an Englishman, a Frenchman, and a Russian—met

at an international medical convention and were discussing who
had accomplished the most during his career.

The Englishman described some delicate brain surgery he had
performed, in which he had helped the patient regain his speech.
He felt that he had not only saved the patient but given him a
renewed desire to live.

The Frenchman then said: "That is much to be admired. But
I have performed a heart transplant, and the patient—father of six
children—lived for more than a year."

The Russian spoke up. "I believe I made medical history," he
said, "when I performed my first operation, removing a man's tonsils."

"What was so unusual about a tonsillectomy?" asked the other
two medical men.

"Ah!" said the Russian. "You must understand that in Russia
our people are deathly afraid to open their mouths. So I had to
approach it from another angle."

*

This story points up how times have changed:

A doctor I know told his nurse to send a blood sample out for a
Wassermann test for a young girl he had just examined. "She's
getting married, you know," he said to the nurse.
"Really?" she replied in surprise. "I didn't even know she was
pregnant."

*

A psychiatrist on a television talk show was asked if he could give
young people any advice on how to have a successful marriage. He
answered: "Yes. Keep your eyes wide open before marriage and
half shut afterward."

*

A doctor had just been introduced to the audience he was to address.
He was described in the introduction as being noble, kind, dedicated,
painstaking, and much beloved by patients and fellow physicians
alike. When he rose to speak, he leaned into the microphone and
said, "However, I do not walk on water."

*

A virus is something originated by a doctor whose wife wanted a diamond ring.

*

"Medicare and Medicaid are the greatest measures yet devised to make the world safe for clerks." [Peter Drucker]

*

The first thing they teach you in medical school is how to check a pulse. The second thing is how to check a credit rating.

*

Physicians, both individually and as part of various groups, are vitally interested in the subject of legal abortions. This story is often told by one faction: Margaret Costanza, a White House adviser to Jimmy Carter, was known for her pro-choice position, which differed from that of the president's. She was heard to comment, "If it were up to the politicians, women would have the right to an abortion, but they'd have to report the pregnancy within forty-eight hours, then be examined by two doctors, two senators, and the Speaker of the House."

*

Before he became a jurist and a writer, Oliver Wendell Holmes was a practicing physician. Some patients questioned whether he was a very serious doctor because, for a while, he had a sign posted in his office that read: Small Fevers Gratefully Received.

*

If you have a patient who winces when you mention what the operation is going to cost, you can always offer to retouch the X rays instead.

*

"We think in youth that our bodies are identical with ourselves and have the same interests, but discover later in life that they are heartless companions who have been accidentally yoked with us, and who are as likely as not, in our extreme sickness or old age, to treat us with less mercy than we would have received at the hands of the worst bandits." [Rebecca West]

*

Tom Masson, a magazine editor, once said, "To feel themselves in the presence of true greatness, many men find it necessary only to be alone." There are many surgeons who would fully understand this.

*

It is easier to like a doctor than an artist, for science reassures, while art disturbs.

*

"A drug is a substance which, if injected into an animal, produces a paper." [Otto Loewi]

*

A doctor told a patient he would have to enter a hospital. The patient refused. "Only a fool donates his body to medical science *before* death," he said. [from *A Life* by Hugh Leonard]

*

There are some gastroenterologists who are awfully quick to suggest to their patients that they undergo a G.I. series or a barium enema or both for diagnostic purposes. In my opinion, anyone who wants to make a living folding parachutes ought to be required to jump frequently.

*

If you asked a doctor what you should give the girl who has everything, chances are he'd say, "Penicillin."

*

Many people, when introduced to a doctor, will immediately ask, "A dentist-doctor or a doctor-doctor?" or, sometimes, "M.D. or Ph.D.?" Some degree of snobbery does exist when it comes to the use of the word *doctor* for other than medical people. For example, I once heard a story about the famous physicist Robert Millikan. He was passing through the foyer of his home and heard the maid answering the telephone. "Yes," she said, "this is Dr. Millikan's residence, but he's not the kind of doctor who does anybody any good."

*

It was Maimonides who told us that it is the job of a doctor "to cure sometimes, to relieve often, to comfort always."

*

We doctors are never as good as our patients say we are when we cure them. And we are never as bad as they say we are when they get our bill.

*

Minor surgery is what they do to someone else.

*

There are, of course, different ways in which a doctor can offer advice and instructions to a patient. One doctor, in talking to a portly patient, told him, "Follow this diet, and in a couple of months I want to see three fourths of you back here for a checkup."

*

Then there's the doctor who discovered what his patient had—and took most of it.

*

When you ask a doctor to tell you what an internist is, she can only define it by telling you what an internist is not. Similarly, we can probably define integrity best by saying what it is not. It is not being slick. It is not being evasive. It is not being arrogant. It is not given to half-truths.

*

Albert Camus, afflicted by tuberculosis, wrote, "Illness is a convent, which has its rules, its austerity, its silences, and its inspirations."

*

"I've got four kids and not one of them will come when I call. They'll probably grow up to be doctors." [Jackie Vernon]

*

The average obstetrician is so busy that I can well believe this story told to me by a friend who was waiting for someone in the lobby of a hospital. Two anxious young fathers-to-be had been pacing back and forth in the lobby for quite a time when a harassed-looking medico came out of the elevator. He was still in his surgical gown, with his mask dangling below his chin. Both young men rushed toward him. "Take it easy, take it easy," he said to them. "You're both fathers. One of you had a girl, and one of you had a boy. But I can't remember which was which."

*

He is not only a fine psychiatrist but one given to good works as well. I'm told he spends one night a week at [name of local hospital] teaching nervous people how to eat Jell-O.

*

The real reason surgeons wear masks has nothing to do with germs. It's so that you can't identify them when you get to the courtroom.

*

"Clearly, in a time when there is a demand for perfect health, perfect sex, and immortality, any open-ended health system will be under strain. When people were threatened with smallpox, they didn't worry about how many orgasms they were having." [Teeling Smith]

*

A man got off a train at a suburban stop and walked over to the nearby office of the local general practitioner, an M.D. he had never met. He told the doctor that his wife was ill, that it was an emergency, and that he would be grateful if the doctor could make a house call. The doctor agreed to go, and together they drove in the doctor's car quite a distance to the outskirts of town. When they drove up the man's driveway, the man said to the doctor, "I know this may seem strange to you, but could I pay you in advance?"

The doctor allowed as how it was, indeed, strange, but said, "If you insist, my fee is thirty-five dollars." The man paid the doctor and then, a bit embarrassed, said, "I think my wife is feeling better now, doctor; you really don't need to come in."

The doctor was amazed and asked for an explanation. "Well, doctor," the man told him, "those bastards at the taxi stand near the station wanted fifty dollars to bring me out here, and I had heard that you were cheaper!"

*

Hans Neumann, M.D., when he was director of preventive medicine for the city of New Haven, Connecticut, was called upon to address a youthful audience on the subject of social diseases. The moderator introduced him in glowing terms, citing his vast experience and background, but used such euphemistic terms as *preventive medicine* and *social diseases* to describe the topic under discussion. After acknowledging the fine introduction, Dr. Neumann faced his audience and said: "Actually, my qualifications for speaking here today could have been given in a single sentence. I am the man responsible for all venereal disease in New Haven."

> *This line could be adapted by doctors in other specialties. For example, a cardiologist could say, "I'm the man responsible for all the heart attacks at Mt. Sinai Hospital," or "I'm the man responsible for all the cirrhosis of the liver in this community," and so on.*

*

He's the kind of surgeon I like. He never operates unless he *really* [pause] needs the money.

*

Will Rogers once said that the best doctor in the world was the veterinarian. He can't ask the patient where it hurts or what's the matter . . . he just has to *know*.

*

Most doctors know themselves to be men of science and have taught their wives to treat them as such. The wife of a doctor friend of mine went into a fabric store to buy some material for a negligee. She asked the clerk for nine yards.

"Madam," he said, "this is very wide material, and you appear to be no more than a size ten or twelve. I really think that two or two and a half yards would be sufficient."

"Oh, no!" said the doctor's wife. "You see, my husband is a scientist. And he'd rather look for it than find it."

*

As is the custom in this country, two strangers shared a hospital room. One had been in and out of hospitals a number of times and felt superior to her roommate when it came to the subject of illness. "Tell me," she inquired, "are you a medical or a surgical patient?" Her roommate said she didn't understand the question.

The knowledgeable one retorted, "What that means is, were you sick when you came in, or did they make you sick after you got here?"

*

During a recent strike of the sanitation-men's union, a homeowner was heard to remark that today's garbage collectors are like today's doctors. "Neither of them," said the homeowner, "will make house calls."

*

A doctor came into a patient's hospital room and told the patient's husband to wait outside while he examined his wife. A few minutes later, the doctor came out and asked a nurse's aide if she could get him a pair of pliers. She did, and he went back into the patient's room. Five minutes later, he came out and asked for a screwdriver, which he again took into the patient's room. When he came out a third time and asked for a hammer, the anxious husband demanded to know what was wrong with his wife. "I don't know yet," said the doctor. "I can't get my bag open."

*

"A good surgeon is a good medical man who can cut." [Thomas Fuller]

*

A new patient confessed to her doctor that she had already consulted a faith healer, a palm reader, and a guru. "And," asked the doctor, "what foolish advice did they give you?"

"They all told me to see you," said the patient.

*

Psychiatrists today have gone back to using shock treatment. They send you the bill in advance.

*

"Last week I sat in my doctor's waiting room so long I finally said

to hell with it. I decided to go home and die a *natural* death instead."
[Phyllis Diller]

*

Just remember that 50 percent of all doctors graduated in the bottom
half of the class.

Lawyers

"One man's justice is another man's injustice." [Ralph Waldo Emer-
son]

*

They say that lawyers are cold, manipulative, without compassion.
I don't believe that, but lots of people do. Take the story of a man
who needs a heart transplant. His doctor tells him he has a choice
between receiving the heart of a twenty-five-year-old Olympic run-
ner and that of a sixty-year-old lawyer. "Easy," says the patient,
"I'll take that of the lawyer." The doctor is amazed. "Why," he
asks, "would you take a sixty-year-old heart rather than one that's
twenty-five?" To which the patient replies, "I want one that's never
been used."

> *This story can, of course, be used in talking about cold-
> hearted Hollywood producers, surgeons, corporate execu-
> tives, real estate agents, IRS auditors, and so on.*

*

"A good and faithful judge prefers what is right to what is expe-
dient." [Horace]

*

Bob Hope accepted an invitation to address a convention of the
American Bar Association. In opening he said: "My being here results
from a slight misunderstanding. I thought I was to talk to the
American *Bra* Association."

*

When a lawyer was asked if he'd like to become a Jehovah's Witness, he replied that even though he hadn't actually seen the accident, he'd like to take the case.

*

Everyone in my family follows the medical profession. They're all lawyers.

*

A priest, a doctor, and a lawyer all arrive in heaven at the same time. Saint Peter tells them they will be assigned places to live, and he first shows the priest his new residence. It's a lovely cottage surrounded by flower beds and a flowing stream. The priest seems pleased. Then he shows the doctor his new home, which is a rather palatial house with a great view. When the foursome get to the lawyer's home, they find it to be a mansion, with a swimming pool, a sauna, a tennis court, and other luxuries.

The doctor and priest express some curiosity about why the lawyer got a residence so vastly superior to theirs. "Well," says Saint Peter, "we get a lot of priests here and quite a few doctors. But this is our first lawyer."

*

"The safety of the people is the highest law." [Cicero]

*

A lawyer who was to give an after-dinner speech received a very impressive introduction. She was described in glowing terms as a woman who was "one in a million," "out of the ordinary," "virtually unique in her profession," and so on. On the way home from the dinner, she remarked to her husband—who had been present—that it was surprising how few extraordinary people there were in the legal profession. "Yes," he replied, "and there is even one less than you believe."

*

I remember that Theodore Roosevelt once told us, "It is difficult to improve our material condition by the best laws, but it is easy enough to ruin it by bad laws."

*

The Italians have a saying, No one likes justice brought home to his own door.

*

Today's Yuppie lawyers don't cry. They just Saab.

*

I'm not going to tell you folks that lawyers are foxy. If you watch the TV shows, you already know this. But the concept does put me in mind of the story about a doctor, a businessman, and a lawyer who attended a funeral in Egypt, where it is still customary upon the death of a loved one for mourners to put some money in the grave with the deceased. The businessman took a one-hundred-dollar bill out of his wallet and placed it on the coffin. Then the doctor did likewise. The lawyer whipped out his checkbook, wrote a check for three hundred dollars, put it on the coffin, and removed the two hundred dollars cash.

*

"A man has to live with himself. He should see to it that he always has good company." [Charles Evans Hughes]

*

The best advice any lawyer can follow is that given by Martin W. Littleton: "Be sure of the facts, know the law, and give them hell."

*

The following passage by Theodore Roosevelt is an excellent way for an industry leader—or any professional or government figure—to reply to criticism that has been leveled against that person or his or her organization:

"It is not the critic who counts, nor the one who points out how the strong man stumbled or how the doer of deeds might have done them better.

"The credit belongs to the man who is actually in the arena, whose face is marred with sweat and dust and blood; who strives valiantly; who errs and comes short again and again; who knows the great enthusiasms, the great devotions, and spends himself in a worthy cause; who, if he wins, knows the triumph of high achievement; and who, if he fails, at least fails while daring greatly, so that his place shall never be with those cold and timid souls who know neither victory nor defeat."

*

It is much better not to have caught a rogue than to catch him and let him go again.

*

Whenever I think of lawyers, I remember the prosecuting attorney who summed up before a jury with these words: "And those, ladies and gentlemen, are the conclusions upon which I base my facts."

*

As every good lawyer knows, it takes wit to pick a lock and steal a horse but wisdom to let them alone.

*

Law cannot persuade where it cannot punish.

*

There is an old Spanish saying that tells us: Fools and the perverse fill the lawyer's purse.

*

Lawyers are very much like painters. They find it easy to turn white into black.

*

It is said by the Italians that he who buys the office of magistrate must of necessity sell justice.

*

"The law is a jealous mistress and requires a long and constant courtship." [Joseph Story]

*

We enact many laws that manufacture criminals, and then a few that punish them." [B. R. Tucker]

*

"Human spirit should be liberated but it should be controlled by a sense of justice." [A. K. Sen]

*

"Our nation is founded on the principle that observance of the law is the eternal safeguard of liberty, and defiance of the law is the surest road to tyranny." [John F. Kennedy]

*

In *Gulliver's Travels*, Swift wrote about lawyers. "Laws," he wrote, "are best explained, interpreted, and applied by those whose interest and abilities lie in perverting, confounding, and eluding them."

*

A doctor, a lawyer, and a banker were on a yacht that sank, and they were faced with a swim through shark-infested waters. The banker went first and was snapped up instantly. The doctor went next and nearly reached shore when he, too, was swallowed up. Came the lawyer's turn and the sharks moved aside to create a neat channel for his safe passage to shore. Later, he was able to explain this miracle to friends. "Professional courtesy," he said.

*

Is there any significance in the fact that attorneys are always described as "practicing"?

*

More than 2,000 years ago, Cato the Elder, one of the chief statesmen of the Roman Republic, told the judges, "Those who do not prevent crimes when they might, encourage them."

*

A good lawyer makes a bad neighbor.

*

"The thing we call law is mainly a device for enforcing respect for custom, and the moral principles which it relies upon to give it dignity are often very dubious and tend to change as readily as the folkways change." [H. L. Mencken]

*

A lawyer and a doctor were arguing about the relative merits of their professions. "I don't say," insisted the doctor, "that all lawyers are thieves. But you'll have to admit that your profession does not make angels of men."

"You're right," answered the lawyer. "We leave that up to you doctors!"

*

"The only point in having laws is to make life work. Otherwise, there will be explosions." [Arnold Toynbee]

*

"At his best, man is the noblest of all animals; separated from law and justice, he is the worst." [Aristotle]

*

"No law is entirely convenient for everyone. This alone is required: that it be good for the majority." [Livy]

*

"The law is a sort of hocus-pocus science that smiles in your face while it picks your pocket." [Charles Macklin]

*

There are three steps in the maturation of a lawyer. He must first get on, then get honor, and then get honest.

*

"If one man is allowed to determine for himself what is law, every man can. That means first chaos, then tyranny." [Justice Felix Frankfurter]

*

Not all legal decisions are logical. The District of Columbia Court of Appeals recently ruled that Breathalyzer tests for drunk drivers are illegal unless the driver is sober enough to give voluntary and informed consent.

Industry Chiefs

"A vital factor in morale is the posture of the chairman. If he is miserable and exhibits his misery, it will filter down through the ranks, and make the whole company miserable. The Chairman must make conscious efforts to be contagiously cheerful and confident." [David Ogilvy]

*

A successful industry leader, asked his formula for success, commented: "Don't learn the tricks of the trade. Learn the trade."

*

Business today is organized like the army, with officers of different grades and importance. Employees don't wear uniforms or have stripes and bars, so they have to find other ways in which their importance can be spotted. One way to distinguish rank is to observe what time a person gets to work. If the individual arrives around ten o'clock in the morning, then you can be sure that person is an executive. If a person usually comes in around nine thirty, it would indicate that he or she has some authority as a manager or as the head of a department. If the employee punches a clock before nine, that individual is a clerk or someone else with some special training. But if a person shows up before eight o'clock in the morning, then he or she is most likely the president of the company.

*

One of my friends, the chairman of a large corporation, told me that he spends most of his time at the office in thinking and little in doing the day-to-day work. I asked him how he justifies this to his board of directors. "I explain," he replied, "that most of the matters before me are uninteresting, unrewarding, and unworthy of my time."

*

What happens all too often in business when you try to fill an executive position is that it takes a year to find the man and then another year to find him out. Then you start all over again.

*

The task of a leader is to fan the spark of curiosity and nurture the seeds of creativity. It is also the leader's job to transmit the conscience of the company, to communicate the excitement inherent in the business, and to promote imaginative and courageous behavior in the individual striving for the corporate good.

*

The trouble with getting to be high up in the business world is that your whole life revolves around protocol, alcohol, and Geritol.

*

A banker has been defined as a man who will lend you money when you don't need it and won't lend it to you when you do.

*

An industry leader, asked for advice on how to be successful, said simply, "A winner never quits, and a quitter never wins."

*

Sam Bronfman, the late CEO of the Seagram Company, entered a crowded conference room and, anxious to get on with the meeting, plopped into the nearest chair. One of his young assistants cried out, "No, no, Mister Sam, you're supposed to sit here at the head of the table!"

"Young man," said Bronfman, "*wherever* I sit is the head of the table!"

*

W. Willard Wirtz once commented, "The divine right of the successful is as false a notion as the divine right of kings." Unfortunately, too many successful men have not yet learned this.

*

Criteria for judging business executives vary from company to company. I lean to the point of view expressed by Eli Ginzberg in *The Development of Human Resources*. He says: "More frequently than not, an executive who gets along easily with others, who does not fight too hard for his position, who is willing to see the point of view of the other fellow, especially if the other fellow is his superior, gains a reputation of being constructive and cooperative. And that he is.

"The question remains, however, what else is he?"

*

One of the things a chairman of the board quickly learns is that the mere act of his being promoted into the position has helped him to acquire a number of business associates whose principal activity is waiting for him to retire.

To illustrate: A chairman was suddenly stricken with an illness that required some surgery, and as he was wheeled from the operating room he was handed a telegram that he managed to open and read. The wire was signed by his company's board of directors, and it read, "We wish you a speedy recovery—by a vote of four to three!"

*

One industry leader was known as a great planner but one who did not care to do the work necessary to follow through on his plans. A critic of his commented, "He sets a beautiful table but is not interested in sitting through the meal, and he's definitely not interested in cleaning up."

*

At his retirement party, the head of a company had this to say: The trouble with having money to burn is that it usually comes after the fire has gone out.

*

As he walked through our offices one day, I heard the president of our company comment that it was his belief that people should work after the age of 65. "I also think," he added, "that it wouldn't do them any harm to work before that either."

*

We all know that many pressured executives have low boiling points. However, in business—as in life generally—you can measure a man by the size of the things that make him angry.

*

The trouble with the top brass in big corporations is that when men are treated like God, they begin to feel they *are* God.

*

A corporate executive, caught in the top-management shuffle that followed the merging of his company with another, was asked what it was like to work for a newly merged outfit. "Well," he said, "it's rather like being a mushroom. First, they keep you in the dark. Then they throw dung all over you. And then they *can* you."

*

The story is told of a corporate head who had to travel frequently on business. Unfortunately, she had a fear of flying. Asked by a reporter whether flying did, indeed, make her nervous, she replied: "No, flying doesn't make me nervous. Only one time, when a flight attendant opened the door to the cockpit and I saw a thousand and one lights and dials and switches and buttons—and over them all hung a statue of Saint Christopher—*that* made me nervous."

*

"Don't envision your own funeral procession as a line of Cadillac limousines with an armored car full of cash bringing up the rear. Either the government will get the bulk of it in estate taxes, or you will have taken advantage of the opportunity to minimize your tax by giving away enough of your money." [Eliot Janeway]

*

Because of urban problems, many businesses have moved to the suburbs. One of the cities that has been hit hard in this respect is Detroit. In fact, at a recent banquet of the Detroit Press Club, a banner in the dining room read, "Will the last company to leave Detroit please turn off the lights?"

*

"If sacrifices are needed, the reasons must be carefully explained. If lifestyles are to be altered, taxes raised, and consumption reduced, we must make every effort to justify these steps to a public that is too often skeptical of our motives and suspicious of our good faith." [David Rockefeller]

*

A man who boasted that he was the dominant factor in his household explained it this way: "My wife is permitted to carry on her illusion of importance by making the unimportant decisions. For example, I let her decide what community we'll live in, what schools the kids will go to, where and when we will take our vacation, and so on. I, on the other hand, decide the *important* things, such as whether to impose import duties on foreign cars, how much money we should allocate for the exploration of outer space, and how to shrink the federal deficit."

*

Although the following line was used in connection with a law firm, you can apply it to your own company, whatever your field of endeavor, if it is appropriate:

President Kennedy appointed to office several men from Adlai Stevenson's Chicago law firm. Mr. Stevenson remarked, "I regret that I have but one law firm to give to my country."

*

Wall Street is the only place where a man can spend one week on the cover of *Time* and the next week doing it.

PROVERBS

Letting the Sages of the Ages Say It for You

The best way to describe a proverb is to say that it is a simple truth that can apply to many different situations and that has been repeated so often it is accepted as truth.

For both the public speaker and the conversationalist, the proverb is an ideal way to punch home a point by saying, in effect, "Look, I'm not the only one who believes this; its wisdom is evidenced by the fact that sages have repeated it through the ages, making it an eternal truth."

It's not important for our purposes here to go into the ways that maxims, platitudes, and proverbs differ. (If you care, *Webster's* will help you understand the slender lines of difference.) This section takes a broad and practical approach to the sort of proverb material you might be able to use in a speech or conversation.

I have not included the hundreds of commonplace proverbs we all learned as children: "A penny saved is a penny earned," "All that glitters is not gold," "Look before you leap," and so on. Your library is full of books containing thousands of such lines. Instead, I have selected only material that can serve an adult speaker addressing a contemporary audience. Do not, however, expect to find here only sayings that you've never heard before. One of the characteristics of the proverb is its familiarity; in fact, the majority of proverbs are very old. "There's many a slip 'twixt the cup and the lip" goes back to an old Greek myth. "Cast not your pearls before swine" can be traced back to the Bible. Some are from inscriptions on the walls of ancient temples, while still others are the punch lines or morals of early fables.

On the other hand, new proverbs are being created all the time. Some come into vogue for a period, then die out; others last, seemingly forever. Many of the longer-lasting proverbs contain some moral or ethical truth, handy to use when a speaker wants to sermonize but is uncomfortable about doing so. The moralistic proverb provides an excellent device for making your point without having to take personal responsibility for it.

Where a proverb is characteristic of a national philosophy (that is, typically Arabian, French, German, and so on), I have indicated its origin—as I know it. In most cases, the first use of a proverb is difficult to ascertain as it may often show up in several languages simultaneously.

Since we rarely know the name of the person who first used a proverb, it isn't necessary to credit the line to anyone when you quote it, although you may want to state the country of origin, when known, if you think it lends some special authority to the point you're making.

As you read through these proverbs, some will instantly strike you as applicable to points you want to make in your talk. In some cases, it will be necessary for you to lead into your proverb with a phrase or sentence of your own creation. For instance, let's assume you have been negotiating to attain certain objectives for a group you represent. In reporting back to your group, you have just advised them that all the objectives have not been achieved yet and that you plan to go on arguing for them. At this point, two proverbs in the following pages might serve you well. "However," you go on to tell your group, *"when you have a stubborn mule, you need a stubborn driver.* And I am just that. I will stubbornly persist in my negotiations, knowing full well—as the old saying goes—that *nothing is impossible to a willing mind.* And I am more than willing to go on trying to reach our objectives."

Or perhaps you are giving a political speech rebutting something your opponent has unjustly accused you of. You might say something such as this, utilizing two proverbs in this section: "I do not plan to spend all my time up here answering the charges that have been made by my opponent. But *even a lion must defend himself against flies.* I do not mind an honest debate; what I object to is the mudslinging. *If I am to be drowned, let it be in clean water."*

Don't hesitate to dot your talk with proverbial sayings, but stop short of making them a noticeable characteristic of your style. Four or five proverbs in a twenty-five minute speech, for example (or a half hour's conversation), help you hammer home your points while at the same time, they establish you as wise and erudite.

*

Anyone can navigate in fine weather.

*

The goose is only plucked feather by feather.

*

It takes four living men to carry one dead man out of the house.

*

To prophesy is extremely difficult, especially with respect to the future.

*

Hope is a good breakfast but a bad supper.

*

As soon as a man is born he begins to die.

*

An old Indian proverb, often quoted by Nehru, tells us that the two greatest causes of unhappiness are: (one) if a person doesn't get what he wants; and (two) if he or she *does*.

*

He who rides on another man's shoulders sees farther than the one who carries him.

*

When you have a stubborn mule, you need a stubborn driver.

*

It is not the same to talk about bulls as it is to be in the bull ring. [Spanish]

*

Everything must have a beginning, but not everything has an end.

*

The one eyed are kings in the land of the blind.

*

The following three proverbs are variations on a theme:

If you hold hands with the frying pan, you run the risk of being burned.
If you lie down with dogs, you get up with fleas.
He who sups with the devil needs a long spoon.

*

No flies ever get into a closed mouth.

*

A thread will tie an honest man better than a rope will tie a rogue. [Scottish]

*

The best peacemaker is a strong stick.

*

He who tells the truth is in the majority, even though he be one. [Middle Eastern]

*

He who talks about what does not concern him will hear something displeasing.

*

He who knows not and knows not that he knows not is a fool—shun him;
He who knows not and knows that he knows not is ignorant—teach him;
He who knows and knows not that he knows is asleep—wake him;
But he who knows and knows that he knows is a wise man—follow him.

*

A hundred friends are not too many; one enemy is. [Russian]

*

Well done is better than well said.

*

Misers make wonderful ancestors.

*

Being content makes poor men rich; discontent makes rich men poor.

*

They who have nothing to trouble them will be troubled at nothing. [Japanese]

*

When you are good to others, you are best to yourself.

*

Admirable is he who can disagree without being disagreeable.

*

The enemy of my enemy is my friend. [Arabian]

*

Only when the well runs dry do we know the value of water.

*

When there are too many cooks in the kitchen, we sometimes fail to get the meal out.

*

"Never measure the height of a mountain until you have reached the top. Then you will see how low it was." [Dag Hammarskjöld]

*

Nothing is impossible to a willing mind.

*

He who is his own enemy cannot be a friend to anyone.

*

When a thing has been done, advice comes too late.

*

Courtesy that is all one-sided cannot last long.

*

There is no such thing as darkness; only a failure to see.

*

It's better to light a small candle than to curse the darkness.

*

One murder makes a villain; millions, a hero.

*

Often, while two dogs are striving for a bone, a third runs away with it.

*

There is a remedy for everything but death. [French]

*

Hate is a bad guide.

*

Even a horse, though he has four feet, occasionally stumbles. [Italian]

*

A good liar has need of a good memory.

*

One cannot ring the bells and also walk in the procession.

*

A door must either be open or shut.

*

Bad news has wings.

*

An ounce of discretion is worth a pound of wisdom.

*

It is harder work getting to hell than to heaven.

*

A foolish consistency is the hobgoblin of little minds.

*

He who knows nothing knows enough if he knows when to be silent.

*

It is better to strive with a stubborn ass than to carry the wood on one's back.

*

A thoroughly wise man knows how to play the fool on occasion.

*

Use it up, wear it out, make it do, or do without. [Colonial maxim]

*

We who do not improve today are bound to grow worse tomorrow.

*

Advice after action is like rain after harvest.

*

You can't judge a ship from the shore.

*

In the final analysis, the foxes all meet at the furrier's.

*

He is lucky who forgets what cannot be mended.

*

In the land of promise, a man may die of hunger.

*

No one knows better where the shoe pinches than the one who wears it.

*

Don't blame the message on the messenger.

*

Well begun is half done.

*

Learned fools are the greatest fools.

*

Thrift is a great form of revenue.

*

An old poacher makes the best gamekeeper.

*

The tree withers long before it falls.

*

No man is a hero to his valet. [German]

*

He who would search for pearls must dive below. [English]

*

A man prepared has half won the battle. [Spanish]

*

They are not all cooks who carry a long knife. [German]

*

If you owe a dog anything, call him "Sir." [Egyptian]

*

Prosperity begets friends; adversity proves them.

*

All war must be for the sake of peace. [Greek]

*

A blind man is no judge of colors.

*

Right is right and wrong is wrong, and it isn't very difficult to tell one from the other.

*

The fewer the words, the better the prayer.

*

A crown is no cure for a headache.

*

All are not asleep who have their eyes shut.

*

Could everything be done twice, everything would be better.

*

He who knows little is confident in everything.

*

It is an equal failing to trust everybody as it is to trust nobody.

*

Creation is seldom without pain.

*

Piety, prudence, wit, and civility are the elements of true nobility.

*

If I am to be drowned, let it be in clean water.

*

If you want to know what a dollar is worth, try to borrow one.

*

Don't be sorry that the bottle is half empty. Be glad that it is half full.

*

The man who doesn't read has no advantage over the man who doesn't know how.

*

Youth lives on hope; old age on remembrance.

*

Open eyes and a closed mouth never did anyone any harm.

*

A father can care for ten children better than ten children can care for one father.

*

Better a red face than a black heart.

*

A man can usually stand his own poverty better than his neighbor's prosperity.

*

Even a lion must defend himself against flies.

*

Fortune gives many too much but no one enough.

*

Deep swimmers and high climbers seldom die in their beds.

*

Work does not make one rich, only round-shouldered. [Russian]

*

Communities begin by building their kitchen. [French]

*

He seeks advice in vain who will not follow it.

*

To be enduring, a peace must be endurable.

*

Patience is the art of hoping.

*

He is like the anchor that is always in the sea yet never learns to swim.

*

He who has been first a novice and then an abbot knows what the boys do behind the altar.

*

If you follow the crowd, you have many companions.

*

By asking for the impossible we obtain the possible.

*

Going on foot is pleasant enough when you have a horse to lead by the bridle.

*

When the house is on fire, it is no time to play chess.

*

Real equality exists only in the cemetery. [German]

*

Profit has a pleasant odor, come whence it will.

*

A jackal is a lion in his own neighborhood. [Bedouin]

*

You can't blame a person for trying to cross a fence where it's lowest.

*

He who builds on the public way must let the people have their say. [German]

*

Larks do not fall ready roasted into the mouth.

*

He has enough to do who holds the handle of the frying pan.

*

If a beard were all, the goat would be king.

*

It is a bad well into which one must put water.

*

Very often, rich parents make poor parents.

*

Only a coward flees from a living enemy—or abuses a dead one.

*

A man suspected is half condemned.

*

When a wolf shows his teeth, he isn't laughing. [Russian]

*

It is foolish to cast nets in a river where there is no fish.

*

When it blows hard, the dirt reaches into high places.

*

To have lost your reputation is to be dead among the living.

*

A danger foreseen is half avoided.

*

A bad compromise is better than a good battle. [Russian]

*

Even the journey of a thousand miles must begin with one step. [Chinese]

*

It's been a long time now since a penny saved was worth writing a proverb about.

*

"Proverbs may not improperly be called the philosophy of the common people." [James Howell]

SPELLBINDERS

---◆◆◆---

Great Orators . . . Memorable Quotes

Platform spellbinders fall into two categories. First, there are those who keep the audience on the edge of its seat because they deliver their message powerfully, sometimes with evangelistic fervor. (*"Ich bin ein Berliner!"*) In the second group are those who, though adequate as speakers, lack the inborn gift of the first group but mesmerize just the same—because of *what* they say or because they enjoy such celebrity status that their words take on added significance.

When speakers have both of these attributes—terrific delivery combined with brilliant words—they are more than public speakers, they are orators. History remembers orators as much for their words as for their deeds. John F. Kennedy, Winston Churchill, and Lee Iacocca are examples of such orators, and in this section I offer a small sample of their memorable quotations. No matter what your personal opinion of these three men may be, you will find in their words a storehouse of usable material: witty lines, humorous stories, and brilliantly phrased gems, many of them adaptable to your own needs.

Examining the excerpts from J.F.K.'s speeches, you notice that his forte was wit but that his compelling style was also characterized by a fearlessness about waxing poetic when the need and the mood of the occasion warranted it. As for content, he never hesitated to ask his audience to join him in reaching for the moon. He asked his listeners to share his vision of the future.

In this century, the true poet laureate of the platform was Winston Churchill. His command of language and prowess in using it surely make him a candidate for the greatest orator in modern times. He had a unique gift for creating a rhetoric that would not be part of the average man's speech; yet while lifting the sights of his audience with exquisite use of language and a dramatic pileup of word upon word ("We shall fight on the beaches, we shall fight on the landing-grounds, we shall fight in the fields and in the streets, we shall fight in the hills. . . ."), he knew enough to avoid phrases that would be difficult for the ear to grasp and comprehend. Unintimidated by the cultural level of his audience, he dared to be poetic, and he awed his listeners with the majesty of his words.

Lee Iacocca tends to go in the other direction. He calls a spade a spade and uses images and analogies that are the common parlance of Everyman and Everywoman. And because his personal conviction is so intense about the matters he addresses from the platform, it is difficult for a listener not to be swayed by his fervor. Although, like John Kennedy, he is known to sometimes use ghostwriters, they are smart enough to pick up not only the flavor but the actual phraseology of Iacocca's unique and earthy form of expression.

In the second group of sought-after public speakers are people such as Henry Kissinger and the late Adlai Stevenson. Neither could cast a spell over an audience the way Kennedy or Churchill could (although Adlai Stevenson came close), but they are men whose words are so profound, so thought provoking that they have been quoted repeatedly. Those who heard Stevenson and Kissinger speak publicly say they will never forget the experience. Both men put me in mind of something Ralph Waldo Emerson wrote: "The eloquent man is he who is no eloquent speaker but who is inwardly drunk with a certain belief."

Adlai Stevenson was the intellectual's speaker; his great strength was with the highly literate. He avoided platitudes even when making campaign speeches, and while using a common sense approach in his speech content, he was always literate and oftentimes profound. He was a master at using anecdotal material in his talks, and his down-to-earth stories helped bridge the gap between his own intellectualism and that of some in his audiences. He also used—to considerable advantage—his ability to laugh at himself by telling humorous, personalized stories.

Henry Kissinger is something else again. His gravelly voice and slight accent do not make for easy transmission through a microphone. Yet audiences hang on his every word, and he is much in demand as a speaker. This doesn't mean that you should use Kissinger as your role model and discount the importance of your own delivery. Unless, of course, in *your* field, you bring the credibility to your remarks that he brings to his. What makes Kissinger such a hot ticket in attracting audiences is a combination of his *opinions* and the credentials that back them up.

A degree of celebrity, along with a quick mind, a facile pen, and something to say, serve to make many people popular on the talk circuit. Gloria Steinem is one such speaker: much in demand, always good on her feet, superb at ad-lib, frequently quoted in the press. While she is not in the same league as Winston Churchill and John Kennedy, you probably aren't either. So it's worth examining how celebrity speakers such as Gloria Steinem make an audience laugh in delight or rise to its feet in applause.

One of Steinem's great assets is her fearlessness. She does not fear offending someone who disagrees with her on a panel nor is she afraid of postplatform repercussions from something she might say. Her courage and forthrightness make her always a delight to hear. In preparing your own talk, consider using a blunt, up-front approach combined with enough humor to make it palatable.

What now follows is a selection of memorable quips and comments made by Kennedy, Churchill, Iacocca, Kissinger, Stevenson, and Steinem.

The ways in which you can use the dozens of items in this section are limited only by your imagination. These wonderful excerpts can also serve you in a secondary way: as standards to which you can aspire in editing your script for quality of expression.

From John F. Kennedy

The problems of the world cannot possibly be solved by skeptics or cynics whose horizons are limited by the obvious realities. We need men who can dream of things that never were . . . and ask, Why not?

Both John and Robert Kennedy were fond of quoting George

Bernard Shaw, who phrased it this way: "Some people see things as they are and ask, Why? I dream dreams that never were and ask, Why not?"

*

Efforts and courage are not enough without purpose and direction.

*

My experience in government is that when things are noncontroversial, beautifully coordinated, and all the rest, it must be that there is not much going on.

*

If men and women are in chains anywhere in the world, then freedom is endangered everywhere.

*

Prestige is not popularity. Prestige is the image which you give of a vital society which persuades other people to follow your leadership.

*

When we got into office, the thing that surprised me most was to find that things were just as bad as we'd been saying they were.

*

At a press conference, a reporter asked President Kennedy how he felt about the fact that the Republican National Committee had adopted a resolution saying he was "pretty much a failure." The president replied, "I assume it passed unanimously."

*

Our goal is to influence history instead of merely observing it.

*

We don't want to be like the leader in the French Revolution who said, "There go my people. I must find out where they are going so I can lead them."

*

The human mind is our fundamental resource.

*

Today . . . every man, woman, and child lives under a nuclear sword of Damocles, hanging by the slenderest of threads, capable of being cut at any moment by accident or miscalculation, or by madness. The weapons of war must be abolished before they abolish us.

*

The more our knowledge increases, the more our ignorance unfolds.

*

I have just received the following telegram from my generous Daddy. It says, "Dear Jack: Don't buy a single vote more than is necessary. I'll be damned if I'm going to pay for a landslide."

*

When President Kennedy was asked to comment on the press's treatment of his administration, he said, "Well, I'm reading more and enjoying it less."

*

Let the word go forth from this time and place to friend and foe alike, that the torch has been passed to a new generation of Americans born to this century and unwilling to witness or permit the slow undoing of those human rights to which we are committed today at home and around the world.

*

Neither smiles nor frowns, neither good intentions nor harsh words, are a substitute for strength.

*

Change is the law of life. And those who look only to the past are certain to miss the future.

*

If we cannot end now our differences, at least we can help make the world safe for diversity. For in the final analysis, our most basic common link is that we all inherit this planet. We all breathe the same air. We all cherish our children's future. And we are all mortal.

*

Let every nation know, whether it wishes us well or ill, that we shall pay any price, bear any burden, meet any hardship, support any friend, oppose any foe, to assure the survival and the success of liberty.

*

We hold the view that the people come first, not the government.

*

Officiating at a ceremony where he was to pull a switch that would activate generators located more than a hundred miles away, President Kennedy commented: "I never know when I press these whether I am going to blow up Massachusetts or start the project."

*

We had an interesting convention in Los Angeles and we ended with a strong Democratic platform which we called "The Rights of Man." The Republican platform has also been presented. I do not know its title, but it has been referred to as "The Power of Positive Thinking."

*

I appreciate your welcome. As the cow said to the Maine farmer, "Thank you for a warm hand on a cold morning."

*

We believe that our society is the best, but that does not mean that it automatically survives.

*

The farmer is the only man in our economy who buys everything he buys at retail, sells everything he sells at wholesale, and pays the freight both ways.

*

In the long history of the world only a few generations have been granted the role of defending freedom in its hour of maximum danger. I do not shrink from this responsibility. I welcome it.

*

Now the trumpet summons us again, not as a call to bear arms, though arms we need; not as a call to battle, though embattled we are; but as a call to bear the burden of a long twilight struggle, a struggle against the common enemies of man—tyranny, poverty, disease, and war itself.

*

On the presidential coat of arms, the American eagle holds in his right talon the olive branch, while in his left is a bundle of arrows. We intend to give equal attention to both.

*

The energy, the faith, the devotion which we bring to this endeavor will light our country and all who serve it, and the glow from that fire can truly light the world.

*

There is always inequity in life. Some men are killed in war and some men are wounded, and some men never leave the country, and some are stationed in the Antarctic and some are stationed in San Francisco. It's very hard in military or in personal life to assure complete equality. Life is unfair.

*

With a good conscience our only sure reward, with history the final judge of our deeds, let us go forth to lead the land we love, asking His blessing and His help, but knowing that here on earth God's work must truly be our own.

*

And so, my fellow Americans, ask not what your country can do for you. Ask what you can do for your country. My fellow citizens of the world, ask not what America will do for you, but what together we can do for the freedom of man.

*

Let both sides explore what problems unite us instead of belaboring those problems which divide us.

*

Actions deferred are all too often opportunities lost.

*

Action and foresight are the only possible preludes to freedom.

*

I do not want it said of our generation, as T. S. Eliot wrote, "These were decent people, their only monument the asphalt road and a thousand lost golf balls." We can do better than that.

*

Those of you who regard my profession of politics with some disdain should remember that it made it possible for me to move from being an obscure lieutenant in the United States Navy to Commander-in-Chief in fourteen years, with very little technical competence.

*

I am concerned with what is on the other side of the moon, but I am also concerned with the condition of life of the man or woman on the other side of the street.

*

A man may die, nations may rise and fall, but an idea lives on. Ideas have endurance without death.

From Winston Churchill

I have always earned my living by the pen and by my tongue.

*

Any clever person can make plans for winning a war if he has no responsibility for carrying them out.

*

Death and sorrow will be the companions of our journey; hardship our garment; constancy and valor our only shield. We must be united, we must be undaunted, we must be inflexible. Our qualities and deeds must burn and glow through the gloom of Europe until they become the veritable beacon of its salvation.

*

Writing a book is an adventure. To begin with, it is a toy and an amusement, then it becomes a master, then it becomes a tyrant. The last phase is that just as you are about to be reconciled to your servitude, you kill the monster, and fling him to the public.

*

In commenting on dictators, Churchill had this to say: "They are afraid of words and thoughts; words spoken abroad, thoughts stirring at home . . . terrify them. A little mouse of thought appears in the room, and even the mightiest potentates are thrown into panic. They make frantic efforts to bar out thoughts and words; they are afraid of the workings of the human mind. Cannons, airplanes, they can manufacture in large quantities; but how are they to quell the natural promptings of human nature, which after all these centuries of trial and progress has inherited a whole armory of potent and indestructible knowledge?"

*

I am certainly not one of those who need to be prodded. In fact, if anything, I am a prod.

*

In commenting upon the horror that English-speaking people have for the one-man power of dictatorships, Churchill said: "They are quite ready to follow a leader for a time, as long as he is serviceable to them; but the idea of handing themselves over, lock, stock, and barrel, body and soul, to one man, and worshiping him as if he were an idol—that has always been odious to the whole theme and nature of our civilization."

*

There are two supreme obligations which rest upon a government. They are of equal importance. One is to strive to prevent war, and the other is to be ready if war should come.

*

Mr. Churchill defined democracy as "the occasional necessity of deferring to the opinions of others."

*

I always avoid prophesying beforehand. It is much better policy to prophesy after the event has already taken place.

*

Civilization will not last, freedom will not survive, peace will not be kept, unless a very large majority of mankind unite together to defend them and show themselves possessed of a constabulary power before which barbaric and atavistic forces will stand in awe.

*

After the battle of Dunkirk, in addressing the House of Commons, Mr. Churchill said: "We shall go on to the end . . . we shall fight on the seas and oceans, we shall fight with growing confidence and growing strength in the air. We shall defend our island, whatever the cost may be. We shall fight on the beaches, we shall fight on the landing-grounds, we shall fight in the fields and in the streets, we shall fight in the hills. We shall never surrender."

*

The finest combination in the world is power and mercy. The worst combination in the world is weakness and strife.

*

Churchill referred to the British victory at Dunkirk as "a miracle of deliverance, achieved by valor, by perseverance, by perfect discipline, by faultless service, by resource, by skill, by unconquerable fidelity."

*

Why is it that from so many lands men look toward us today? It is certainly not because we have gained advantages in a race of armaments, or have scored a point by some deeply planned diplomatic intrigue, or because we exhibit the blatancy and terrorism of ruthless power. It is because we stand on the side of the general need.

*

The day will come when the joy bells will ring again throughout Europe, and when victorious nations, masters not only of their foes but of themselves, will plan and build in justice, in tradition, and in freedom a house of many mansions where there will be room for all.

*

I have derived continued benefit from criticism at all periods of my life, and I do not remember any time when I was ever short of it.

*

I have nothing to offer but blood, toil, tears, and sweat.

*

Churchill was modest on the subject of the important role he played in inspiring his nation during World War II. "It was the nation and the race dwelling around the globe," he said, "that had the lion's heart. I had the luck to be called upon to give the roar. I also hope I sometimes suggested to the lion the right place to use his claws."

*

In referring to one of the members in the House of Commons: "The Honorable Member is never lucky in the coincidence of his facts with the truth."

*

It is a fine thing to be honest, but it is also very important to be right.

*

If the British Empire is fated to pass from life into history, we must hope it will not be by the slow processes of dispersion and decay, but in some supreme exertion for freedom, for right, and for truth.

*

"Can peace, goodwill, and confidence be built upon submission to wrongdoing backed by force? One may put this question in the largest form. Has any benefit or progress ever been achieved by the human race by submission to organized and calculated violence?

As we look back over the long story of the nations, we must see that, on the contrary, their glory has been founded upon the spirit of resistance to tyranny and injustice, especially when these evils seemed to be backed by heavier force.

*

I have always urged fighting wars and other contentions with might and main till overwhelming victory, and then offering the hand of friendship to the vanquished.

*

Come then: let us to the task, to the battle, to the toil—each to our part, each to our station. Fill the armies, rule the air, pour out the munitions, strangle the U-boats, sweep the mines, plow the land, build the ships, guard the streets, succor the wounded, uplift the downcast, and honor the brave. Let us go forward together. There is not a week, nor a day, nor an hour to lose.

*

I am ready to meet my Maker. Whether my Maker is prepared for the great ordeal of meeting me is another matter.

From Lee A. Iacocca

In any kind of competition, the first thing you do is protect yourself. In baseball, the batter protects the plate, and in basketball you protect the lane. In business, you protect your trade secrets. There is nothing wrong with protecting yourself. It's irresponsible and stupid not to.

> In the above comment, Lee Iacocca was referring to pro-
> tectionism in foreign trade. After quoting him, however,
> you might then lead into such other subjects as secrecy in
> time of war, the media, the First Amendment, information
> about movies, new products in the development stage, and
> so on.

*

In a commencement address delivered by Iacocca, he recommended to the graduates that they "use [your] new degree and your common sense to kick America off dead center.

"A little righteous anger really brings out the best in the American personality. Our nation was born when fifty-six patriots got mad enough to sign the Declaration of Independence. We put a man on the moon because Sputnik made us mad at being number two in space. Getting mad in a constructive way is good for the soul—and the country."

*

I am not a jingoist or a saber rattler. I don't believe we need to dominate the world economically, militarily, or any other way. I don't believe in rigging the trade rules to make sure American companies win. But I don't believe in being a patsy either.

*

American entrepreneurship, which used to be based on building better mousetraps, seems to be giving way to leveraged buy-outs and junk bonds. It's becoming a great big Monopoly game with real money. If this keeps up, Wall Street is going to foul its own nest, and we'll all be the losers. The American securities market lubricates our whole economy. We can't afford to . . . let it be manipulated by people out for a quick and dirty buck.

*

If you don't like what you read in the newspaper, you can always crumple up the paper and wrap the fish with it. And if you don't like what's on the tube, you can just hit the button. It's all in your hands—literally.

*

Three years before Desert Storm, Lee Iacocca made this comment: "Take the Persian Gulf problem today. I don't know how we got there, but the specter of the U.S. Navy's making sure Kuwaiti tankers can get safely to Japan carrying oil at fifteen dollars a barrel is a little laughable. It probably costs the U.S. five dollars a barrel to keep the Japanese industrial machine going so that the Japanese can export their industrial goods back to the United States. That's really stretching common sense."

*

Life is full of all sorts of cycles. Some of them are predictable—night follows day; fall follows summer; tides follow the moon. Those are the ones God takes care of. Then there are the ones people take care of: business cycles, energy cycles, automotive cycles. Those we manage to screw up but good.

From Henry A. Kissinger

The longer I am out of office, the more infallible I appear to myself.

*

Existing trends may sometimes appear bleak, but let us not forget that they are the result of decisions by free societies and can therefore be reversed by free decisions.

*

This prediction was made by Kissinger in an address in Pretoria before the South African Institute of International Affairs:
"The history of the remainder of this century will be full of dramatic events, and much of the history of that period will be made on this continent. Your beautiful and dramatic country will be a major actor in the unfolding drama."

*

This job has done wonders for my paranoia. Now I really *have* enemies!

*

After a speech about the Middle East that Kissinger gave at the Center for Strategic & International Studies at Georgetown University, he made this extemporaneous remark: "For a nation with a narrow margin of survival, the dividing line between arrogance and panic, between self-assurance and hysteria, can be very narrow. I would urge some compassion and understanding and a resumption of dialogue."

*

Experience has taught that moral idealism and geopolitical insight are not alternatives but complementary; our civilization may not survive unless we possess *both* in full measure.

*

Democracies have no forum for addressing the future in a concrete way, let alone harmonizing disagreements or implementing common policies.

*

Most of the American public view this country as being relatively unaffected by international economic developments. Our political process has not yet adjusted to the reality that the United States is becoming more integrated into an international economy that is becoming more global.

*

Henry Kissinger has said that modern women leaders are more likely to be protectors than conquerors, that they "tend toward preserving the good and important, but do not conquer new worlds and push off into the future."

*

Both Britain and America have learned that whatever their histories, their futures are part of the common destiny of freedom.

*

Although not known as a man given to excess modesty, Kissinger, when he was President Nixon's adviser for national security affairs, commented: "In the exercise of power, intelligence is not all that important and is often useless. Just as a leader doesn't need intelligence, a man in my job doesn't need too much of it, either."

*

When asked how it felt to have become something of a celebrity, Kissinger commented, "Now when I bore people at a cocktail party, they think it's their fault."

*

Power is the great aphrodisiac.

From Adlai Stevenson

After his defeat in the 1952 presidential campaign, Stevenson commented in an address to a group of reporters: "I have great faith in the people. As to their wisdom, well, Coca-Cola still outsells champagne."

*

If some catastrophe destroyed the things that we have built, we could rebuild them. But if through some catastrophe we lost faith in the principles by which we came to birth and by which we live, we could never return to greatness.

*

I am not sure what it means when one says he is a conservative in fiscal affairs and a liberal in human affairs. I assume what it means is that you will strongly recommend the building of a great many schools to accommodate the needs of our children, but not provide the money.

*

Progress is what happens when impossibility yields to necessity.

*

In replying to a criticism that the wit in his speeches was too highbrow, Stevenson said: "If it is a crime to trust the people's common sense and native intelligence, I gladly plead guilty. I've just been trying to give the customers the right change. That seems to be novel and effete."

*

Those who benefit by the vested privileges or injustices of an existing order always resent and resist change.

*

I pray that the imagination we unlock for defense and arms and outer space may be unlocked as well for grace and beauty in our daily lives. As an economy, we need it. As a society, we shall perish without it.

*

Shortly after being defeated by Eisenhower, Stevenson was late in arriving at an affair where he was scheduled to give a talk. It seems that he had been held up by a military parade. He explained this to his audience and then went on to remark, "Military heroes are always getting in my way."

*

We Americans do not fear the winds of change and the winds of freedom which are blowing across so much of the world. To us they make a wonderful sound; and as the seeds they carry take root and grow, we will feel that America's great purpose in this world is being fulfilled.

*

On accepting the presidential nomination of the Democratic Party in 1952, Governor Stevenson said: "When the tumult and the shouting die, when the bands are gone and the lights are dimmed, there is the stark responsibility in an hour of history haunted with those gaunt, grim specters of strife, dissension, and ruthless, inscrutable, hostile power abroad."

*

In his eulogy for Eleanor Roosevelt, Mr. Stevenson described her as "a woman who spoke for the good toward which man aspires, in a world which has seen too much of the evil of which man is capable."

*

During the Cuban missile crisis in 1962, the Russians argued that the threat to peace had been caused not by the Soviet Union in secretly installing weapons in Cuba but by the United States. To which Mr. Stevenson replied, "This is the first time that I have ever heard it said that the crime is not the burglary, but the discovery of the burglar."

*

It is only by intense thought, by great effort, by burning idealism, and by unlimited sacrifice that freedom has prevailed. And the efforts which were first necessary to create it are fully as necessary to sustain it in our own day.

*

Freedom and security are indivisible . . . any society which chooses
one, loses both.

*

My opponents say that America cannot afford to be strong. I say
that America cannot afford to be weak.

*

After losing to Eisenhower in 1952, Stevenson remarked: "I felt like
a little boy who had stubbed his toe in the dark. He was too old
to cry, but it hurt too much to laugh."

*

Let us proclaim our faith in the future of man. Of good heart and
good cheer, faithful to ourselves and our traditions, we can lift the
cause of freedom, the cause of free men, so high no power on earth
can tear it down.

*

We travel together, passengers on a little spaceship, dependent on
its vulnerable supplies of air and soil . . . preserved from annihi-
lation only by the care, the work, and I will say the love, we give
our fragile craft.

*

Every man has a right to be heard. But no man has the right to
strangle democracy with a single set of vocal cords.

*

No nation, however powerful, can subdue all the tides of history
to its will.

*

Stevenson, deeply grieved by the death of his good friend Eleanor
Roosevelt, said this: "Yesterday I said I had lost more than a friend;
I had lost an inspiration. She would rather light candles than curse
the darkness, and her glow has warmed the world."

*

I say to you that the anatomy of patriotism is complex. But surely intolerance and public irresponsibility cannot be cloaked in the shining armor of rectitude and of righteousness. Nor can the denial of the right to hold ideas that are different, the freedom of man to think as he pleases. To strike freedom of the mind with the fist of patriotism is an old and ugly subtlety.

*

Peace cannot be won as a war is won. Peace, like religion and the good life, is the task of each new day; it must be worked at in little things and in big things, so long as breath we draw.

*

I utterly reject the argument that we ought to grant all men their rights just because if we do not, we shall give Soviet Russia a propaganda weapon. This concept is itself tainted with Communist wiliness. It insultingly suggests that were it not for the Communists, we would not do what is right. The answer to this argument is that we must do what is right for right's sake alone.

*

We are trying to construct a civilized world for man. This aim may appear one of high generality. But so are such phrases as the "defense of national interest" . . . or "the white man's burden," or any of the other catch phrases with which men have gone out with good conscience to plunder and maim their neighbors.

*

Our prayer is that men everywhere will learn, finally, to live as brothers, to respect each other's differences, to heal each other's wounds, to promote each other's progress, and to benefit from each other's knowledge.

*

No one can be certain about the meaning of peace. But we all can be certain about the meaning of war.

From Gloria Steinem

Gloria Steinem was delivering an address at Wesleyan University when a male student streaked naked through the auditorium. Always a quick thinker on her feet, Steinem interrupted her prepared remarks to say, "For men, liberation may be taking their clothes off; for women it's *not* having to take our clothes off."

*

The importance of words is their power to exclude. *Man, mankind, the family of man* have made women feel left out, usually with good reason.

*

In reflecting on the feminist movement: "We look at how far we've come, and then we know—there can be no turning back." [from *Outrageous Acts & Everyday Rebellions*]

*

There is no subject that feminism doesn't transform.

*

Hans Conried, the actor, and Gloria Steinem were guests on the same episode of the Dick Cavett TV show. They disagreed strongly about something and Conried said, "If you were a man, I'd punch you in the nose."

"Why don't you?" she answered. "At least then you'd be taking me seriously."

> *This story can be used as a lead-in to almost any speech that explores the subjects of women in business or women in politics.*

*

If he has "ring around the collar," let him wash his neck.

From Barbara Bush

By most definitions, the word *spellbinder* would not be applied to Barbara Bush. But she made public speaking history when she addressed the graduating class of Wellesley College in the spring of 1990. Not only did she bring the audience to its feet, but the following excerpt from her speech was picked up by the media all over the United States and abroad. It is a wonderful quotation that you might want to pick up and use (giving due credit) in one of your own talks.

"Somewhere out in this audience may even be someone who will one day follow in my footsteps, and preside over the White House as the president's spouse. I wish him well."

WISDOM OF THE EAST

Worldly Comments on Life
From India and China

In their centuries-long quest for the meaning of life, Indian and Chinese writers, philosophers, seers, poets, teachers, and astrologers have made bounteous contributions to the world in the form of pithy expressions that are as relevant and sagacious today as they were hundreds and even thousands of years ago. This rich treasury of wisdom offers you, in your role as public speaker, an opportunity to present to your audience philosophical and worldly points of view, phrased in succinct and readily understandable language.

The Western world's growing interest in Indian gurus and Chinese philosophers has gained momentum in recent years, and audiences grow uncommonly attentive when a speaker supports or summarizes his beliefs with quotations drawn from the wisdom of the East. This section contains material as old as Confucius and as contemporary as party slogans from the rulers of the People's Republic. Its beauty lies in the fact that even a fourth-century saying—"The tail of China is large and will not be wagged"—might have been uttered yesterday. And a thousand-year-old toast—"May you live in interesting times!"—proves as serviceable at your next cocktail party as when it was first used.

The pragmatic philosophies of India and China both concentrate on day-to-day worldly wisdom, suggesting interpretations of life and telling us how best to live it. In the case of India, Western attitudes toward her contributions to world civilization have not always been generous. Yet, in addition to the philosophy of Buddhism with its emphasis on self-examination and inquiry, India, particularly the creative Hindu mind, has been the source of a great deal of imaginative literature, including most animal fables as we know them and many of our own popular childhood fairy tales. From both Hinduism and Buddhism come the philosophy of nonviolence and the rejection of materialism. Many of the sayings given here are characterized by Hindu morality and mirror the ethos and folklore of the people.

Although this Indian wisdom, passed down both orally and through the literature, searches for a way of life that provides peace of mind, the Chinese philosophies, particularly those stemming from Confucianism, concentrate on human values and human relationships. Through the centuries, Chinese thought—nonmystical, enduring, humanistic—has focused on matters of personal conduct. The Chinese do not strive for originality. Rather, they seek eternal truths that are reflected in the philosophical attitudes of the people and in their adherence to older and more traditional ways of viewing the world.

You need not be giving a speech about the East to use the material in this section. No matter what the subject of your planned talk, read these comments. One or more of them may well serve to summarize or urge upon listeners a point of view you wish to convey and permit you to do it in a style that is erudite, concise, and of contemporary interest. Since some of the comments that follow have the flavor of proverbs, you may find it helpful to reread the material that opens the section on proverbs.

There is no need to justify to the audience your use of Eastern logic. People associate wise sayings with the Chinese and also, if to a lesser degree, with the teachings of the Indian guru or pundit. However, should time permit and should you feel that you want to relieve a serious moment with a light touch, there is a delightful story with which you can follow up your use of any of the material in this section and, in so doing, explain why you have looked to the East to make your point.

If you use a Chinese quotation, you might lead into the story this way: "Whatever opinion you may have of the People's Republic, I'm sure you'll agree that ancient Chinese knowledge and wisdom are profound. Which puts me in mind of a story I heard just the other day. . . ."

If you use an Indian selection from this section, you might

introduce the story in this way: "When one thinks about the wisdom we have garnered from the Hindus, it's easy to understand why so many great men—including Goethe and Schopenhauer—found inspiration in Indian philosophies. Sometimes, I think we have a tendency to forget how much knowledge came to the Western world from the East. Which reminds me of a story I heard the other day about China—another Eastern country whose wisdom is much admired. . . ."

And then you can tell this story: A man in Connecticut wanted to go to the People's Republic of China. He went to the East Norwalk railroad station and asked the clerk for a ticket to Beijing. "We wouldn't have a Beijing ticket here," the clerk told him. "We're just a small commuter station. Why don't you try the station at South Norwalk, which is much larger?" So the man went to South Norwalk and asked the clerk for a ticket to Beijing. "Beijing?" repeated the clerk. "Let me see if we go there." He checked his schedules. "Nope," he said, "we go to Greenwich and Stamford but not to Beijing." Then, scratching his head, he said, "You might be able to get it at Grand Central Station in New York City. That's the biggest railroad center in the East."

So the man went to Grand Central Station, waited a long time in line, and when he got to the window, he asked for a ticket to Beijing. "Forget it!" said the clerk. "We don't get any of the good trains out of here. They get 'em all out of Penn Station, on the other side of the city. Maybe you should try there."

So the man went to Penn Station, and when he asked for a ticket to Beijing, the clerk said, "We don't have it, and I can assure you that you won't get it anywhere around here. The only place you're going to get a railroad ticket to Beijing is in Moscow." So the man flew to Moscow and went to the railroad station and asked for a ticket to Beijing—and got it. Off to the People's Republic of China he went, where he spent a couple of weeks sight-seeing and doing some business, and when he was ready to go home he went to the railroad station in Beijing and asked the clerk for a ticket to Norwalk, Connecticut. "Yes, indeed," said the Chinese ticket clerk. "*East* Norwalk or *South* Norwalk?"

And now, to add a philosophical flavor to your speech, here are more than a hundred bits of wisdom from the East.

From India

Sarcasm is the last weapon of the defeated wit.

*

In the friendship of asses, look out for kicks.

*

Neither too much talk nor too great a silence, neither continuous rain nor continuous sunshine, is desirable. But while the weather is not at your command, your tongue is.

*

Fate and self-help share equally in shaping our destiny.

*

It is easy for the shopkeeper to promise full weight when he has not agreed to sell.

*

Men grind a knife because they dislike it blunt, but when they have sharpened it, it cuts their fingers. In a similar manner, men seek wealth because they dislike poverty, but when they amass it, they often find it brings them pain.

*

What is impertinence? When the jackal is born in August and there is a flood in September and the jackal pup says: "Good gracious! I never saw such a high flood!"

*

At least the ambitious man dies for fame. The glutton dies only for his belly.

*

The crow is capable of learning the walk of the goose. But in doing so it loses its own.

*

Do not trouble to preserve your hair if you plan to cut off your head.

*

The cricket mounted on a bundle of twigs says, "I am the owner of all this wealth." His position lasts until the first jolt.

*

Tricks and treachery are the practice of fools who have not the wit to be honest.

*

Genius without education is like silver in the mine.

*

The truth seeker's battle goes on day and night; as long as life lasts, it never ceases.

*

What can't be cured must be endured.

*

If a man dies for charity and duty to his neighbor, the world calls him noble. If he dies for gain, the world calls him lowly. The dying is the same; it is up to you to choose your path to it.

*

Only from subjective knowledge is it possible to proceed to objective knowledge.

*

Speech is not mere breath. It is supposed to have meaning. Take away that and you cannot distinguish it from the chirping of birds.

*

You don't ask a blind man's opinion of a picture. Nor do you invite a deaf man to a concert. But blindness and deafness are not only physical. There is a blindness and deafness of the mind as well. You should not, therefore, ask those afflicted with such infirmities to discuss philosophies with you.

*

As a man in a dream can form a thousand sorts of shapes, so by contemplation is the forgotten truth resprung.

*

Learn to be careful of what you say. That which goes out of your mouth goes into someone's ear.

*

It is possible to buy brains and muscle. But you cannot buy loyalty, which can only be earned.

*

Life is not a continuum of pleasant choices but of inevitable problems that call for strength, determination, and hard work.

*

When a man says he would like to do good for humanity, ask him how well he gets on with his family.

*

The reason more progress is not made in improving the human race is that the improvers do not all begin with themselves.

*

A word to the wise is sufficient, but a word to the foolish is often one too many.

*

Though a gem be cast into the dirt, its purity cannot be sullied; though a good man lives in a vile place, his heart cannot be depraved.

*

In lighting a candle, we seek to illuminate a dark chamber. In reading a book, we seek to enlighten the heart.

*

Truth crushed to earth will rise again, but it takes its time in doing so, and error creates a great deal of mischief meanwhile. Thus, all good people should labor to keep truth on its feet.

*

Kindness is never wasted. If it has no effect on the recipient, at least it benefits the bestower.

*

Though your fields yield many bushels of corn, you can eat but a pint a day; though your house be ever so large, you can sleep on but eight feet at night.

*

If you long for wealth and position, ask whether you are willing to work yourself to death for it.

*

Virtue beautifies.

*

Given three men with equal skill, he who plays for the sake of the game will play well. He who stakes his daughter will be nervous. And he who plays for gold will lose his wits.

*

Should you find that your well-meant counsels are not heeded, depart quietly.

*

The great man usually stands apart from the crowd. But part of his greatness is that he takes no credit for his exceptionality.

*

Perfect trust requires no pledges.

*

To the mediocre, mediocrity appears great.

*

The best remedies are found by those who suffer.

*

The masses value money; honest men, fame; virtuous men, resolution; and sages, the soul.

*

Too many men seek ways to spend their leisure when they have not yet learned to adapt themselves to the natural conditions of their existence.

*

"The world has no place for the weak in spirit." [Mahatma Gandhi]

*

He who talks about his inferiors hasn't any.

*

A thirsty man must go to the well, for the well will never come to him.

*

The way to overcome the angry man is with gentleness, the evil man with goodness, the miser with generosity, and the liar with truth.

*

Blaming your faults on your nature does not change the nature of your faults.

*

If you have faith, you can believe a common piece of stone to be a god; otherwise, it is nothing but a stone.

*

Keep seven cubits away from a horse and fourteen from a drunkard but as far as you can from a bastard.

*

The grass suffers in the fight of the tiger and the buffalo.

*

A falsehood uttered for the sake of a righteous end ceases to be a falsehood.

*

The folly of one man is the fortune of another.

*

One works on his own salvation by serving his fellow man.

*

It is ironic that age slows one down. For the older one grows, the more eager is he to work fast, lest time run out.

*

It is the spirit of the quest that determines its outcome.

*

The truly great man seeks not gain. Neither does he indulge himself in despising those who do.

*

To be eclipsed by someone need not destroy you. The sunshine seems all the brighter when the moon's shadow has passed away.

*

A man without morals is like a letter without a stamp—it will go nowhere.

*

And when your life's tale is finished, who will be the hero?

From China

Sometimes, to deviate an inch is to lose a thousand miles.

*

Though man cannot reach perfection in a hundred years, he can fall in a day with time to spare.

*

It is better to go than send.

*

Scholars are their country's treasure and the richest ornaments of the feast.

*

Would you know politics, read history.

*

Just scales and full measure injure no man.

*

It is worthier to do a kindness at home than to go far in order to burn incense.

*

One generation plants the trees; another sits in their shade.

*

Unskilled fools quarrel with their tools.

*

As meat is the cure of hunger, so is study the cure of ignorance.

*

In enacting laws, rigor is indispensable; in executing them, mercy.

*

If you would see the valley, you must climb the mountain.

*

The greater the favor, the greater the obligation.

*

"From each according to ability; to each according to work." [saying of the People's Republic of China]

*

Only when there is harmony in the home can we have peace in the world.

*

If you suspect a man, don't employ him; if you employ a man, don't suspect him.

*

It is easier to govern a kingdom than to rule one's family.

*

To rise early three mornings is to gain a day of time.

*

Think not any vice trivial, and so practice it; think not any virtue trivial, and so neglect it.

*

He who cannot achieve cannot be happy.

*

No flower can remain in full bloom for more than ten days. No man can last longer than ten years in power.

*

Dig a well before you are thirsty.

*

"We must learn to look at problems all-sidedly, seeing the reverse as well as the obverse side of things. In given conditions, a bad thing can lead to good results and a good thing to bad results." [The Little Red Book of Mao Tse-tung]

*

What is the use of running if you are on the wrong road?

*

He that takes medicine and neglects diet, wastes the skill of the physician.

*

Rats know the ways of rats.

*

The best cure for drunkenness is, while sober, to observe a drunken man.

*

A people without faith in themselves cannot survive.

*

If you don't want anyone to know it, don't do it.

*

It is too late to pull the rein when the horse has gained the brink of the precipice.

*

If a man does not receive guests at home, he will meet with very few hosts abroad.

*

If you continually grind a bar of iron, you will eventually make a needle of it.

*

It is difficult to satisfy one's appetite by painting pictures of cakes.

*

Examine the neighborhood before you choose your house.

*

The tongue is like a sharp knife. It can kill without drawing blood.

*

It is easier to visit friends than to live with them.

*

If good luck comes, who doesn't?
If good luck does not come, who does?

*

The best way to avoid punishment is to fear it.

*

To know the truth is easy; but oh, how difficult to follow it!

*

It is easy to go from economy to extravagance. It is hard to go from extravagance to economy.

*

Preserve the old, but know the new.

*

A cat is as brave as a lion—behind his own door.

*

If you wish to know everything about a man's mind, listen to his words.

*

Falling hurts least those who fly low.

*

He that pursues two hares at once catches neither.

*

Only step after step is the ladder ascended.

*

Gold has its price. Learning is priceless.

*

If you travel by boat, be prepared for a ducking.

*

A whitewashed crow will not remain white for long.

*

One dog barks at something, and a hundred bark at his sound.

*

Should you wish to know the road through the mountains, ask those who have already trodden it.

*

Tigers and deer do not stroll together. The crow does not roost with the phoenix. So, too, is a man known by his friends.

*

It is the beautiful bird that gets caged.

*

The Great Wall stands; the builder is gone.

*

> *The philosopher Confucius, reviled in Mao Tse-tung's China as a reactionary feudalist, made a comeback after the death of Mao. Then the post-Mao order once again hailed Confucius as a great and glorious philosopher. Here are some examples of Confucian thought:*

It is easy to act but difficult to know.

*

Failure is the first step toward success.

*

A diamond cannot be perfected without friction, and people cannot be perfected without trials.

*

A thief is a thief whether he steals a diamond or a cucumber.

*

It is only in winter that the pine and cypress are known to be evergreens.

> *This can be followed by a form of contemporary "translation": It is only in adversity that men are known for what they really are.*

*

The tail of China is large and will not be wagged.

CLOSINGS

Getting Off While You're Still Ahead

A long-winded speaker was once interrupted by a member of his audience, who shouted: "Enough! Enough! I don't agree! Let me answer you!" To which the speaker retorted, "You may speak for the present generation, sir, but I speak for posterity." "Yes," countered the man in the audience, "and it seems you are determined to speak until your constituency arrives!"

The single worst and most often committed crime against audiences is that of speaking too long. No matter that a man is brilliant; if he is also long in the tongue, his brilliance is bound to lose some of its shine. And, of course, there is nothing more painful than a speaker with only a couple of things to say—who doesn't stop when he's already said them.

On the other hand, a good speech delivered with snap and variety, with changes of pace and good humor, can make a platform hero of even an ordinary man—provided he knows when to get off!

The best time to get off is when you've said all you need say (but not all you *could* say) to make your points. Then, when you're still ahead, wind up with a line, an anecdote, a proverb, a quotation, or some other memorable piece of copy that leaves your audience laughing or thoughtful—depending upon the subject of your address.

One of the great advantages of ending with a laugh—and this can be done even with serious speeches by using stories or fables that reaffirm your main point cleverly rather than by repetition—

is that the laughter and applause you'll win from your audience as you sit down give the impression that you are being applauded for your entire speech. And what happens during your last few seconds on the platform will have a strong bearing on what they take away with them when it's all over.

So if you want to go away popular, appreciated, and applauded, leave 'em laughing. If this isn't possible, if the occasion is such that humor is out of place, then leave 'em with the best line or paragraph in your speech, some eloquently phrased comment that will make them cheer you for your sensitivity and depth.

This section on closings offers you some proven, successful ways to end a talk. But you might find the right closing for your speech anywhere in this book. Every section offers possibilities. Be sure to go through it again, page by page, scanning the material for a suitable thought with which to make your exit. There are some fine possibilities in the section on fables and in The Fifteen Best Speech Bits I've Ever Heard. Many superb exit lines are to be found in the section on proverbs. And, of course, use the Subject Index if you're seeking closing material on a specific topic.

It may seem to you that the amount of time spent in selecting the right closing is out of proportion to the time you've spent on the entire talk. Not so. These final words are of such importance that no amount of time devoted to finding them is too much. Remember: All the work, all the research, all the worrying, all the pruning and editing and rehearsing that have gone into preparing for your appearance on the platform will pay off during that single moment when you make your exit amid the cheers, the whistles, the laughter, and that burst of final applause.

*

Samuel Johnson was discussing with one of his students a report the student had just given. Dr. Johnson told the student: "I found your speech to be good—and original. However, the part that was good was not original. And the part that was original, was not good."

I hope you will not go away saying the same about my talk.

*

Well, as an old Texas friend of mine used to say, "If you haven't struck oil in the first half hour, stop *boring.*"

*

In conclusion, I would like to offer you a quotation from Louis D. Brandeis. Said Mr. Brandeis, "Nine tenths of the serious controversies which arise in life result from misunderstanding, result from one man not knowing the facts which to the other man seem important, or otherwise failing to appreciate his point of view."
I have attempted today to present some of the facts that seem important to me, to give you my point of view. If in examining these facts and viewpoints we can be brought a bit closer to the solution of our mutual problems, then my appearance here today will have been worthwhile.

> *The Brandeis quotation could be followed by any number of concluding statements. The one given here is merely an example.*

*

Well, it was nice being here with a group of such extinguished-looking gentlemen.

*

> *If you have been urging your audience to take some action or to address some problem that involves risk and requires courage, you might use this quotation from Julius Caesar:*

"Cowards die many times before their deaths. The valiant never taste of death but once."

*

It has been said that those who know the most say the least, and those who know the least say the most. Lest I be numbered among the latter, I will now conclude my remarks.

*

Will Rogers, invited to sit in on the business session of an organization that did not ordinarily permit the presence of outsiders, remarked when the meeting was over: "I agreed to repeat nothing and I'll keep my promise. But I gotta admit I heard nothing worth repeating."
I hope this audience will not feel that way about the material presented here by our panel.

*

I hope you leave here pleased and stimulated by what you've heard at this meeting. Some people come away from this type of presentation very much inspired; others just wake up refreshed.

*

And so in closing let me say that as we go into the coming months, we can either ride up the escalator or walk up two steps at a time and be there ahead of what we know is coming.

*

A closing quotation that urges some stocktaking about the way we have been creating ecological problems:

"We human beings are rushing forward unthinkingly through days of incredible accomplishments, of glory and of tragedy, our eyes seeking the stars—or fixed too often upon each other in hatred and conflict. We have forgotten the earth, forgotten it in the sense that we fail to regard it as the source of our life." [Henry Fairfield Osborn]

*

Calvin Coolidge was once heard to remark, "If you don't say anything, you won't be called upon to repeat it."

Well, I cannot be sure whether I have uttered any thoughts that will bear repeating, but I certainly hope that I have.

*

"The *great* commitment all too easily obscures the *little* one. But without the humility and warmth which you have to develop . . . to the few with whom you are personally involved, you will never be able to do anything for the many. Love . . . would remain powerless against the negative forces within you if it were not tamed by the yoke of human intimacy and warmed by its tenderness." [Dag Hammarskjöld]

*

I have talked a good deal up here about change. But I fully realize that change is not as easy to accept as one might think. Most people have something of the attitude of the lady who attended a lecture of Werner Von Braun's on the subject of putting a man on the moon. When the lecture was over, he made the mistake that most speakers make—he asked if there were any questions.

The woman's hand shot up, and Dr. Von Braun called on her for her question.

"Why," asked the woman, "can't you forget about getting people on the moon, and stay home and watch television like the good Lord intended for you to do?"

*

Our speeches are over, and now we will ask you to fill out the papers [or questionnaires] you have been given. Please keep this in mind: Legibility is a virtue! And profanity will be accepted only if it has artistic merit or redeeming social value.

*

Different cultures define character in different ways. I like this definition by an Indian professor, Sir Phiroze Sethna: "Character is a complex of many great qualities of the heart and mind but it always includes love of truth, initiative, courage, grit, tenacity of purpose, fair play, a balanced judgment, quick and at the same time sound decision, and a high sense of duty."

I hope that my remarks here today have bred in you a determination to pursue at least some of these personal qualities.

*

Robert Benchley is credited with having been the first to use this line: "I must get out of these wet clothes and into a dry martini."

I think I hear the luncheon whistle, so let's head for those dry martinis.

*

For the most part, we have done away with capital punishment. But still, at meetings such as this all over the country, a lot of people are put to death by *elocution*. So let me spare you such a fate and conclude my remarks.

*

The recipe for a successful speech should include plenty of shortening.

*

This quotation from H. G. Barnett's book Innovation *gives you a thought-provoking conclusion if you have presented new or innovative ideas:*

"Innovation is the linkage or fusion of two or more elements that have not been previously joined in this fashion, so that the result is a qualitatively distinct whole. It's like a genetic cross or hybrid: it is totally different from either of its parents, but it resembles both of them in some respects."

*

I think I had better conclude before I become like the speaker who appeared on a program where Will Rogers was the moderator. This speaker had continued well beyond his allotted time, and when he finally sat down, Will Rogers rose and said, "You have just heard from that famous Chinese orator, On Too-long."

*

If I've held your interest with a good speech, then this is a good place to stop; and if it's been a bad speech, then this is a *helluva* good place to stop!

*

"America's first frontier was the fabled open land to the west. Our challenge was to settle a rich but harsh environment. The first frontier closed at the turn of this century, and a second—the industrial or technological—frontier opened to replace it. The challenge became mastery of the environment we had usurped in pursuit of material affluence. With some exceptions, that challenge has now been met. Today, as concern for the environment increases and we realize the limits of world resources, we are witnessing, symbolically at least, the closing of this second great frontier.

"Even now the new third frontier is opening. It is a frontier of social and individual change, the exact dimensions of which are still unclear but whose rough outline is discernible. It is the frontier of the person, exploring in community with others the next stage of human possibility. Challenges along our past frontiers were external: in one case, mastery of the land; in the second, manipulation of technology. The challenge of the third frontier is primarily an internal one—realizing our collective human potential." [Duane S. Elgin]

*

In conclusion, I would like to read to you a short passage written by a famous physician, William Osler, who was as brilliant a philosopher as he was a doctor. Dr. Osler wrote, "Though little, *the master word* looms large in meaning. It is the 'open sesame' to every portal, the great equalizer, the philosopher's stone which transmutes all base metal of humanity into gold. The stupid it will make bright, the bright brilliant, and the brilliant steady. To youth it brings hope, to the middle-aged confidence, to the aged repose. It is directly responsible for all advances in medicine during the past twenty-five years. Not only has it been the touchstone of progress, but it is the measure of success in everyday life. And the master word is *work*."

> *If you are trying to inspire your audience to pursue some given objectives, you can then go on to conclude with a sentence or two in which you urge them to work, and work hard, on behalf of those objectives.*

*

You have been a fine audience. I thank you for your attentiveness and hope it has been worth your while. As Wilson Mizner once said, "A good listener is not only popular everywhere, but after a while he knows something."

*

In concluding, I would like to borrow from John W. Gardner's book *Excellence*. Gardner tells us that "Mankind is not divided into two categories, those who are creative and those who are not. There are degrees of the attribute. It is the rare individual who has it in his power to achieve the highest reaches of creativity. But many could achieve fairly impressive levels of creativity under favorable circumstances. And quite a high proportion of the population could show some creativity some of the time, in some aspect of their lives."

In describing further the characteristics of the creative person,

Gardner goes on to say, "Unlike the rest of us, he does not persist stubbornly and unproductively in one approach to a problem."

Why have I read these excerpts? Because it is going to take creativity to solve the problems we have been discussing here today. And it is my opinion that this audience is made up of enough people who can lend various aspects of their creativity to finding and executing solutions.

*

When John D. Rockefeller III was chairman of the board of trustees of the Population Council, he said something in a speech that sums up my final thought, and I can do no better than to quote him directly:

"Man is more than animal. He has mental, emotional, and spiritual needs that go far beyond bare necessities, creature comforts, and material resources. Every man deserves at least the chance to lead a life of satisfaction and purpose, to achieve in life more than mere existence.

"Even if science by some magic could show the way to feed new billions of people, we still would not have solved the population problem. The *quality* of life cannot be omitted from the solution. Indeed, there can be no true solution until society can offer every individual an opportunity—in the fullest sense—to live as well as to survive."

*

When a speaker says, "Well, to make a long story short," it's too late.

I hope we have not arrived at a point where it is already too late. For I have just about come to my conclusions.

*

It has been my job to speak, and yours to listen. I do hope we finished at the same time.

*

In the late nineteenth century, a famous man wrote these words: "If we would only testify to the truth as we see it, it would turn out at once that there are hundreds, thousands, even millions of men just as we are, who see the truth as we do, are afraid, as we are, of seeming to be singular by confessing it, and are only waiting, again as we are, for someone to proclaim it."

The man who wrote that was Leo Tolstoy.

As Americans, we may not agree with other theories and ideas of that famous Russian; but I, for one, cannot help but agree with those words. And I have attempted today to "testify to the truth" as I see it.

*

I have presented many facts in my talk, and I would like, if you will bear with me, to draw some conclusions from these facts. For even with all the facts at hand, it is possible for people to come to different—and sometimes erroneous—conclusions.

*

It's rather like the Eskimo who went on a visit for the first time to New York. When he came back to Eskimo-land, he had a long, narrow package, wrapped in gift paper and tied with a big ribbon. His wife asked him what it was, and he told her it was a present for her. She opened it, and inside was a long length of pipe. She thanked him and then asked him again, "But what is it?"

"It's a great invention," he said. "They use it in New York. You prop it upright in the bedroom, one end on the floor and the other end at the ceiling. When you have a very cold night, you rap on it and you get heat."

*

I have taken a good deal of your time here today. Hopefully, you have had some to spare. After all, what is time really for? Let me answer my own question by quoting Max Kaplan, the author of Leisure in America.

Mr. Kaplan wrote: "The average middle-class home in America has in it enough vacuum cleaners, dishwashers, clothes scrubbers, and other gadgets to equal the energy of ninety male servants. This 'supplements' time, providing the American style of life.

"In addition," continues Mr. Kaplan, "we have at our disposal better lights, frozen foods, telephones in all colors, unpaid-for cars, paper-covered books, and countless other paraphernalia that enrich time, helping us to save it, pass it, spend it, kill it, or use it for a variety of purposes."

*

I hope I have made some small contribution to the subject under discussion today, particularly since it is the only area in which I enjoy any sort of expertise at all. There are so many other subjects about which I know absolutely nothing—like sports. I know so little about sports that when I was asked what I thought of the Indianapolis 500, I said I thought they were all guilty.

If you happen to be on a program where some sports figure is also scheduled to speak or to be introduced, you can use the above bit with a different lead-in: "I'm amazed that I'm even in the same room with a prominent sports figure. I know so little about sports. . . ."

*

A Southern minister whose sermon had developed the point that salvation is free—as free as the water we drink—was then obliged to complain that the collection was scandalously small that day. A member of the congregation rose up to remind the minister that he had said salvation was as free as water.

"Indeed it is," replied the minister, "but when we pipe it to you, you have to pay for the plumbing."

This can be used if you are a speaker who must end by asking your audience for something: money, pledges, signatures on a petition, action, or whatever.

*

It has been said that a good orator implies a good audience. From where I stand, you have been a fine audience indeed. And if you have found my oration to be good, then that, too, is a credit to all of you.

*

"I have talked a good deal about creativity and I want to make one final point—absolving myself from any impression you may have gained that I think I can make creativity happen. I cannot, and anyone who tells you he can is kidding himself. I think creativity can easily be managed to death. On the other hand, it can also be

starved to death—or worked to death. The most valuable contribution that a good manager can make is to create an environment
in which creativity can flourish without being managed, starved, or
worked to death." [Stephen O. Frankfurt]

*

Permit me to end with a passage from William Saroyan:
    "What can a man do to move along in some kind of grace
through his days and years? Well, there are a million ways of putting
it, but it always comes to pretty much the one way—he can do his
best, in accordance with his laws, and in keeping with his truth,
in favor of himself, and on behalf of his expectation to see it all
through in the best possible style, with some meaning, and without
harm to anybody else."

*

If nothing else, the speeches here today have pointed up how many
problems we have and how much unhappiness accompanies these
problems. This, despite the fact that most Americans have many
material possessions. As Archibald MacLeish once said, "We have
more in our garages and kitchens and cellars today than Louis XIV
had in the whole of Versailles!"

*

In talking about life under the sea, an oceanographer once commented that it was one thing to glimpse a new world and quite
another to establish permanent outposts in it and work and live in
it. The same might be said about our explorations of outer space.
    There is a world of difference between theory and application.
I have offered you my theories. I do not for a minute suggest that
their applications will be quite so simple to come by.

*

In the year 50 B.C., someone inscribed upon an ancient wall these
words: "Conversation is the image of the mind. As the mind is, so
is the talk."
    In my talk today, I have tried to reveal—not hide—what is on
my mind. I know that my words will not, like the quotation I just
gave you, live more than two thousand years. But if they give you
food for thought, I will be satisfied.

*

Well, I have been going on and on for quite a bit, and I imagine you are all anxious to go eat. So I will end by telling you a remark I heard at a party last Saturday night. A couple I know had been hoisting the martinis rather steadily for quite some time. Finally, I heard the lady say to her mate: "Honey, you'd better stop drinking. Your face is getting awfully blurred."

I'm afraid your faces are also getting a bit blurred, so I had better knock it off. Thank you for your kind attention and for the invitation to address you.

*

Mark Twain once said that between him and Rudyard Kipling he felt—and I quote—"We have all the knowledge in the world."

Perhaps the last speaker and I gave the impression of having all the knowledge in the world, on both sides of the question; but I assure you that such is not the case. In fact, we will now throw the floor open to discussion so that you can learn firsthand how much knowledge we lack.

*

Of course, you may not agree with my diagnosis as I have expounded on it up here. A story is making the rounds about the three scientists who were working with some highly dangerous radioactive material when a big explosion occurred in their laboratory. They were examined by the company physician, who looked very grave and said: "Gentlemen, I have bad news. Each of you has but two months to live. But since the accident happened on company time, the company is willing to grant whatever last wishes you may have for the ends of your lives."

The first scientist was an Englishman, and he pondered for a few minutes and then said: "I rather imagine I would like to spend the end of my days back in old England. I shall just sit in my club and read the London *Times* and talk politics with my chums."

The second scientist was a Russian, and he told the doctor: "My family lives on the outskirts of Leningrad, and I would like to be with them, sharing the community pleasures, visiting the Hermitage and enjoying party lectures on the radio."

The doctor then asked the third scientist, who was a New

Yorker, for his last wish. "Well, to tell you the truth," he replied, "I'd like to get a second opinion from another doctor."

You are, of course, free to look for other opinions.

*

I once heard something attributed to Frank Lloyd Wright. "Early in life," he is reputed to have said, "I had to choose between honest arrogance and hypocritical humility. I chose honest arrogance and have seen no reason to change."

I didn't have to make that choice early in life. But in preparing my opinions for presentation here today, it was a choice I had to come to grips with. Like Frank Lloyd Wright, I chose honest arrogance—as I imagine you detected in my remarks—and I hope you will find it in your hearts to forgive me for it.

*

I may not have come off as being very tactful in my remarks. But I share the feelings of Sir Frank Medlicott, an English solicitor who once made this statement: "Some people mistake weakness for tact. If they are silent when they ought to speak and so feign an agreement they do not feel, they call it being tactful. Cowardice would be a much better name. Tact is an active quality that is not exercised by merely making a dash for cover. Be sure, when you think you are being extremely tactful, that you are not in reality running away from something you ought to face."

I have done my best to face the facts as I see them.

*

During the course of this meeting, we have heard a great deal about what is new in our field. The fact that there is so much that is new reminded me of something the physicist Robert Oppenheimer once said: "One thing that is new is the prevalence of newness, the changing scale and scope of change itself, so that the world alters as we walk in it, so that the years of man's life measure not some small growth or rearrangement or moderation of what he learned in childhood, but a great upheaval."

I, too, feel that what we are experiencing is a great upheaval.

*

Let me read you a quotation. It is from a man named John Jay Chapman: "So long as there is any subject which men may not freely discuss, they are timid upon *all* subjects. They wear an iron crown and talk in whispers."

We have not spoken here today in whispers. We have talked freely, which may leave us open to outside criticism. But I would rather have that than wear an iron crown.

*

I have given you a lot of good news today about our company [school, hospital, institution]. But we are never satisfied—that would be complacency. Maybe that's precisely what has *made* us so successful.

*

We may face some difficult days ahead in this wizardless world, but with the concerned goodwill of those who recognize that we share a mutual goal, this struggle can indeed be won." [David Rockefeller]

> *If talking to company employees, stockholders, university staff, or even party workers in a political campaign, this quotation can be followed by a comment like this:*

"I know we have the goodwill. And that we share a mutual goal. And so I believe our objectives can be won. Let's all pitch in and win *big*."

*

Today is the first day of the rest of your life.

*

We haven't agreed on many things here today. But in taking a fifteen-minute break now, I'm sure we'll all agree on one thing: At the rest room, incoming traffic has the right-of-way.

*

I have now come to a point where I want to tell you something I was once taught, although the lesson is something I have a tendency to forget. I was taught that the four most important words in our language are *What is your opinion?* The three most important words are *If you please.* The two most important are *Thank you,* and the single most important word is *you*. I was also taught that the *least* important word is *I*.

I—if I may once again use that least important word—have not adhered closely to this belief, having tortured the word *I* perhaps needlessly. But now, in opening the meeting to a discussion from the floor, I want to ask, "If you please, what is your opinion?" to hear what *you* have to say—and, finally, to say, "Thank you."

*

I am reminded of the story of a Boy Scout who showed up at his troop meeting with a black eye. When his scoutmaster asked him what had happened, he replied that he had tried to help a little old lady across the street. "How in the world," asked the scoutmaster, "could you get a black eye doing that?" To which the scout replied, "She didn't want to go."

I am a bit like the Boy Scout. I have been trying—not too subtly, I fear—to lead you across the street. And I have detected a bit of resistance to going. However, even if we have come halfway together, I will be pleased.

*

In closing, I would like to tell you something that Pierre Curie, the Nobel Prize-winning chemist, once said. "Humanity," said Curie, "surely needs practical men who make the best of their work for their own interest, without forgetting the general interest. But it needs also dreamers, for whom the unselfish following of a purpose is so imperative that it becomes impossible for them to devote much attention to their own material benefit."

Perhaps the ideas I have expressed up here today have not been in the realm of practicality. But I hope that I have set some of you to dreaming—and that you will find your dreams so insistent that you want to make them a lifetime goal.

*

In conclusion, I would like to point out something that John W. Gardner, when he was the head of Common Cause, stated so beautifully. "We must never forget," said Mr. Gardner, "that though the word may be popular, the consequences of true creativity can never be assured of popularity. New ways threaten the old, and those who are wedded to the old may prove highly intolerant. Our affection is generally reserved for innovators long dead."

*

George Eliot once remarked, "Blessed is the man who, having nothing to say, refrains from giving us wordy evidence of the fact."

I have that comment in mind as I come to the end of my talk. I have no more to say.

*

On a plane bound for Europe, the pilot's voice suddenly came over the public address system:

"Ladies and gentlemen," the pilot said, "I have two pieces of news for you. One of them is good, and one of them is not so good. So I'll tell you the bad news first. The bad news is that we are lost: We don't have any idea where we are. But as I told you, there's good news, too. The good news is that we have a two-hundred-mile-an-hour tail wind."

> *From this story, you can bridge into some final comments in which you state that there are times when it seems that the story sums up the current state of American society [or of universities, youth, Congress, and so on]. We don't know where we are going, but, quite clearly, we are getting there awfully fast.*

*

We have covered a lot of territory here today; but then, we appear to be headed for a time in history when we may all end up like the man who refused to become a specialist because there were so many wonderful things to know in our great bustling world.

"I am a generalist," he said, "and my purpose is to know less and less about more and more, until I know absolutely nothing about absolutely everything."

*

"Everything has an end—except a sausage, which has two." So goes an old Danish proverb. Well, this talk is not a sausage, although it may have seemed hammy in certain spots. So it has come, at last, to its end.

*

Albert Szent-Györgyi, a Hungarian-born chemist who won a Nobel prize in 1937, once said, "I find myself running, impatiently, to my laboratory every morning at an early hour. My work is not finished when I leave my workbench in the afternoon. I go on thinking about my problems all the time, and my brain must continue to think about them even when I sleep, for I wake up sometimes in the middle of the night, with answers to questions that have been puzzling me. I think that without such concentration and devotion, nothing serious can be achieved, be it in the arts or in the sciences."

I leave you with that thought as I conclude my comments here today. As you go about your own work, I would urge you to ask yourself whether Szent-Györgyi's type of concentration and devotion might have an impact on the success of your own activities.

*

You may know that it was Hubert Humphrey who ran for the presidency against Richard Nixon. What you may not know is that Mr. Humphrey, in conversation or on the platform, was not particularly known for his brevity. In fact, it was reported that Muriel Humphrey once said to her husband, "Hubert, a speech doesn't have to be eternal to be immortal."

Keeping that in mind I will come to some very quick conclusions.

*

As we leave here tonight, let me give you this reminder: Rule number one is, don't sweat the small stuff. Rule number two is, it's *all* small stuff.

*

A good quotation if you're talking to party workers during a political campaign:

An Indian philosopher once said that "no man knows what he is capable of achieving so long as he does not rouse himself for a heroic effort."

I know that in the campaign ahead we will witness great heroic effort by all of you, and I want to thank you in advance, no matter the outcome.

*

If your talk is to be followed by a question-and-answer period, you might open it by saying, "And now ladies and gentlemen, ask me any question at all. If I know the answer, I will answer you. If I don't know the answer, I will answer anyhow."

*

"Our main business is not to see what lies dimly at a distance, but to do what lies clearly at hand." [Thomas Carlyle]

*

I once heard that someone had written a book called *An Unbiased Opinion of the Civil War, From a Southern Point of View.*

I fear that my own comments up here today have been equally unbiased.

*

It's been a privilege to talk to you, and although I don't expect you to fly out of here on the wings of my inspiration, if a bit of posthypnotic suggestion manages to take, our time together will have been well spent.

Or, the same thought might be conveyed with these words:

Those are my final words on this subject. I do not expect them to live in history alongside those of Neil Armstrong, the first man on the moon, who said, "One small step for a man, one giant leap for mankind." But if you remember even the gist of my message, my time here today will have been well spent.

*

And in conclusion let me remind you of something Victor Hugo once said, "Initiative is doing the right thing without being told."

*

And finally, let me give you the first law of wing walking: Never let go of what you've got until you've got hold of something else.

*

Sometimes, as you get well into your talk, you may find that audience attention appears to be lagging. If this hap-

pens, interrupt your prepared remarks with either of the following:

"I don't mind all of you going to sleep, but at least you could say, 'Good night!' "

   Or:

"Am I in the right room? Or is this the place where they're having the reading of the will?"

                              *

The best speeches are those that have good beginnings and good endings—close together.

                              *

As I near the end of my remarks, I am reminded of the little girl in school who was asked to spell *banana*.

   "I can spell *banana*," she told the teacher, "but I never know when to stop."

   I'm told that I sometimes have the same problem.

                              *

And now I will tell you something my father once told me. He said:

   If you want to be seen, stand up.
   If you want to be heard, speak up.
   If you want to be loved, shut up and sit down.

AUDIO AND VISUAL AIDS

Making Them Work Harder for You

I once conducted a course for business executives who wanted to improve their public speaking techniques as well as their ability to make presentations in front of large groups. One evening, I invited my good friend José Quintero, the famous Broadway director who won the Pulitzer Prize for his brilliant direction of Eugene O'Neill's *Long Day's Journey Into Night*, to appear as our guest lecturer.

The subject of the session was "The Use of Visuals," and I launched the program by asking Mr. Quintero how a speaker could make the most of them. "I can tell you in five words," he replied. *"Make love to your visuals!"*

Mr. Quintero then demonstrated what he meant. As though he were holding on to something precious, he put his arm firmly around a stack of cards that rested on an easel beside him. Then he drew the audience's attention to the waiting visuals by quietly announcing that he was "about to reveal some dramatic and telling facts." He paused to let this sink in; and as he took his arm from the cards, he straightened them carefully, almost lovingly. By now, all eyes were glued to the easel. Slowly, he removed the cover card, revealing his first visual. Without any rush at all, he read off the headline, lending emphasis to each word by gently tapping it with his index finger. Before continuing with the material on the card, he moved in front of the easel, completely hiding the visual from the audience, and repeated the headline. Only then did he move aside and permit the audience to see what the balance of the card contained.

What a contrast to the average speaker, who rattles off the words on the visual aids—often in a mumble that communicates that person's own disinterest in the message—and then casts each card aside as though glad to be rid of it!

If the nature and subject matter of your talk suggest a need for visual material, be sure to use it in a way that enhances your message. All too often, even capable speakers do themselves a disservice by hiding behind their props, using them as crutches. Many speakers seem unaware that their visuals are not truly helping them but are working against the spoken message.

The advice in this section is based on hundreds of separate experiences in using visuals with speeches and presentations of various types, presentations designed to convince an audience of a point of view, to rebut an opposing viewpoint, to make a sale, to get agreement for action on a proposal, to describe an experience or an accomplishment, to teach, to preach, or to entertain. The suggestions cover visuals that can be designed in advance of the presentation, not drawings or blackboard demonstrations created right before the audience. But even such on-the-spot visual aids can benefit from some of the techniques described here.

• *Decide what types of visuals to use.* This may be the most important decision you make regarding this aspect of your presentation. Too many speakers take the easy way out and settle for a slide presentation. I say easy because the slides are shown in a darkened or semidarkened room (permitting the speaker to hide) and are flashed on a screen that is physically out of reach of the podium ("You see," the speaker would almost seem to say, "they're not really related to me!"). The speaker need only turn the script over to a visual designer and say, "Make me some slides," and when they arrive in their neat little frames, fait accompli, no one will deny that they look professional and unassailable.

All these factors help to separate the presenter from the audience, impersonalize the presentation, and give the audience a chance to doze. Unless you are an unusually gifted speaker or have a message of gut concern to the audience, the turning off of the lights before the slides go on is tacit permission to the listener to turn off his or her cortex.

• *Never use slides unless the audience is too large for more intimate visual aids.* You may properly ask, "How large is 'too large'?" I have used 40- by 50-inch charts before an audience of forty people, and because the charts were designed with the size of the audience in mind, everyone in the room could see everything. Of course, the seating arrangement in the auditorium or conference room also determines visibility. Whether a group of forty persons is able to see your "live" visuals in a theater-type room with the seats fixed in place depends on how far apart the rows are and how they are staggered as well as on the size of the lettering and pictures on your cards. (If you have a choice, avoid such a theater arrangement for forty people or fewer.) If you can arrange for a long conference table—or better yet, two or three tables with chairs clustered around them—you can easily seat forty people so that they will be able to see your charts. With fewer than forty people, never put your audience in the dark, and never mechanize your visuals.

If your audience is large and you have no alternative but to use slides, there are ways to avoid the pitfalls of darkness. I'll tell you about them later on. Of course, motion pictures or tape, which usually has a sound track as well as a moving image, is another matter entirely. For reasons that you can guess, a good motion picture provides an excellent change of pace and can actually wake up a sluggish audience. But most speakers have neither the money nor the time to create, or have someone create for them, a motion picture film that can be used to strengthen their talk. (There are, of course, exceptions. For example, campus recruiters for large companies are often supplied with short films to supplement their oral presentations.)

• *If you use presentation cards or flip charts, don't let them fight you.* A visual is supposed to help you get across your message. If it fails to do that, it has no reason for being. Visuals also serve to remind speakers of points they wish to make if they are not reading a complete script. There is nothing wrong with this, provided it does not become the sole purpose of the visual.

Here are some thoughts to keep in mind when designing and producing your presentation cards or charts:

• *Your visual must reinforce your message by adding to it or making it more memorable.* If the visual is saying one thing while you are saying another, one of you is going to lose out. It just isn't possible for the audience to think two different things at the same time, so whichever has a stronger appeal—your voice or the material on the card—will win. Usually the visual wins, so it's best to avoid this kind of infighting by making sure that nothing on your visual aid takes the audience away from you.

Let me give you an example. Suppose you are giving a speech to a dozen college seniors, and your talk is designed to encourage them to join Teach for America (TFA), a sort of domestic education equivalent of the Peace Corps. You have just made this statement: "It is not only what you can do in Teach for America, but what TFA can do for you."

You are using visuals in your presentation, and if some or all of them are in the form of flip cards, you might go on to say, "Let's examine both aspects of that statement." You might want to use two cards to help your audience follow—*and remember*—the arguments you are going to present. One card might be headlined YOU AND TEACH FOR AMERICA; and the other card, TEACH FOR AMERICA AND YOU. On the first card, under your heading, these key phrases might appear centered:

1. Teach your specialty
2. Fight illiteracy
3. Break the poverty cycle
4. Improve U.S. standard of living
5. Give hope to young people

On the second card, perhaps these points are lettered:

1. Develop independence—*yours*
2. Gain job experience
3. Discover your strengths
4. Discover your weaknesses
5. Make lifelong friends

Since these are only key phrases designed to help the audience remember the ten points, you will no doubt amplify each item in your speech. If your amplification is brief, you can put each set of five points on a single card. But audiences have a tendency to leave the speaker and read ahead, so if you're going to spend several minutes on each idea, you would do well to list each point separately and use a total of ten cards. You might also illustrate each point with a suitable drawing or photograph.

Another good technique if you use only two cards is to cover each lettered item with a thin but opaque piece of paper, which you then rip off as you get ready to talk about it. This helps build suspense and interest in your talk. It also creates an automatic summary of each group of five points when all the covering papers have been removed.

• *Beware of the pitfalls in creating such visuals.* Three major mistakes are commonly made in designing flip cards or, for that matter, slides. First, there is the tendency to put complete sentences, even paragraphs, on the visuals, which provide the speaker with a talking script but alienate the audience. If you put too much copy on a card, the lettering is bound to be small, and your audience is less likely to be able to make out the words. More important, if your audience is reading the sentences or paragraphs, they're not listening to you unless you're saying precisely the same words. In which case, if everything being said is in writing, who needs *you?* Why not just send your cards? On the other hand, if the cards carry one set of sentences and you speak different sentences (thus giving the impression that you are not dependent upon your aids), you're creating confusion in the mind of the listener-viewer. *So use only key words!*

The second pitfall is the tendency to let an overeager art director overdesign the visual aid, so the design aspects—multicolors or fancy lettering—detract from the message. A visual aid should not be a test of the artist's design talents; *it is a test of the artist's ability to communicate visually.* This doesn't mean that you shouldn't use color in your flip charts. On the contrary, there is no reason to limit yourself to black or to a single color, provided the color or colors help get the message across. *Just be certain each card doesn't become a circus poster.*

The third danger in designing visual aids is illegibility. Fancy script, tiny type, too little space between lines of copy, reverse type (white lettering on black or colored background)—all these tend to make the copy on a visual inaccessible to the viewer. Nothing is more frustrating than to have a speaker say, "As you can see from these figures," and for the audience not to be able to see anything at all because the visual has been designed for close-up reading and not for audience absorption. The more the people in the audience have to strain to see, the less likely they will be to concentrate on what you're saying. And when they discover that they really can't see anything, they usually give up trying. Even worse, they may also give up listening.

• *Visuals should be alive—otherwise, they're deadly.* If you need to use a large number of visuals (whether they are flip cards or slides), make sure they offer some variety. If they all follow a single format and are unrelieved by illustration or proper use of color, they can act as a soporific. There are a number of ways to make your visuals more interesting without letting them take over. One approach is to introduce a visual theme in the form of color or illustration.

A color theme would work this way: Assume you have eight major concepts to visualize along with a number of other subfactors. You can assign a color to each of the eight concepts—red, green, blue, orange, purple, yellow, brown, and magenta. Each idea (or each section) would then utilize only the color assigned to it, plus the color of the lettering—probably black or sepia. Charts, graphs, illustrations, and other similar items would use the assigned color. When the next idea is presented, the audience knows immediately that it has to shift gears because the color has changed. If the eight points are to be summarized at the end, you might have the summary done in all eight colors. Or if this is too gaudy because of the amount of copy, each of the eight numbers that precede the summary lines could pick up the previously used color.

Color can also enhance your visuals if you use it only for illustrations. In such a case, the lettering could be in black, sepia, or some other legible color.

Another way to make your visuals come alive is to use only pictures—perhaps photographs, if available—and let the speech do the talking while the pictures reinforce your words. For example, if you are giving a talk to raise funds for children in underdeveloped countries, your text might call for you to say, "Last year, ten thousand of these children under the age of five died of protein deficiency." As you say the words *these children*, you flip your chart to reveal a blowup of a child clearly suffering from malnutrition.

Still another way to enliven your visuals, particularly if you must show a large number of graphs or statistical information, is to humanize the statistics by turning them into people or things.

Let's say you want to tell your audience that the consumption of pickles in this country has increased steadily during the last decade. Instead of using a graph with lines and numbers, show a small mound of pickles for the year of lowest consumption; more and more pickles for the years when the consumption increases; and, finally, pickles tumbling off the chart for the year of maximum consumption. If you are talking about people instead of pickles, you might use stick figures or heads. If you are talking about housing construction, you could use small houses, roofs with TV antennae, or some other symbol of a house that would appeal to your particular audience.

• *If you have to use slides, they have to be good.* With flip cards, you can quickly sense whether the audience is paying attention. If interest lags at any point, you can skip a section of the cards and cover that material verbally only. Or you can interrupt the card presentation by walking in front of your easel and expanding on some point without visual assistance. You can even break into your own presentation with some ad lib designed to elicit audience response, such as this: "You know, I had a very talented young man assigned to work out these visuals—I'm sure he had every reason to be a bit on the arrogant side. Sometimes, however, he carried it a little far. One morning I stopped by to see how my charts were progressing, and as I entered his office, I said, 'Beautiful morning!' To which he replied, 'Thank you!' "

Slides are another story entirely. Once the lights are dimmed and your slides begin to flash on the screen, you are enslaved by them. This is particularly true if you are using a projectionist in a booth who will change slides in accordance with your script, as arranged during rehearsal. The slides simply have to be right, and they have to be good.

What can you do to ensure a successful slide presentation? As with flip cards and charts, make sure that everything you want the audience to read is legible; use color so that it lends variety but does not take over; work to have each visual reinforce your message, not fight it; use key words only and avoid body copy; and humanize your graphs and statistics.

Here is another bit of advice dictated by experience. Group your slides together so that they are all used in one segment of your talk rather than being scattered throughout the presentation. If you use one slide here, a couple there, you're literally keeping your audience in the dark throughout your presentation. On the other hand, if you use all your slides during one segment of your presentation, the audience is in the dark only part of the time, and the slides can give you a good change of pace. When the lights go on again and the focus of attention returns to you, you will be speaking to an audience that has just had its interest renewed by the introduction of something new in the proceedings.

Another way to make the slide portion of your talk heighten interest is to use a large number of slides within any given slide period and flash them on the screen in rapid succession. My rule is fifteen seconds or less for each slide. I realize that this is not always possible. If there is statistical information to be presented against a particular slide ("This slide shows you how our corporation spent its gross income last year") and if you need more than fifteen seconds to tick off such information, you will have to keep the slide on longer. But you should then consider breaking up the slide into several shorter ones or using a "pop on" technique where slide A shows one fact; slide B shows the same fact plus one other; slide C shows everything that was on A and B plus a third fact; and so on. In this manner, you can eventually show on a single slide (the last in the grouping) all the material needed to explain your point. At the same time, you will have kept up the action while building to a climax.

• *What other visual devices can improve a presentation?* The list is as big as your imagination and depends, naturally, on the context and purpose of your talk. If you're introducing this season's line of men's shirts to a group of salespeople, you might have every item in the line on display behind you and stand beside each one as you describe it. If you're a physician talking about anatomy, perhaps you'll want a skeleton with removable parts. If you're an ecologist talking about how modern packaging clutters the environment, you could stand in front of twenty tables, each displaying different types of packages, and weave your talk around this visual material. If you're a hair stylist addressing a group of beauty shop owners, you might want to use live models.

Apart from such special devices, there are several of a more general nature that have proved uncommonly successful in practice.

One spectacular technique requires a room with corkboards all around it. Failing this, you can have special boards cut for you that can take tacks or two-sided tape, and place these boards around two, three, or four sides of the room to create "a wall within a wall." Tack up all your visuals sequentially on the boards, and then cover them with large sheets of paper or cloth. As you give your talk, remove the coverings from the various sections of your displayed material (or if you wish to stand in one place and speak from a podium up front, have an assistant remove the coverings as you address the audience). When you have finished your presentation, your audience will literally be surrounded by a visual summary of your talk.

A reversal of this technique offers you an excellent way to build up your visuals to a dramatic close. Instead of starting with all the visuals already in place, begin with blank walls or boards. Have an assistant tack up or tape up each visual as you talk about it. The tacking up of every point (either in key words or pictures) should be done *after* the point is made, not before, in order not to kill the suspense of your narration. When you are ready for a summary or conclusions, you can move around the walls, using the posted visuals as aids in ticking off the points you have covered verbally. By the time you return to the lectern, you will have paved the way for your closing lines.

There are a number of variations on these techniques for revealing or building up your presentation with visual props. For example, another way to "reveal" is to use a series of horizontal venetian blinds, and as each point is made, turn down another slat of the blind on which key words are lettered. A more condensed version of the "buildup" device involves using a flannel board—a flocked display board to which cards of all shapes and sizes (some with pictures mounted on them, some with lettering) will easily and firmly adhere. The cards are affixed on the back with a magnetic gum, which you can buy wherever you purchase the flannel board. One or two such boards are usually sufficient to hold all the visual materials a speaker might want to pop on during an average-length presentation. Of course, all the suggestions made previously for design of flip card visuals apply equally to the pictures and lettering used in this type of buildup.

Finally, a couple of short thoughts on using your visual aids to greatest advantage. Keep in mind that you're on the program to speak to the assembled audience, not to have a conversation with your visuals. It is surprising how often speakers unwittingly turn their backs on their audiences and address their visual material, face-to-face. This doesn't make the people out front curious about what's going on up there; it just turns them off.

Remember, since the audience has come to hear *you*, it just doesn't make sense to let your visual aids upstage you. After all, even if you do "make love to them," your visuals are still only supporting players. *You* are the star of the program!

Are there ways in which your *audio* aids can also be made to work harder for you? You bet. First of all, if you consider using audio aids, don't limit your thinking to the sound track of a film that might be part of your presentation. There is virtually no end to the imaginative ways in which sound can enhance your talk. Here's an example of how far out you can go in using sound to intrigue your audience and reinforce your message.

I was working for a subsidiary of Lorimar Telepictures when I became acquainted with Lee Rich, then president of Lorimar, the company that produced "Dallas," "Knots Landing," "Falcon Crest," and other successful TV series. Lee is a terrific speaker, and when his schedule permits, he needs no help from anyone in putting together a blockbuster presentation. But there was a time when Lorimar as a corporation was moving ahead at breakneck speed, selling syndications and foreign rights to their TV series, producing motion pictures, expanding through mergers and acquisitions, and so on. Lee had accepted an invitation to be the keynote speaker at an annual conference of the Advertising Research Foundation, and as the date of his talk approached, he realized that his hectic schedule dictated he get some scripting help. I flew to the West Coast and had a number of meetings with Lee, whose input was far greater than that of many executives who work with a "ghost." I came back East inspired and determined to help him give an unforgettable speech. Some 2,000 people had preregistered for this conference, and it was expected that most of them would attend the luncheon where Lee was to deliver his talk.

He had been asked to speak on the subject of a producer's responsibilities to society when creating programs for television, and we agreed the title of his talk should be "Am I My Brother's Keeper?" Lee told me he wanted to start off with a bang.

As I reviewed the material that would go into the speech, I was impressed by some facts Lee had given me. He wanted to make the point that "you can lead a horse to water, but you cannot make him drink." Translation: You can lead a viewer to culture, but you cannot make him watch. I had at hand some comparative figures on viewing habits that showed what had happened when two much-advertised programs had recently been aired on the same night at the same hour. One of those programs was about incest, until that time a taboo that couldn't even be talked about on television. The show got an incredibly large audience: It was seen, wholly or in part, by sixty million viewers. In the greater New York area, two and a half million people watched it.

At precisely the time the show was airing, Mozart's *Magic Flute* was being telecast on another station. It was a superb production, and much print and on-air advertising had been calling it to the attention of potential viewers. But Mozart got a mere 1.9 rating against a 39.6 rating for the show on incest. Lee Rich wanted to present these figures along with others that showed sex and titillation winning out over "culture" every time.

Of course, the easy way to have made the point would have been to show some slides with numbers or maybe a graph. But I was not going to do that for Lee Rich. Here's how he began his speech: He walked to the microphone and stood silent for a few seconds. Suddenly the sounds of the Vienna Philharmonic playing the overture to the *Magic Flute* filled every corner of the ballroom. The audience was stunned and intrigued. Lee stood silent. The overture continued. The audience went on wondering. Then the music slowly faded as Lee began speaking. "That," he said softly, "was the overture to Mozart's *Magic Flute*, which most of you undoubtedly recognized. It is not unconnected to what I will say here today. I'll get back to Mozart in a little while." When he got to the point in his speech where he gave the ratings of Mozart versus incest, he referred to the beauty of the music and the extraordinary quality of the TV production on the night it was telecast opposite the much-viewed competition.

Not only did Lee's unusual introduction make the audience wonder and care about what he was going to say, but no one at that luncheon could possibly ever forget the point it made. The audio was no mere gimmick. *It was used to reinforce the message.* It *was* the message.

I once had a speaker start by showing an early film of the Beatles in concert. Another time, I opened the annual meeting of a large company with a Salvation Army band marching down the aisle and playing Christmas music. I once had a speaker begin his presentation with the room in darkness and amplifiers bringing to the audience the voices of Franklin D. Roosevelt and Winston Churchill uttering the opinions expressed on page 126 of this book.

All of these, of course, are theatrical devices. But why not? A speech *is* theater, and there's no reason why you shouldn't make use of the many audio possibilities that are available to you as a performer. One caution, however: You do not merely want to hit the mule over the head just to get his attention (see story on page 15). What the audience hears should never be extraneous to your message. Your audio should, in some way, be connected to your theme or to some significant point you wish to make. Or borrowing from the ways in which Hollywood uses a sound track, you may want to use your audio to set a mood or set the stage for what's ahead. So when preparing your speech or presentation, think *sound*.

Well integrated and used imaginatively, your audio devices, like your visuals, can emphasize, explain, sharpen, and reinforce your rhetoric to make you a speaker an audience won't easily forget.

GUARANTEED APPLAUSE

The Fifteen Best Speech Bits I've Ever Heard

Ever so rarely, one hears a story or a line that is virtually timeless and almost certain to evoke the desired audience reaction—provided, of course, that the speaker delivers the material in such a way that his listeners fully understand both the punch line and what went before it. (Obviously, an audience can't be expected to respond to something it hasn't heard well enough to absorb.) I've heard hundreds and hundreds of talks. And of the thousands of stories, allegories, and punch lines in them, there are only a handful of such bits I'd be willing to include in this category of immortals.

I've used each of these gems a number of times in speeches I've ghosted. And sitting in on the deliveries, I've never known any of them to fail. Nor did they receive mere trickles of response; they got everything from 100 percent applause or laughter to standing ovations. Each of these items offers numerous possibilities for adaptation to special situations. And each of them is a winner that can also be used in social situations—to make a point, offer advice, help a flagging conversation come alive. Here are my candidates for the top bits ever delivered from a platform.

*

1. Russian Fable

I think I can best make my point by telling you an old Russian fable. A small bird lay freezing to death on a country road in Russia. A peasant came along, saw the dying bird, and thought to himself, if only I had something—anything—in which to wrap this bird, I might save its life, for surely it is freezing to death. Unfortunately, he had nothing on him that he could spare.

Nearby he caught sight of some cow droppings, and in desperation he thought, perhaps if I wrap the bird in that, it will warm it enough to save its life. He picked up the bird, wrapped it in the cow dung, laid it gently on the ground, and went on his way. Sure enough, the dung began to warm the bird, and it started to come to life again. The bird felt so overjoyed at being warm again that it attempted to sing. But all it could emit in its weakened condition were some low, pitiful notes.

Just then, another peasant came along. He heard the bird's attempt at song and thought, Poor bird, it's strangulating in that cow dung. So he picked it up, removed the dung, laid the bird back on the ground, and—confident that he had saved its life—went on his way. Shortly thereafter, the bird died of the cold.

There are three morals to this fable. The first one is: It isn't necessarily your enemies who put you in it. The second one is: It isn't necessarily your friends who get you out of it. And the third moral is: When you're in it up to here, for God's sake, don't sing!

There are many ways in which this Russian fable can be used in a talk. It might be used to summarize what has gone before. Or it can be used after giving advice to people whose business or industry is beset by regulatory problems. It can be used appropriately when talking to, or about, politicians. Or it can be used at the tail end of a talk after saying something such as this: "I have been asked to give you my thoughts on [subject], which I have tried to do. And now, I'd like to throw in a piece of gratuitous advice, in the form of a Russian fable." As you go through the draft of your own speech, perhaps you will find an even better way to work in this story.

*

2. Always A Better Way

A brave young man had just finished his period of training as a member of the Royal Canadian Mounted Police. Before he went off into the wilderness on his first assignment, his fellow Mounties gave him a farewell party. As a going-away gift, they presented him with a complete martini-making set: a bottle of Canadian gin, some vermouth, a martini mixer, a stirrer, even a bottle of olives. The new Mountie thanked his friends most graciously, but he commented that he really didn't see a martini setup as a very appropriate gift for someone going off alone, into virtually unsettled territory, to search out a wanted criminal.

"Ah!" said one of his friends, a more experienced Mountie. "You'll find it to be a very important part of your equipment indeed. You may be out there in the vast wilderness, totally alone, for weeks or maybe even months. Sooner or later, you will yearn for the sound of another human voice. Then you will remember your martini set. You'll take it out, start to make yourself a martini, and in ten seconds flat there'll be someone at your shoulder saying, 'That's not the way to make a martini!' "

> This is a most serviceable story because it can so easily be adapted to a host of activities other than martini making. For example, a speaker might have occasion to say: "You may not like the way we planned this program. At meetings such as this, there is always someone who knows a better way. And that reminds me of the story about the young Canadian Mountie who. . . ."
>
> In addition to being awfully good in public speech, it's also an infallible way to put down someone who says to you, "That's not the way to build a fire!" or "That's not the way to barbecue chicken!" or to handle any of those other situations in which people make it clear that they believe their way is better than yours.

*

3. Eager Beaver

When Woodrow Wilson was governor of New Jersey, a very ambitious young civil servant called him at his home at 3:30 one morning and said in an urgent voice, "Mr. Governor, I'm sorry to wake you, but your state auditor has just died, and I would like to know if I can take his place."

Mr. Wilson thought that over for a moment and then replied dryly, "Well, I guess it's all right with me if it's all right with the undertaker."

> Although this story is credited to Woodrow Wilson (there is no way of proving or disproving that he actually said it), it can be adapted to almost any political candidate: "People are so anxious to work on George Bush's team that, just the other day, an eager young politician got through the White House switchboard to him at 3:30 A.M. and said, 'Mr. President, sir, I heard that a member of your staff has just died, and I wonder if. . . .' " The story can also be used to make a point about the many people who might be vying for a position on the board of directors of a big business firm or for a position on the board of a museum, school, or civic organization. Or it can be nicely adapted to refer to staff members of a college or university who are eager for promotion. In fact, there is almost no competitive situation in which the eagerness of the competitors cannot be teased with this anecdote.

*

4. Appearances Deceive

A lumber camp had advertised for help, and one morning a skinny little guy swaggered into the camp looking for the senior honcho in charge of lumberjacks. When he found him, the big, burly outdoorsman sneered at the runty applicant and told him to get out. "My ax," he said, "weighs more than you do. Scram!"

But the little fellow wouldn't give up and pleaded for an opportunity to show what he could do. Finally, the head lumberjack said: "Okay, here's my ax. Let's see you do your stuff on that baby sapling." In less than two minutes, the small tree was down.

"Great!" said the number one lumberjack. "Over there's a redwood that's a hundred years old. Let's see what you can do with that one." In five minutes that tree, too, was down. The head lumberjack was amazed. "I can't believe it," he said. "Where did you ever learn to chop trees like that?"

"In the Sahara Forest," replied the skinny little man.

"You mean," the lumberjack said, "the Sahara Desert."

"Sure," said the little man, "now!"

This is an excellent story to use if you yourself are slight of build and are addressing an audience shortly after having been promoted into a new position. Follow the story with a line such as this: "So don't be misled by my size. I took on this assignment because I felt I could do the job, and I plan to surprise all the skeptics." In any situation in which you want the audience to realize that "appearances can be deceptive or misleading," this story gives you an excellent way to make your point without appearing to sermonize.

*

5. Dig This One

The story is told of an industrialist who went to Latin America to build a manufacturing plant. After several years of constructing the expensive facility and launching the new business, he discovered that it was taking too long for raw materials to arrive from the other side of the mountain to where his new factory was located.

The solution seemed to be to build a tunnel through the mountain to cut down the transit time for carrying supplies to the manufacturing facility. The entrepreneur consulted with the major engineering firms in this underdeveloped country, asking each to submit an estimate for designing and constructing such a tunnel. When the estimates came in, the figures were so high that the industrialist felt he could not possibly finance such a venture.

He gave the matter much thought and then, knowing that local labor was very cheap and in good supply, hired two hundred laborers. He put one half to work digging through the mountain on one side and one hundred digging on the other side. "This way," he told his friends, "if they meet in the middle, I'll have a tunnel. If they *don't* meet, I'll have *two* tunnels!"

> *This tale can be told to illustrate any number of points:*
> *"Ingenuity will often accomplish the impossible."*
> *"Big minds may seek big solutions to problems, but some-times it's toil and sweat that provide the best answer."*
> *"Management may have a pretty good notion of how to solve the problems, but without labor, nothing will happen."*
> *"If you're going to operate your business abroad, you had better be ready to meet some unusual situations—and go prepared to handle those situations with imagination."*

*

6. What Can You Do For Me Lately?

One government agency often under attack by consumerists is the Federal Communications Commission. Of course, not all the FCC's problems come from consumerists. When Newton Minow was head of the agency, he complained that his chief problem came from his mother. She called him up and said: "Newton, since you've been in that job, the television programs have really got much better. But can't you do anything about the TV dinners?"

> *Although this very effective anecdote takes off on a gov-ernment agency, it is easy to bridge from the punch line to other operational groups. After giving Mrs. Minow's comment, you might say something such as this: "We have the same problem in our business. After we put into effect all the quality controls, updated distribution, improved warranties, and easy-replacement policies that customers have been yelling about, they call us up and ask, "But how come you didn't lower the price?"*
> *This anecdote is effective whenever you want to make the point that you simply can't do enough for certain people. And whether or not your audience is familiar with the problems of the FCC or has ever heard of Newton*

Minow makes no difference, audiences seem to get the point just the same.

*

7. Woman's Ad-Lib

A woman motorist was doing seventy miles an hour on a highway with a fifty-five-mile speed limit. She happened to glance in her rearview mirror and spotted two state troopers on motorcycles as they pulled out from behind a billboard she had just passed. They seemed to be catching up with her, so she put her foot down on the gas and zoomed up to eighty miles an hour, with the cops in hot pursuit.

Down the road she spotted a service station. Gunning the motor, she roared into the station, drew to a screaming halt, jumped out of her car, and dashed into the ladies' room.

After a little while, she came out and saw the troopers flanking her car. She walked brightly over to where they were waiting and, with a big grin on her face, said, "You didn't think I'd make it, did you?"

> This story is effective if you or some other speaker is late in arriving or if the program is off to a late start. Then you might preface the story with a comment on how "our lateness in getting started puts me in mind of the woman motorist. . . ."
>
> However, the story has a fine track record in other situations as well. For example, you can use it at the end of your talk, after which you might say something to this effect: "We promised you this session would be over by noon, and I'm sure some, listening to me prattle on, didn't think we'd make it. Well, I have come to the end, and we have made it—just in time for lunch."
>
> In reviewing your own proposed talk, use a bit of imagination to find other ways in which this story might serve you. A speaker talking about his industry's self-regulation—which was, perhaps, late in getting organized—could tie in with the punch line. A company president

addressing his stockholders could use the tag line as an amusing way of getting across the point that the company had a profit and dividend objective and that maybe some "didn't think we'd make it." In fact, any situation in which there is doubt about whether an individual or a group or an organization "might make it" provides a perfect opportunity to use this certain laugh getter.

*

8. Big Bargain

At the time of the first walk on the moon, a reporter asked one of the astronauts if he had been nervous when he was strapped into his seat before going into space.

"Well," the astronaut said, "of course I was. Who wouldn't be? There I was, sitting on top of 9,999 parts and bits—each of which had been made by the lowest bidder!"

This quickie rejoinder gets a big hand, whether the audience is made up of businesspeople, students, or anyone else. And it can easily be juggled into a place in your talk, whether your topic is the economy, the high cost of living, free enterprise, nervousness, reality testing, psychoanalysis, bargains, science, or education facilities.

*

9. Presidential Suite

I have to tell you about the terrible experience I had when I got in town last night. I arrived at the hotel, went to the registration desk, and found that no room had been reserved for me, even though I had written ahead for one.

I was a bit irritated and explained to the registration clerk that I was scheduled to speak here today, and it was essential that I have a place to sleep. There was a long line behind me, and the clerk was very harassed, and he said: "Look, we'd certainly give you a room if we had one. There simply isn't a vacant room anywhere in the hotel."

I told him that I simply couldn't believe that. "Do you mean to say," I asked, "that if President Bush showed up, you'd turn him away? Wouldn't you manage to find him a room?"

"Well," admitted the clerk, "I guess if Mr. Bush showed up, we'd find a room for him somehow."

"Great!" I said. "Give me his room. He's not coming!"

This is an excellent story to use if you are speaking in a big and busy city that is not your hometown or if you're attending a convention at a crowded resort. Everyone who goes to large meetings out of town has, at some time, had the experience of finding the hotel overbooked. It's also a pretty good story if you're abroad and speaking to a foreign audience that doesn't mind a bit of good-natured ribbing about its overworked hotel facilities.

This anecdote is especially good as an opener, but it can also be used elsewhere in your talk. For example, if you're speaking to an audience in a city other than your own and want to say some nice things about the town, you might comment on the lovely airport, the friendly taxi drivers, the scenery, the downtown skyline, or a host of other appropriate things. Then, you might follow by saying: "However, I did have a bit of a scare when I arrived at the hotel last night. The clerk told me. . . ."

Here's yet another way to use it. If you come from a big city such as New York, where out of towners find the natives less than friendly, you might run it in along these lines: "Yes, your city is delightful to look at, great to be in, and I must say I have found people to be a lot friendlier than you might find them to be when you come to visit me in [speaker's hometown]. Why, just last week one of my friends was in from out of town, and when he arrived at his hotel. . . ."

The story can also be adapted to an airline reservation that the computer failed to acknowledge. ("I guess if Mr. Bush showed up, we'd find a seat for him somewhere on the plane.")

*

10. Thou Shalt Not Swear

A young boy was pulling a loaded wagon down the road when the wheels fell off. "I'll be damned," said the boy. He spent some time putting the wheels back on and went on his way. Very soon, the wheels fell off again. "I'll be damned!" he cried out.

A minister was passing by and heard the boy's remark. He stopped and said to the boy: "You shouldn't swear when something like that happens. What you should say is 'Praise the Lord.'"

The boy replaced the wheels once more and went on his way, the minister riding alongside the wagon. But in no time at all, the wheels fell off again. "Praise the Lord!" shouted the boy. The wheels leapt off the ground and reattached themselves to the wagon.

"I'll be damned!" cried the minister.

> *This story might then be followed by a comment such as this: "And, frankly, that's how I felt when I heard the news about. . . ." Or it can be used as an opener if the audience is, unexpectedly, S.R.O. Any place in your talk where you deal with a truly surprising event or piece of information could offer an opportunity to break in with this laugh getter. If you prefer, you can change the wagon wheels to the hubcaps on an automobile.*

*

11. Positive Thinking

A scientist, unjustly accused and convicted of a major crime, found himself incarcerated with a long-term sentence in a jail in the midst of the desert. His cellmate turned out to be another scientist. Determined to escape, the first man tried to convince his coprofessional to make the attempt with him, but the man refused. After much planning and with the undetected help of other inmates, our scientist made his escape.

But the heat of the desert, the lack of food and water, and his inability to locate another human being anywhere drove him almost mad, and he was forced to turn around and return to the jail. He reported his terrible experience to the other scientist, who surprised him by saying, "Yes, I know; I tried it and failed, too, for the same reasons."

The first scientist responded bitterly, "For heaven's sake, man, when you knew I was going to make a break for it, why didn't you tell me what it was like out there?"

To which his cellmate replied, with a shrug of the shoulders, "Who publishes negative results?"

> One need not be a scientist or be addressing scientists to use this story. I have heard it bring roars of laughter from media people, from students, and from businesspeople. In fact, I wrote it into a business executive's speech in the following manner. He was giving an annual report to the stockholders of the company he headed. First, he told all the good things that had happened to the company that year. Then, he said: "Now, maybe you think everything in the last twelve months has been almost too good to be true. And perhaps you are remembering that great story about the scientist unjustly accused. . . ." When the business executive said, "Who publishes negative results?" he all but brought down the house. And with the audience still laughing and chuckling, he went on to say, "I'm going to give you all the results of our last year's operation— including a few negative ones." After that, he presented the less happy side of the annual ledger. I truly think his stockholders took the bad news in good grace because of the delightful lead-in.
>
> Similarly, the tale can be told by any appointed or elected official reporting to his community on a mixed bag of results from a specific program or campaign. It can be employed successfully by almost anyone—doctors, teachers, publishers, manufacturers, store executives, and, of course, researchers—reporting on some study or program that was recently concluded, with or without "negative results."

*

12. Taking Off On Management Consultants

Leo Rosten, writing in the old Saturday Review, *told the following story about "an unknown wit, analyzing the*

*operations of a symphony orchestra for technical effi-
ciency." However, the story would apply to any situation
in which a management consultant is called upon to evaluate a business, a university, a hospital, a government
agency, or any other institution. Rosten stated that the
following report on the orchestra was submitted:*

"All twelve violins were playing identical notes; this is unnecessary and wasteful duplication. The violin section could be cut
drastically, saving considerable labor costs.

"The oboe players had absolutely nothing to do for long periods
of time. They just sat in their chairs. Their number should be
reduced. Compositions involving the oboe can be rewritten so that
the work is spread out more evenly, thus eliminating costly 'peaks'
and 'valleys' of oboe productivity.

"I noted a recurring repetition of certain musical passages. What
useful purpose is served by repeating on the horns what has already
been produced by the strings?

"Were all such redundant passages eliminated, the concert time
(two hours) could easily be reduced to forty minutes. This would
also eliminate the need for a time-wasting intermission.

"Something should be done about the shocking obsolescence of
equipment. The program notes informed me that the first violinist's
instrument was several hundred years old. If normal depreciation
schedules had been applied, the value of this instrument would
have been reduced to zero, and a more modern and efficient violin
could easily have been purchased."

*As a speaker, you might then go on to warn your audience
to beware of arithmetic—because you cannot always make
music with it.*

*

13. The Last Word

A man pulled off the highway and went into a roadside diner to
have lunch. He ordered a hamburger, a cup of coffee, and a piece
of pie. As his lunch was set before him, three rough-looking guys

in leather jackets, motorcycle helmets, and boots entered the diner and sat down beside him at the counter. One grabbed his hamburger and ate it. Another grabbed his coffee and drank it, and the third tasted his pie, then mashed the rest of it on the plate.

The man said nothing, got up, paid the cashier for the food, and walked out. The three guys turned to the cashier, and one said: "Not much of a man, is he?"

"He's not much of a driver, either," said the cashier. "He just ran his truck over three motorcycles."

> These are just some of the points you can lead into from the truck driver story:
> "Silence speaks louder than words, particularly when accompanied by action."
> "Speak softly—even better, not at all—and carry a big stick."
> "It isn't always the loudmouth who has the last word."
> "Getting even; having the last word; tit for tat; a soft answer doesn't always turn away wrath—or hide it."
> If you can't find a place for this tale in your talk, save it. Tell it later, at lunch or over drinks or out on the golf course. I guarantee the laughter.

*

14. True Power

William Wrigley, Jr., the chewing gum magnate who amassed a great fortune, was traveling on a train with a friend who asked him why he continued to spend millions of dollars on advertising.

"Your gum is already known the world over," argued his friend. "Why don't you save the millions you are spending on advertising?"

Wrigley thought a moment and then asked, "How fast is this train going?"

"About sixty-five miles an hour," replied his friend.

"Then why doesn't the railway company remove the engine and let the train travel on its own momentum?" asked Wrigley.

If you are in advertising or marketing, this story might

then be followed by this line: "Advertising is the engine that fuels the economy." If you're a university or hospital administrator talking to the staff: "Administration is the engine that drives this whole operation. Without it, the work of the so-called professional staff would come to a halt." In politics: "Were it not for the workers behind the scenes, everything would cease. We are the engine that drives the whole political campaign."

*

15. One-Upmanship

Three stores on the main street in town stood side by side. They all sold the same type of merchandise. One day the owner of the store at one end put up this sign: ROCK BOTTOM PRICES.

This prompted the storekeeper at the other end to hang up a sign reading: LOWEST PRICES IN TOWN.

The owner of the store in the middle was thrown by these aggressive maneuvers until he had a bright idea. He put up his own sign, which proclaimed, MAIN ENTRANCE.

This "Main Entrance" story can be used to make any number of points:
"There is always a way to beat out the competition."
"We have to find a way to write 'main entrance' on our product line."
"Like the retailer in the story, we find ourselves between a rock and a hard place."
"It ain't over till it's over."

REHEARSALS

You're in Show Biz, So Do As the Professionals Do

Every professional actor rehearses. It is suicide for an amateur to take to the platform without it. Rehearsal is your insurance policy against sounding unprepared or unfamiliar with your subject matter.

After all his years in show business, Bob Hope still rehearses. So do Meryl Streep and Al Pacino and Carol Burnett and Dustin Hoffman and every other successful performer. Perhaps the only people in show business who don't have an opportunity to rehearse are TV's news anchors. That's because the news breaks quickly, there's little time for the script to be written, and because these people do it day in and day out until they develop a personal, proven technique. And even such daily practice does not always make perfect.

As a public speaker, you, too, are in show business. And like every show-biz performer, you face an expectant, sometimes critical audience that may even have paid to come to the meeting. Once you're center stage, there is no director, no time to redo a "take," and little sympathy if you fall flat on your face. So do not even *think* of giving an important speech without rehearsals. And the more the better.

The principal benefit of rehearsals is that you develop familiarity with your script *as spoken*. Familiarity breeds confidence. If you've rehearsed enough, it will be possible for you to look at your typed copy while delivering your talk but still look up occasionally to

make eye contact with the audience. The more familiar you become
with where the words are on the page, the less likely that you will
have to search for your place when your eyes return to the script
after a glance at those out front.

Here are ten excellent reasons for you to rehearse:

1. *You need to read out loud.* When an advertising agency or
theatrical producer holds a casting session, the waiting room of the
casting department is usually filled with professional actors vying
for roles. Each is given a script before being auditioned, and were
you to wander through that room, you would hear the quiet sound
of all those applicants rehearsing their scripts out loud—talking to
themselves. Why, you might wonder, don't they speak the lines
silently, within their heads? Why do they actually give voice to
them? The answer lies in the fact that there is a vast difference
between the two methods and would-be performers learned that
fact in drama school. The out-loud rehearsal helps the actor *feel*
the words and the rhythm. It helps the actor hear which words
need to be pronounced more slowly in order to have them understood. It prevents stumbling during delivery and, in your case as a
public speaker, helps you avoid that awful pitfall: having an audience
think you are unfamiliar with your own material.

2. *You can edit to the spoken word.* By the time you are ready
for a rehearsal, you will have edited your written talk several times
(see Step 10 in the *Simmons System,* pages 27–35). But only when
you speak the words out loud will you discover which parts of your
talk seem to drag or need a pick-me-up. That's a clear signal for
you to doctor your script with more quips, quotations, or one-liners.
Mark the needy spots on your script, and when the rehearsal is
over, settle back with this book and explore some of the possibilities
you may have missed. Using the Subject Index can prove surprisingly
helpful as you may discover some unexpected treasures that you
overlooked before you had specific holes to fill.

3. *You discover the value of tape recording your rehearsal.*
Unless you are a seasoned and frequent public speaker, recording
your rehearsal is the way to go. When you play it back and hear
your own delivery, you know as well as any speech coach where
you need to speed up or slow down, where to phrase more carefully
or sometimes even repeat a few words or a whole sentence for
impact. It suggests places where you might want to speak more

loudly for emphasis or whisper for effect. You soon find out how varying the speed with which you deliver your talk, as well as changes in your projection from soft to adamant, works for you in keeping the audience alert and attentive.

4. *You gauge the humor.* When you rehearse, if you have an audience of one or maybe a few colleagues, you might fail to get the laughter you expected from a story or quip. Don't feel you need to delete that part of your talk. Every stand-up comic will tell you that humor is more likely to bring forth laughter when told to an audience of many rather than to an individual. If your humorous bit was picked up from this book, be assured that it *has* worked for someone, somewhere, and if told well and audibly, if you don't swallow or mangle the punch line, it should work for you, too. And that's the advantage of rehearsals. They help you get the feel of the joke or one-liner until you are quite comfortable about the way you deliver it.

5. *You perfect your delivery.* Many speakers have a tendency to drop their pitch at the end of a sentence because that's the way we normally speak in conversation. Doing this in a speech can hurt your delivery. While it's desirable to vary your tempo and cadence, it's always a poor idea to swallow the end of a sentence. Some speakers blame their ghostwriters for having given them poor material that failed to get a response from listeners when the real problem was that part of the audience never heard the end of the sentence. And they were so busy asking their neighbors what it was the speaker said that the next lines were completely lost as well! So though you might drop your voice at the end of a sentence while at the dinner table, don't do it on the platform. Recording your rehearsal enables you to hear whether this is a problem that you want to correct.

6. *You can edit to fit your allotted time.* You will know well in advance how much time is allotted to you on the program. Don't plan to race through your presentation to conform to the time you've been given. This makes all parts of your talk difficult to follow and does not allow you adequate time to project your own style and personality. Instead, after timing your speech in rehearsal, eliminate as much as necessary to bring your talk into the required time frame.

The time allocated to you should not be taken lightly, and keep in mind that it's meant to be the *outside* time. You may have precisely twenty-five minutes before the waiters are due to arrive and make a noisy performance of their own as they set the tables. Or there may be another speaker who is forced to cram his remarks into minimal time because you ran over your own allotted period.

Racing through your talk gives the audience the impression that you're bored with your own material and want to get it over with. That could well turn them off. A relaxed but inspired speaker communicates to the listeners that what is being said is important, perhaps even vital, both to the speaker and to the audience.

7. *You learn to use the microphone.* The success of a speech can sometimes depend upon how well a speaker uses the microphone. Faulty use of the mike can defeat even a brilliant script and adequate rehearsals. Failure to get across even 1 percent of a sentence can have unfortunate results if that 1 percent contains the key to the whole line or to the punch line.

Here are a few fundamental tips on correct use of a microphone: Rocking back and forth while speaking, or alternating between standing straight up and leaning on the lectern, produces an uneven projection: The audience hears you shouting and whispering in turns.

If you use visuals and turn to the screen to discuss something being projected, remember that the mike won't pick you up unless it's a neck mike.

If at all possible, get on the platform *before* your meeting begins, preferably with a technician at hand (and a projectionist, if your performance calls for one), and familiarize yourself with the equipment: the podium light, the remote switch for slides, the height of the mike relative to your height, even the glass of water. Knowing where everything is and how everything works prevents fumbling and stumbling.

8. *You can decide whether to use a professional director.* In Inside Tips From the Author (page 1), I mentioned that even theatrical directors are sometimes willing to take on the free-lance job of directing a person who is going to give an important speech and wants professional help in preparing for it. Such available expertise is not always prohibitively expensive, because a director at leisure is sometimes happy to pick up a little pocket money for a couple of hours' work. If you don't live in one of the cities where theater is a staple of the area, think about contacting the director of a regional theater or even a local semipro drama group.

If you work for an advertising agency or if your company retains such an agency, there will be at least one or perhaps many people on staff who direct and produce television commercials. Those people are usually superb directors, as they understand the basics of communication to large audiences, and they know how to make every second count. Getting such a pro to sit in on one of your rehearsals and make suggestions can be of inestimable value in improving your delivery.

9. *You can avoid the 8:00 A.M. editing session.* Unless the program chairperson tells you at the last minute that your time on the platform has just been cut from twenty minutes to ten, don't, for pity's sake, try to cut or edit your speech the morning you're to deliver it. Ninety-nine times out of a hundred, the person who does this does it out of nervousness or a sudden lack of confidence and ends up with a talk that doesn't track well, ideas that don't segue into each other, and an impression among the audience that this speaker inadvertently left out a sentence or more.

For better or worse, make up your mind at the time of your final rehearsal that you're going to live with your script as edited at that time.

10. *You should keep clear of well-intentioned friends.* It's almost always a bad idea to go out with friends or colleagues the night before your speech and describe to them the jokes and anecdotes and philosophical lines you plan to use in your talk the next day. Everyone likes to show how smart he is, make Brownie points. Everyone likes to play at being the Savior—the person who saves you at the last second from making a fool of yourself.

Generally, people find it easier and more satisfying to say, "I don't like it" or "Better take that out!" or maybe even "Let me give you a better punch line!" rather than "It's great . . . go with it!" That's a human trait, and it's never done any speaker any good. The ideas, the quotations, the stories you tell a large audience gathered in goodwill, in a receptive mood, with some degree of respect and awe for the speaker, will get a vastly different response from the one you might get over drinks with a couple of friends. Your script was not written for them. If you truly want their input, get it early on. Then you'll have plenty of time to calmly evaluate its merits rather than chop up a good talk at the last minute.

Finally, if you worry that too many rehearsals may turn you into the performer who "walks through" the lines because they've been mouthed too often, worry not! You will not be repeating your performance hundreds of times like a matinee idol. The rehearsals you do are a far cry from the eight performances a week, month after month, that are necessary for theatrical performers.

How many rehearsals? As many as you need to feel satisfied with your finally edited script, to feel confident about your delivery, and to be convinced that your audio and visual aids (if you use any) will work as planned. But if I had to give you a number—and if you are not Lee Iacocca, Ann Richards, or Mario Cuomo—I'd say not less than four rehearsals, with one of those being a final run-through with a script that satisfies you.

When the time comes for rehearsals, you should consider the possibility, unlikely as it is, that another speaker on your program might use one of the anecdotes or jokes that you have included in your script. In the many years I've been involved with speakers and speechwriting, I've known this to happen only twice, and it is quite unlikely that it will happen to you. Just the same, unless you are the only speaker on the program, you should consider it to be a possibility.

The best way to avoid such duplication of material is to ask the chairperson or the individual who invited you to be on the program to provide you with advance copies of the talks others plan to give. You won't necessarily get them. Many speakers refuse to release their speeches before they are delivered from the platform. Should you be asked to release yours, I advise you to eliminate your jokes from any advance copy that you give to anyone other than your projectionist. Seasoned speakers usually do this. (For more on this subject, see page 3.)

If someone ahead of you on the program tells a story that you had planned to use, you have two choices. If the story is not essential to the point you want to make, merely eliminate it. However, if the story leads to a point you wish to make, or amplifies the point, or emphasizes it, refer to the previous speaker and say something such as this: "I think [name of speaker] made a good point when she [or he] told you the story about [identify story or its punchline]. She [or he] was making my point—namely, that [continue with your prepared script].

Don't lose any sleep over the possibility of someone using your material. To repeat, it is not likely to happen. In the event that it does, don't let it throw you. If neither of the above options works for you, just be gracious and say something such as this: "I'm glad that [name of speaker] told my joke for me—the one about [subject of joke or its punch line]. She [or he] is a much better joke teller than I am, and I'm glad that the point has been made for me. [Repeat the point of the joke that leads into the next part of your speech.]

EXTRA MILEAGE FROM YOUR SPEECH

Provocative Titles and Good Publicity

If the speech you are invited to make comes ready-made with a title—and if it also happens to be a *good* one—count yourself lucky. Most often, you'll be told the subject of your talk (or asked to pick one yourself), and it will be up to you to come up with the title along with the script.

Devising a title isn't difficult. Almost any climactic sentence right out of the speech text could probably serve as a handle. But an exciting and provocative title—and by that I mean one that arouses interest, anger, laughter, agreement, disagreement, or just plain curiosity—is going to help bring in a larger audience and get you press coverage and other publicity when the talk is over. Here are some considerations when creating your title:

• *Should you create your title before or after you write the speech?* There's no rule, and it doesn't matter. Obviously, if a title occurs to you at the outset, you will have it in mind while thinking through your talk; and as you write the script, you'll be able to "prove out" the title, or make it fulfill its promise. But most speakers change titles several times before they settle on one, and often the best titles come right out of the script after it's been committed to paper.

• *How do you think up an exciting title?* Once in a while, it will just come to you—which isn't as miraculous as it sounds. All those weeks of planning, researching, and thinking through your speech will have left your unconscious with a residue of ideas that will be stimulated into consciousness as you seek a title line to summarize your basic thesis or woo an audience. Sometimes, one of your favorite lines or phrases in the script will seem to stand out every time you read it, and you may feel it has enough built-in interest to make a good headline. But often you will need some special stimulus to get yourself thinking in the right direction. I usually start by "checking my p's and q's." Let me explain. I keep an index card in my desk drawer that has these words on it:

For Titles, Check These P's & Q's

Provoke	Praise
Question	Quip
Predict	Paraphrase
Quote	Pique Curiosity

With these eight "clues" in front of me, I then go through my speech text several times, looking for ways to provoke interest or disagreement, ask a question, make a prediction, pick up a quotation, come out in praise of an idea or a person, use humor, take off on someone's phraseology (maybe my own), or arouse curiosity concerning the subject of my talk.

These examples will show you the sorts of titles that could result from "checking your p's and q's":

Provoke

Let's Do Away With S.A.T.s
Clean Needles for Drug Addicts
Our Town's Zoning Laws Are Discriminatory

Question

Why Socialized Medicine?
Is Made in USA Passé?
Should We Return to Capital Punishment?

Predict

A Service Economy: Trend of the Future
We're Going to Destroy Every River in the Land!
Japan Will Soon Own America

Quote

"Ask What You Can Do for Your Country"
"Creativity Is the Sudden Cessation of Stupidity"
Recycling: "An Idea Whose Time Has Come"

Praise

Long Live Woody Allen!
How Group Therapy Cut My Weight in Half
A.A. to the Rescue!

Quip

It Only Hurts When I Laugh: The Story of My Bypass Operation
My Son the Nurse
Equal Rights for the Better Half

Paraphrase

Caveat Vendor—Let the Seller Beware!
A Funny Thing Happened to Me on the Way to the Senate [a
    talk by a defeated candidate]
How to Fail in the Stock Market Without Really Trying

Pique
Curiosity

A New Payout Plan for Stockholders
Ten Reasons Why Socialized Medicine Has Failed in Canada
Why I Am Resigning the Presidency [of the company; or the
    university; or the club, and so on]

• *Should a speech title be long or short?* If the program chairperson advises you that the title of your talk should be "one line"
or "eight words or less," tell that person to forget it! As with a book

or play, the important thing is whether the words fulfill their function as a title, not whether they conform to someone's concept of proper length. One of the most successful and best-publicized talks ever given by Stephen O. Frankfurt when he was the youthful president of the Young & Rubicam Advertising Agency was titled: "Stephen O. Frankfurt Presents Ed Sullivan, Arthur Godfrey, and Andy Warhol in 'The Decline and Fall of the Holy Grail.' " Although all the members of the Hollywood Radio and Television Society, before whom the talk was to be given, knew that Sullivan, Godfrey, and Warhol were not going to appear, Mr. Frankfurt's advance notices, which gave only the title and divulged nothing of the talk's content, brought out a record-breaking crowd. The title had twenty words in it, but it did a fine job of arousing curiosity and suggesting to the audience that this would be an amusing talk.

Very short titles can also be effective and stand out in a printed program. I remember one clever twist involving a short title. The membership chairman of the New York Sales Executives Club was listed among the speakers at one of the club luncheons. Next to his name on the program appeared only the words *An Appeal.* Knowing that the membership chairman's job was to increase membership, the audience was understandably restless and barely tolerant when it came time for him to make his remarks. Were it not that the door prizes were still to be awarded, it is likely that many in the audience would have walked out at that point.

After a somber introduction that included the general chairman's plea for careful attention to this serious part of the program, the membership chairman stood up, conspicuously organized a thick sheaf of papers he held in his hand, waited for total silence in the room, and—dramatically gripping the microphone—cried, "Join!" and sat down. The applause was thunderous.

Once you've decided on your title, here are some more tips:

• *Play devil's advocate with yourself.* Try to determine if the title is the right sort for the members of your potential audience. Is your title on target for their age, education, orientation? Why are they there? For a laugh? To learn? To debate? What are their problems? What is likely to make them angry? What will make them laugh? Most of all, ask yourself if the audience, as best you can create its profile, is likely to be responsive to a talk that is heralded in advance with the headline you've selected.

• *The title gives you a big advantage over the rest of your script.*
You need not say the title unless you choose to do so. Everything
else in your speech should be written for the *ear*, but your title
can be created for the *eye*. The person who introduces you to the
audience will probably state your speech title, and that is the only
time it will be voiced. Therefore, the title words you pick need not
necessarily "be you"; that is, they need not be words you would
be likely to use in talking. On the other hand, your title should
also *read* well because it will appear in programs, advance notices,
press reports, and so on.

So approach the title problem as if you had written a book,
magazine article, play, or movie. And whatever title you go with,
remember that you owe it to your audience to either explain it or
make it "pay out" during the talk. Otherwise, some members of
the audience may feel they didn't get what they were led to expect.

• *You can expand the audience for your message by publicizing
your speech*—before and after the talk is delivered. After all, you've
worked long and hard to put together a meaningful and perhaps
important speech. Why let it die after delivery? The hardest work
is behind you. You deserve extra mileage for your efforts, and
publicity is the way to get it.

• *The notices about your talk should go out far enough in advance
to ensure a large audience*—large in terms of filling the room in
which you will speak. It's depressing to speaker *and* audience if
only a few seats in the room are occupied. You're better off with
a small room and an overflow crowd than with a large auditorium
only one-third filled.

When you accept your invitation to speak, ask the person who
invited you how large an audience can be expected and what means
will be used to publicize your talk in advance. Customarily, the
sponsoring group sends out a mail announcement of your forthcom-
ing appearance. If the audience is to be drawn from the general
public, a notice or advance press release is also sent to local newspapers. If the audience is to be a specialized one, then press releases
will usually go to relevant trade or professional publications. These
advance releases should contain some clue as to the content of your
proposed talk as well as a bit of biographical information.

If you are not familiar with the publicity capabilities of the
group sponsoring your talk, ask to see the press releases and advance
notices before they go out and request that your name be added to

the mailing list. This is perfectly permissible and will give you a firsthand check on when the advance publicity has gone out. If you get close to the speaking date and have not received any notices in the mail, don't hesitate to phone the program chairperson with a polite inquiry. Even well-intentioned groups sometimes slip up between plan and follow-through. If you're going to take seriously the job of preparing an outstanding speech, you have every right to expect the sponsoring group to deliver an audience.

Other ways to stimulate interest and build audiences include making phone calls to local club chairpeople, posting bulletin board notices in clubs and business offices where potential audience members might see them, and sending announcements to local radio stations for use on their "community billboard of the air" or in their public service announcements.

• *After the speech is over and the applause has died down, you can enjoy an extra payout and give longer life to your words by using some of the techniques employed by professional public relations people.* Here are the most frequently used devices:

Press releases containing the most important ideas in your talk are a "must." They should open with a dramatic statement or a provocative passage taken from your text, much as a newspaper story opens with the most significant aspect of the event. All the newsworthy parts of your talk should be quoted in the release, and a bit of biographical information should establish your credentials as a speaker on this particular subject. The releases should be made available to members of the press immediately after your talk (or just before it if reporters have imminent deadlines). Have the sponsoring group or someone from your staff—not you—make phone calls alerting the press to these releases.

Press conferences give you an opportunity to amplify or expand on some of your speech ideas in person. However, in order to get members of the press and radio to attend such a conference, you must be a VIP or the subject matter of your talk must be of vital concern to their reading or listening audiences. Of course, in small towns that have only one newspaper, it is relatively easy to arrange a press interview at the newspaper's offices. If your remarks could be of significance in cities other than the one where you are speaking, be sure that members of the national press corps (AP and the TV and cable networks) have also been invited to your conference.

Copies of your complete text can carry your message into many homes, offices, and classrooms if they are made available to interested people. They can also get added attention from people who heard you talk and want to give further thought to your comments or pass them along to others in their organizations. There are several good ways to distribute such copies:

1. Make copies of your talk available to everyone who heard you speak. The copies should either be stacked at the back of the room and distributed when your address is over or mailed to audience members who leave their names and addresses.
2. Mail copies of the complete text to outstanding scholars or leaders in your field, along with a short note from you inviting their comments.
3. Send copies to radio and television commentators and to the editors of appropriate print media.

Reprints of your talk in booklet form can be used for mailing purposes instead of the less expensive (and less impressive) "duplicated" variety. While the ordinary photocopied or office-reproduced copies convey a feeling of immediacy (and are therefore excellent for the press), the printed booklet lends an air of importance to the text. Your talk in printed form, along with a covering letter, could make an excellent mailing piece to prospects, clients, community leaders, or any other group you wish to reach with your ideas.

Magazine reprints of your speech bring still another audience to your message. If there is a magazine in your field or specialty whose readership could be interested in your comments, send a copy of your talk to the editor and offer to edit the copy for publication should the magazine agree to carry it. If your talk is heavily dependent on visual material, an interested editor will usually offer you assistance in turning your visuals into print-worthy illustrations. Otherwise, the editing is usually a simple job and well worth the small amount of additional work on your part, since your ideas might then be carried to many times the number of people who heard you speak.

Repeating your talk before other groups is still another way to increase the return on your investment in time and effort. Once you know that you have a good speech and that you've been successful in communicating your ideas to an audience, it becomes easier and easier to deliver that same talk, sometimes with minor variations to suit your new listeners. I know several famous personalities who have given the same speech, or variations of it, to as many as fifteen or twenty different audiences. (Of course, during an election campaign, politicians frequently give the same speech over and over again to every audience they address.) There is nothing wrong with this. If your message is still valid, if the audience hasn't heard the talk before, and if you can fulfill a program need, why not put all that hard work to use again? Just be sure you don't go stale and "walk through" your tenth delivery. Your audience will at once detect your own boredom.

A digest of your speech, picking up the salient ideas and the most readable phrases, can bring the essence of your address to still other audiences. Writing such a digest is not difficult; it's a pick-and-choose process, with perhaps some new sentences to bridge ideas and tie them together. The digest can be used as a mailing to clients, prospects, friends, and association members or as an interoffice or interstaff communication.

Whatever reprint techniques you use, be certain to obtain the widest possible distribution. Think in terms of mailing lists to VIPs, campus and student publications, the Chamber of Commerce, the staffs of schools, fraternal organizations such as Kiwanis and Rotary groups, and trade and professional associations. And don't forget the employees of your own company!

All your thought and work in creating a great speech and finding a title worthy of it will pay off many times over. If you have used the material in this book to spice up your text and make it memorable, and if you have sharpened and rehearsed your delivery as described in the Rehearsals section, you are bound to experience the thrill that every public speaker knows when the audience breaks into spontaneous and sustained applause. Long after you have left the platform, you will hear the sound of this acclaim ringing in your ears.

And with the right sort of publicity, you will continue to get calls and mail from people who have an opportunity to read or hear about your speech—or, better yet, to read the speech itself. Don't be surprised if months after you make your platform appearance, someone writes you for a copy of "that fine talk I've heard so much about and would like to read for myself." Chalk it up as one of the justly deserved rewards that come to every public speaker who has learned how easy it is to be the life of the podium.

BIOGRAPHICAL INDEX

How to Authenticate
Your Speech

This index contains a thumbnail identification of each person quoted directly in *How to Be the Life of the Podium*.

You may, in going through the book, find quotations you would like to include in your talk, but perhaps the persons quoted are unfamiliar or only vaguely familiar to you. By checking their thumbnail biographies here, you can find out when they lived (or, if still alive, their age) and their principal claims to fame. Should you need more information, you can, of course, refer to such library sources as *Who's Who* and various biographical dictionaries and encyclopedias. But the chances are that the data you find here will be sufficient for the average reference.

Sometimes you may feel that a person quoted might be unfamiliar to your audience. That shouldn't stop you from using the quotation. You can identify the person with a brief reference, such as "Otto Loewi, the German pharmacologist who won the Nobel Prize, once said . . ." or "Edwin Land, who—as you probably know—invented the Polaroid camera, was once known to remark. . . ." Even with so brief an identification, your audience will accept the fact that the person quoted has acceptable credentials for fame.

There may be other instances where you like a quotation but prefer not to use the name of the person who first made the quoted statement. It is perfectly proper for you to use the passage without

specific credit, provided you indicate that you are quoting someone—
that the passage is not original with you. The way to handle a
situation such as this is to say, "A well-known banker once said
. . ." or "More than two hundred years ago, a philosopher expressed
it this way. . . ."

Being clued in on a few facts about the person you're quoting
will give you greater self-confidence in using this material. It will
also establish for your audience that you are well-read and well-
prepared for your platform appearance. All this is bound to reflect
favorably upon your reputation as a speaker and will give your
listeners additional reason to respect your points of view.

ACTON, JOHN EMERICH EDWARD DALBERG, 1st Baron
(1834–1902) Professor of modern history, Cambridge. Leader of
Roman Catholics hostile to doctrine of papal infallibility.

ADDISON, JOSEPH (1672–1719) English essayist, poet, statesman.
Contributor, *The Tatler* and *The Spectator*.

ALEXANDER THE GREAT (Alexander III) (356–323 B.C.) Ruler of
Greece. Founded Alexandria, conquered Thrace and Illyria, destroyed Thebes.

ARCHIMEDES (c. 287–212 B.C.) Greek mathematician and inventor.
Known for work in mechanics and hydrostatics. Discovered
principle of buoyancy while seeking gold in King Hieron's crown
and shouted "Eureka!" (I have found it).

ARISTOTLE (384–322 B.C.) Greek philosopher; tutored Alexander
the Great. Author, *Sophisms*, *Metaphysics*, and other works.

ARMOUR, RICHARD (1906–   ) Educator, author, lecturer. Served
with U.S. State Department. Authored *It All Started With Co-
lumbus*, *Golf Is a Four-Letter Word*, and other humorous works.

ARMSTRONG, NEIL A. (1930–   ) Chairman, CTA, Inc. since 1982.
Former NASA astronaut. Commander, Apollo rocket flight to
the moon, 1969. Pilot's license at age 16, naval aviator in Korea.

AUDEN, W. H. (for Wystan Hugh) (1907–1973) Naturalized American
poet born in England. Known for prose, plays (with Isherwood),
and essays of criticism.

AURELIUS, MARCUS (A.D. 121–180) Roman emperor from 161 to
180 and Stoic philosopher.

BACKER, WILLIAM MONTAGUE (1926–   ) Advertising agency
executive, cofounder and president Backer & Spielvogel. President, executive creative director, Backer Spielvogel Bates
Worldwide. Composer (with others) "Teach the World to Sing."

BAKER, RUSSELL WAYNE (1925–   ) Journalist, author, columnist. Won Pulitzer Prize for autobiography *Growing Up*.

BARCLAY, ALBAN WILLIAM (1877–1956) Immensely popular U.S. vice president under Harry Truman, 1948–52. Served seven consecutive terms as member of House of Representatives from Kentucky; three terms as U.S. Senator.

BARNETT, HOMER GARNER (1906–   ) Educator and anthropologist. Author, *Innovation: The Basis of Cultural Change* (McGraw-Hill, 1953).

BARNUM, P. T. (for Phineas Taylor) (1810–1891) American showman. Brought Jenny Lind to United States. Opened "The Greatest Show on Earth" in Brooklyn, 1871. Merged with Bailey to form Barnum & Bailey Circus. Exhibited the dwarf Tom Thumb and Jumbo, huge African elephant. Circus acquired by Ringling Bros. after Barnum's death.

BEAME, ABRAHAM ("Abe") (1906–   ) Former Democratic mayor of New York City. Had strong accounting and financial background.

BEECHAM, SIR THOMAS (1879–1961) English conductor and impresario. Son of manufacturer of Beecham's pills. Initiated and conducted New Symphony and Beecham Symphony concert orchestras in London. Made many U.S. tours.

BEGIN, MENACHEM (1913–   ) Israeli politician and prime minister since 1977. With Anwar el Sadat of Egypt, awarded Nobel Peace prize in 1978.

BELASCO, DAVID (1859–1931) Dramatist and producer. Owner Belasco Theater, New York City. Noted for realistic stage settings, lighting effects.

BENCHLEY, ROBERT CHARLES (1889–1945) American humorist on staff of *N.Y. Tribune, Vanity Fair, New York World, Life, New Yorker*. Author, numerous books and radio scripts.

BERNBACH, WILLIAM (1911–1982) Advertising executive, leader of the "creative revolution" of the 1960s in advertising. Founder, Doyle, Dane, Bernbach, which became tenth largest U.S. ad agency by the time of his death.

BERRA, LAWRENCE PETER ("Yogi") (1925–   ) Professional baseball player with N.Y. Yankees, 1946–63. Coach, N.Y. Mets, 1965–75; manager, N.Y. Mets, 1975.

BILLINGS, JOHN SHAW (1838–1913) Physician and librarian. Chief Librarian, New York Public Library, 1896–1913.

BLUESTONE, NAOMI, M.D. Public health physician, Department of Health, New York City.

BOND, EDWARD L. (1913–   ) Advertising executive. Former CEO of Young & Rubicam, Inc.

BOORSTIN, DANIEL (1914–   ) Author, educator, historian, State Department official. Wrote *What Happened to the American Dream, The Sociology of the Absurd,* and others.

BORGE, VICTOR (1909–   ) American, born in Denmark, who began as a serious pianist but turned his comic talents to a form of showmanship, mixing stand-up comedy with humorous piano performances.

BOVET, DANIEL, M.D. (1907–   ) Italian physiologist and biochemist who won Nobel prize in physiology and medicine in 1957.

BRANDEIS, LOUIS DEMBITZ (1856–1941) American jurist and U.S. Supreme Court Justice. Author, *The Curse of Bigness.*

BREZHNEV, LEONID I. (1906–1982) Russian politician; president of the U.S.S.R., 1960–64; 1977–82. First Secretary of the Communist Party, 1964–82.

BRONFMAN, SAMUEL (1891–1971) Canadian distillery company executive; founder of the Seagram Company.

BROOKS, MEL (Melvin Kaminsky) (1926–   ) Actor, producer, director, writer. Wrote and directed *Blazing Saddles, Young Frankenstein.* Wrote TV scripts for "Your Show of Shows," "Caesar's Hour," "Get Smart."

BRYAN, WILLIAM JENNINGS (1860–1925) American lawyer and political leader; known as "the Commoner." Thrice defeated in bid for presidency.

BURKE, EDMUND (1729–1797) British statesman, orator, and political pamphleteer. Served in Parliament and advocated liberal treatment of the colonies.

BURNS, GEORGE (1896–   ) Vaudeville comedian, TV, radio, movie performer. Married Gracie Allen and formed comedy team. Played straight man to Gracie's hare-brained antics. At age 80, became a national institution when he returned to movies. Oscar for role in *Sunshine Boys.*

BUSH, GEORGE HERBERT WALKER (1924–   ) Forty-first president (1989–   ). Vice-president of the United States, 1981–89. U.S. representative to U.N.; Director CIA; U.S. liaison officer, Peking; Congressman from Texas. Cofounder, director, Zapata Petroleum Corp.

CAESAR, JULIUS (Gaius Julius) (100 B.C.–44 B.C.) Roman general and statesman. Patrician by birth, he formed the First Triumvirate of Rome. Elected consul and proconsul in Gaul and Illyricum. Led his army across the Rubicon, fought the Roman general Pompey, conquered Italy. Brought Cleopatra to Rome. Murdered by a group of nobles including Brutus and Cassius.

CAMUS, ALBERT (1913–1960) French novelist, essayist, playwright. Active in French Resistance during World War II. Won Nobel prize for literature, 1957.

CAPOTE, TRUMAN (1924–1984) Southern author; born New Orleans. Wrote *Breakfast at Tiffany's, Other Voices, Other Rooms, In Cold Blood, Thanksgiving Visitor,* others.

CAPP, AL (1909–1979) Cartoonist, columnist, author of comic strip "Li'l Abner."

CARLYLE, THOMAS (1795–1881) Scottish essayist, historian, lecturer. Attacked shams and corruption. Author, *Past and Present, Oliver Cromwell.*

CARNEGIE, DALE (1888–1955) Writer and instructor in public speaking. Author, *How to Win Friends and Influence People.*

CARROLL, LEWIS (pseudonym of Charles Lutwidge Dodgson) (1832–1898) English mathematician and writer. Author, *Alice's Adventures in Wonderland, Through the Looking Glass.*

CARSON, JOHNNY (1925–   ) Affable midwestern television personality whose sly wit, nonchalant manner, and youthful good looks have contributed to his enormous popularity as host of the "Tonight" show, which he took over from Jack Paar in 1962.

CARTER, JAMES EARL, JR. ("Jimmy") (1924–   ) Thirty-ninth president of the United States, 1977–1980. Born Plains, Ga., served in navy; later governor of Georgia from 1971 to 1975.

CATO, MARCUS PORCIUS (known as Cato the Elder and Cato the Censor) (234–149 B.C.) Roman statesman who attempted to restore morals of early Republic by legislation.

CELLER, EMANUEL (1921–1981) Elected to House of Representatives from New York; became ranking majority leader in the early 1970s. Served on House Judiciary Committee.

CHAPMAN, JOHN JAY (1862–1933) American essayist, playwright, lawyer. Author, *Emerson and Other Essays.*

CHESTERTON, G. K. (for Gilbert Keith) (1874–1936) English journalist and writer who contributed to American and English journals. Became Roman Catholic, and wrote in defense of Catholicism, including *Heretics, The Scandal of Father Brown, The Uses of Diversity.*

CHIAT, JAY (1931–   ) Advertising agency executive. Founder, Jay Chiat & Associates. Chairman, Chiat, Day and Chiat/Day/Mojo.

CHURCHILL, SIR WINSTON LEONARD SPENCER (1874–1965) British statesman and author. Prime Minister, 1940–45 and 1951–55. Led country to victory in World War II.

CICERO, MARCUS TULLIUS (106–43 B.C.) Roman orator, statesman, philosopher. Famous for orations against Catiline.

CLARK, MARK WAYNE (1896–1984) Five-star army general famous for his World War II victories in Italy. Allied chief, Italy, 1944–45. Chief, U.S. Forces in Austria, 1945–47.

COCTEAU, JEAN (1889–1963) French poet, novelist, playwright, and noted graphic artist and designer. Considered one of the most creative artists of the twentieth century.

COLTON, CHARLES CALBE (1780?–1832) English clergyman, sportsman, wine merchant. Author, *Lacon*.

CONFUCIUS (551–479 B.C.) Latinized form of Kung Fu-tse ("Philosopher Kung") Chinese utilitarian philosopher born in Ku-fow, State of Lu (now Shantung Province) who called himself "a transmitter, not an originator." Prime minister of Lu. Wandered twelve years from state to state teaching morals, family system, social reforms. His maxims became a guide for people's daily lives.

CONRAD, JOSEPH (1857–1924) Novelist. Seaman in French and British merchant marine. Many of his stories have seagoing background. Wrote *Lord Jim*, *The Nigger of the Narcissus*, *Arrow of Gold*, *The Rover*.

CONRIED, HANS (1917–1982) American comic actor of stage, screen, TV. Played in *My Friend Irma*, *Senator Was Indiscreet*, *Mrs. Parkington*, *Bus Stop*, *Oh God, Book II*, others.

COOLIDGE, CALVIN (1872–1933) Thirtieth president of the United States. Lawyer, state senator, and two-term governor of Massachusetts. Elected vice-president in 1921; became president after death of Warren Harding, 1923.

COSTANZA, MARGARET (1932–   ) Presidential assistant to Jimmy Carter. Resigned midterm because of differences with president's policies regarding women.

CUNNINGHAM, MARY ELIZABETH (1951–   ) Venture capital company executive. Formerly V.P. Strategic Planning, Bendix Corp. and Executive V.P. for Strategic Planning, Joseph Seagram & Sons. Author, *Powerplay*.

CURIE, PIERRE (1859–1906) French chemist. Known especially for work with his wife on radioactivity, leading to their discovery of the elements polonium and radium. Won Nobel prize in physics, 1903.

DALI, SALVADOR (1904–1989) Spanish painter. Associated with ultramodern schools, notably futurism, constructivism, cubism, abstract irrationalism, and surrealism. A leader of the surrealist school.

DARWIN, CHARLES (1809–1882) The great naturalist. Educated for the ministry but sailed on a surveying expedition to Australia and the South American coasts, gathering data on flora, fauna, and geology. Wrote the results of his studies on inbreeding and his theory of evolution by natural selection. His *Origin of Species by Means of Natural Selection* created a storm of controversy. *The Descent of Man* proposed that the human race derived from an animal of the anthropoid group.

DEAN, JAY HANNA ("Dizzy") (1911–1974) Baseball player who disliked his given name and chose to be known by his nickname. Played for St. Louis Cardinals.

DE GAULLE, CHARLES (1890–1970) French soldier and president of the Fifth Republic, 1958–69. As general in World War II, refused to accept France's capitulation to the Germans. Headed Provisional Free France in England and French Committee of National Liberation. Returned to France in 1944 and became interim president; then elected president in 1959.

DEMOSTHENES (384–322 B.C.) Athenian statesman, regarded as greatest of Greek orators. Attacked Philip of Macedon in series of orations. Advocated Athenian alliance with Thebes against Philip. Exiled, then recalled. Fled Athens and took poison to avoid capture when Antipater and Craterus took the city.

DEPEW, CHAUNCEY MITCHELL (1834–1928) Lawyer and U.S. Senator. President, N.Y. Central Railroad, 1885–99. Renowned after-dinner speaker.

DE VRIES, PETER (1910–   ) Writer, editor, novelist. Staff of *New Yorker* magazine. Author, *The Tunnel of Love* and many others.

DEWAR, THOMAS ROBERT (1864–1930) First Baron Dewar of Homestall. British distiller, sportsman, and raconteur. Author, *Ramble Around the Globe.*

DIEBOLD, JOHN (1926–   ) Consultant and author. Internationally recognized leader in the fields of technology and management. Chairman and founder of The Diebold Group, Inc., a management consulting firm. Books include *Automation, The Role of Business in Society,* and *Managing Information.*

DILLER, PHYLLIS (1917–   ) Actress, comedienne, and TV personality. Author, *Phyllis Diller Tells All About Fang, Phyllis Diller's Marriage Manual.*

DIOGENES (412?–323 B.C.) Greek Cynic philosopher who rejected social conventions, lived in a tub, and went through the streets with a lantern "looking for an honest man."

DISRAELI, BENJAMIN (1804–1881) Prime minister of Great Britain, 1868 and 1874–80; author; and intimate friend of Queen Victoria. On own responsibility, purchased for British government an interest in Suez Canal.

DOSTOYEVSKI, FYODOR MIKHAYLOVICH (1821–1881) Russian novelist. Arrested and convicted of conspiracy against the government. Sentenced to be shot, but reprieved at the last moment. Sent to Siberia. Author numerous works including *Crime and Punishment, The Idiot, The Brothers Karamazov.*

DRUCKER, PETER (1909–   ) Writer, educator, economist, lecturer. Wrote *Concept of the Corporation, The Future of Industrial Man, Managing for Results.*

DULLES, JOHN FOSTER (1888–1959) Lawyer; U.S. Secretary of State, 1953–59. American representative at Berlin Debt Conferences, 1933.

DUNNE, FINLEY PETER (1867–1936) American humorist and newspaperman. Editor, *Chicago Journal.* Creator of saloon keeper–philosopher Mr. Dooley.

DUVALL, KENNETH KEITH (1900–   ) American banker. President and director, First National Bank of Appleton, Wis., and director, Merchandise National Bank of Chicago.

DYSTEL, OSCAR (1912–   ) Publishing executive associated with *Sports Illustrated, Esquire, Colliers,* and Bantam Books.

EDISON, THOMAS ALVA (1847–1931) American inventor who patented more than 1,000 inventions, including the phonograph, automatic telegraph repeater, mimeograph, the Ediphone, and the incandescent electric lamp.

EINSTEIN, ALBERT (1879–1955) Theoretical physicist. Deprived of German citizenship, property confiscated by Nazis, became U.S. citizen. Enunciated Theory of Relativity. Nobel prize for physics; author papers, books, including *Why War?,* written with Freud.

ELGIN, DUANE S. Social policy analyst formerly associated with Stanford Research Institute.

ELIOT, CHARLES WILLIAM (1834–1926) Mathematician; president, Harvard University, 1869–1909. Editor, *Harvard Classics*. Author, *The Happy Life*.

ELIOT, GEORGE (pseudonym of Mary Ann Evans) (1819–1880) English novelist. Friend of Spencer, Carlyle, Martineau. With George Henry Lewes, formed an irregular relationship she regarded as marriage. Best-known works include *Mill on the Floss, Silas Marner, Adam Bede, Agatha,* and *Daniel Deronda*.

ELIOT, T. S. (for Thomas Stearns) (1888–1965) Poet, essayist, and critic born in St. Louis, Mo., who became a naturalized British citizen. Won Nobel prize for literature, 1948.

ELLIOTT, OSBORN (1924–) Editor, *Newsweek*. After many years as a *Time* editor, moved to *Newsweek* in 1955 where he was managing editor, editor, editor in chief, president, CEO, and board chairman.

EMERSON, RALPH WALDO (1803–1882) Essayist, poet, Unitarian minister, and antislavery lecturer. Author, *The Conduct of Life*.

EPSTEIN, JOSEPH (1917–) Educator, philosopher, professor at Columbia University and Amherst College. Wrote *The Virtues of Ambition*.

FALKLAND, LUCIUS CARY (1610–1643) English writer and son of lord deputy of Ireland. Inherited a fortune and devoted himself to literature. M.P., eloquent for constitutional liberty. Secretary of State, 1642.

FERNANDES, MILLOR (1924–) Brazilian playwright, painter, author, and humorist.

FITZGERALD, F. SCOTT (1896–1940) American fiction writer. Attended Princeton, served in World War I as an officer. Author *This Side of Paradise, The Beautiful and Damned, The Great Gatsby, Taps at Reveille,* others.

FOLEY, PAUL (1914–1983) Advertising executive and writer. Chairman of the Board of Directors and CEO, The Interpublic Group of Companies.

FRANCE, ANATOLE (pseudonym of Jacques-Anatole François Thibault) (1844–1924) French novelist, critic, poet, playwright. Eminent satirist and humorist. Nobel prize in literature.

FRANCIS THE FIRST (originally Francis Stephen) (1708–1765) Holy Roman emperor married to Maria Theresa of Austria with whom he was coregent of that country. Chosen emperor in 1745.

FRANKFURT, STEPHEN OWEN (1931–) Communications executive; President, Young & Rubicam Advertising Agency at age

36; CEO Frankfurt Communications International; Director, Kenyon & Eckhardt; President, Frankfurt, Gips, Balkind. One of the leaders of the "Creative Revolution" of the 1960s.

FRANKFURTER, FELIX (1882–1965) American jurist born in Vienna. Professor, Harvard Law School. Associate Justice, U.S. Supreme Court, 1939–62.

FRANKLIN, BENJAMIN (1706–1790) American statesman, scientist, and philosopher. Wrote satires under name of Silence Dogood. Published *Poor Richard's Almanack* under name of Richard Saunders. Many articles on political, economic, religious, philosophical, and scientific subjects. Invented the Franklin stove, bifocal spectacles, and the lightning rod.

FREUD, SIGMUND (1856–1939) Austrian neurologist, founder of modern psychoanalysis. Believed dreams to be unconscious representations of repressed desires. Forced to leave Vienna by the Nazi regime, he took up residence in London, where he lived until his death.

GALSWORTHY, JOHN (1867–1933) English novelist and playwright. Also nonpracticing lawyer. Best known for *The Forsyte Saga*. Awarded Nobel prize in literature, 1932.

GANDHI, MOHANDAS KARAMCHAND (called "Mahatma," i.e., "great soul") (1869–1948) Hindu nationalist and spiritual leader. Studied law in London. Introduced passive resistance. Organizer of politico-religious movement of noncooperation with British in India and twice imprisoned for advocating social reforms.

GARDNER, JOHN W. (1912–   ) Secretary, Department of Health, Education, and Welfare, 1965–68. Founder, Common Cause. Director, Woodrow Wilson Foundation.

GERSTENBERG, RICHARD C. (1909–   ) Automotive executive who came up through the ranks to become Chairman of the Board of General Motors.

GHOSE, AUROBINDO (1872–1950) Indian Yoga philosopher. Prominent in nationalist movement. Editor various periodicals. Led life of a Yogi.

GIAMATTI, A. BARTLETT (formal first name Angelo) (1938–1990) University administrator and baseball executive. President, Yale University 1978–86. President of the National League 1986–90. Baseball Commissioner in 1990 until his death.

GINZBERG, ELI (1911–   ) Economist, educator, government consultant, author. Served in Departments of Labor, Defense, Commerce, and State in 1950s and 1960s. Wrote a number of books, including *The Development of Human Resources* (McGraw-Hill, 1966).

GLENN, JOHN HERSCHEL, Jr. (1921–   ) Astronaut; first American in orbit, 1962. Circled the earth three times in Mercury capsule *Friendship 7.* Elected U.S. Senator from Ohio in 1975; still serving in that role.

GOETHE, JOHANN WOLFGANG VON (1749–1832) German poet and writer. Author, *Faust, Egmont,* others. Inaugurated German literary movement known as Sturm und Drang.

GOLDMAN, WILLIAM (1931–   ) Screenwriter. *Harper, Butch Cassidy & the Sundance Kid, The Great Waldo Pepper, All the President's Men, The Marathon Man, A Bridge Too Far,* others.

GOLDWYN, SAMUEL (née Goldfish) (1882–1974) Motion picture producer and founder of Metro-Goldwyn-Mayer Corp. Pioneer in hiring famous writers to do film scripts.

GORBACHEV, MIKHAIL SERGEYEVICH (1931–   ) Soviet politician who began as a machine operator and rose to presidency of USSR. Introduced *perestroika* and *glasnost.* Chairman, Congress of People's Deputies of the USSR. Wrote *A Time for Peace* and *Peace Has No Alternatives.*

GOSSAGE, HOWARD (1919–1970) West Coast advertising agent. Cofounder, Wiener & Gossage Advertising Agency.

GRAHAM, MARTHA (1893–1991) American dancer and choreographer. Recipient numerous awards. Formed Martha Graham Dance Company, which toured the world.

GRAVES, CHARLES (1899–   ) British chronicler, historian, and world traveler. Author, *Fourteen Islands in the Sun* and *The Rich Man's Guide to Europe* (Prentice-Hall, 1966).

GUBER, (HOWARD) PETER (1942–   ) American film producer. Became famous when he ran a major film studio at age 29 and produced *Missing, Flashdance.*

GUINAN, "TEXAS" (born Mary Louise Cecille Guinan) (?–1933) Screen, stage, and vaudeville actress and nightclub hostess. Made ten movies between 1917 and 1933.

HAIG, ALEXANDER M., Jr. (1924–   ) Army officer. Vice Chief of Staff, U.S. Army. Assistant to President Nixon and Chief of White House Staff, 1973–74. Supreme Allied Commander Europe, SHAPE, 1974. Secretary of State under President Reagan.

HAMILTON, ALEXANDER (1755–1804) American lawyer and statesman. Served in American Revolution. Secretary and aide-de-camp to Washington. Member, Continental Congress. Supported new constitution in his articles in *The Federalist*. First U.S. Secretary of the Treasury. Mortally wounded in a duel with Aaron Burr.

HAMILTON, EDITH (1867–1963) American classical scholar and writer. Specialist in Greek, Roman, and Hebrew philosophy. Author, *The Greek Way*.

HAMMARSKJÖLD, DAG (1905–1961) Swedish diplomat and first Secretary General of the United Nations. Killed in plane crash while on U.N. mission to Northern Rhodesia.

HARDING, WARREN G. (Gamaliel) (1865–1923) Twenty-ninth president of the United States (1921–23). Lieutenant Governor, U.S. Senator from Ohio. Owned and edited *Marion* (Ohio) *Star*. Favored protective tariffs.

HARPER, MARION (1916–1989) Oklahoma-born, made his mark on Madison Avenue, first in research, then as CEO of McCann-Erickson, later at Interpublic, which became a dominant agency in advertising when Harper introduced the concept of putting competing agencies under one corporate umbrella. His unauthorized biography was published in 1982 by Crain Books. Entitled *Marion Harper: The Man Who Built Interpublic*, it was written by Russell Johnston.

HAYES, HELEN (Mrs. Charles MacArthur; Helen H. Brown) (1900–   ) Actress, star of Broadway, Hollywood, and radio. Considered the "first lady of the American theater." Won Oscars for *The Sin of Madelon Claudet, Airport*. Also starred in *Anastasia, Arrowsmith*. Awarded Medal of Freedom.

HAZARD, ELLISON LOCKWOOD (1911–   ) Business leader and president of Continental Can Co., which he joined in 1934.

HEMINGWAY, ERNEST (1899–1961) American journalist, novelist, and short-story writer. Served with French and Italian armies in World War I. Foreign correspondent. Awarded Nobel prize in literature, 1954. Author, many books of short stories, poems, novels, including *The Sun Also Rises, Men Without Women, A Farewell to Arms, For Whom the Bell Tolls, The Old Man and the Sea*.

HEROPHILUS (circa 300 B.C.) Greek anatomist and surgeon. Founder of first school of anatomy in Alexandria. First to conduct postmortems.

HIROHITO (1901–1990) Japanese ruler. Emperor of Japan 1926–90. Surrendered to U.S. at end of World War II.

HOBSON, JOHN (1858–1940) English economist. Author, *Problems of Poverty, The Evolution of Modern Capitalism.*

HOFFER, ERIC (1902–1983) Author, *The True Believer, Reflections on the Human Condition,* and other works.

HOLMES, OLIVER WENDELL (1809–1894) American man of letters and sometimes practicing physician. Professor of anatomy at Dartmouth. Author, *The Autocrat of the Breakfast Table, The Chamber'd Nautilus.*

HOPE, BOB (1903–   ) Stage, radio, film, TV actor/comedian. Entertained U.S. armed services overseas for forty years.

HORACE (Quintus Horatius Flaccus) (65–8 B.C.) Roman lyric poet and satirist. Educated in Rome and Athens. Commanded legion in republican army. Favorite of Emperor Augustus. Wrote satires, epodes, odes, epistles, and *Ars Poetica.*

HOROWITZ, VLADIMIR (1904–1989) American pianist of Russian birth who made his U.S. debut with the New York Philharmonic in 1928.

HOWELL, JAMES THEODORE, M.D. (1919–   ) Internist, Medical Service Chief at Henry Ford Hospital, Detroit. Associated with Medic Alert, Association of American Medical Colleges, Health & Fitness, Inc.

HUBBARD, ELBERT GREEN (1856–1915) American writer, editor, and printer. Wrote for *The Philistine,* a monthly magazine in which he expressed his homely, common sense philosophy. Went down with the *Lusitania.*

HUGHES, CHARLES EVANS (1865–1948) American jurist. Practiced law in New York City. Governor, New York; Associate Justice, then Chief Justice, U.S. Supreme Court. Unsuccessful candidate for presidency against Wilson. Secretary of State; member, Hague Tribunal.

HUGO, VICTOR-MARIE (1802–1885) French playwright, novelist, and poet, and leader of the Romantic movement in French literature. Author, *Les Misérables.*

HUMPHREY, HUBERT HORATIO (1911–1978) U.S. vice-president under Johnson, 1965–69. Democratic candidate for presidency, 1968. Senator from Minnesota, 1949–64; 1970–78.

IACOCCA, LEE (for Lido) **ANTHONY** (1924–   ) Automotive manufacturing executive. Thirty-two years in sales, marketing, then presidency of Ford Motor Co. until fired by Henry Ford. Became CEO of Chrysler Corp. Credited with turning around that company when on the brink of bankruptcy. Coauthor, *Iacocca: An*

Autobiography, Talking Straight. Former chairman, Statue of Liberty-Ellis Island Centennial Committee.

JACKSON, JESSE LOUIS (1941–   ) Baptist clergyman and civic leader. One of the founders of the Southern Christian Leadership Conference. Active in Black Coalition for United Community Action.

JAMES, WILLIAM (1842–1910) American psychologist and philosopher. Taught anatomy, physiology, and hygiene as well as philosophy at Harvard. One of the founders of pragmatism.

JANEWAY, ELIOT (1913–   ) Economist and syndicated columnist. Worked as staffer on both *Time* and *Newsweek.* Author, *You and Your Money.*

JARRELL, RANDALL (1914–1965) American poet, essayist, and teacher. Author, *Blood for a Stranger; Little Friend, Little Friend.*

JEFFERSON, THOMAS (1743–1826) Third president of the United States, 1801–09. Drafted and signed the Declaration of Independence.

JOHNSON, LYNDON BAINES (1908–1973) Thirty-sixth president of the United States. Succeeded to presidency upon assassination of President Kennedy, 1963. Elected president in 1964.

JOHNSON, SAMUEL (1709–1784) English lexicographer, critic, and conversationalist. Known as Dr. Johnson (held LLD degree). Edited *The Rambler.*

JONES, ERNEST, M.D. (1879–1958) Britain's foremost psychoanalyst and biographer of Sigmund Freud. President of the International Psychoanalytical Association.

KAEL, PAULINE (1919–   ) Film critic, *New Yorker* magazine since 1968. Author, *I Lost It at the Movies, Kiss Kiss Bang Bang.* Guggenheim fellow.

KAPLAN, MAX (1911–   ) Director of Arts Center, Boston University. Author, *Leisure in America: A Social Inquiry* (Wiley, 1960) and *Music in the City.*

KELMENSON, LEO-ARTHUR (1927–   ) President and CEO, Kenyon & Eckhardt; chairman of the executive committee and director, Bozell Advertising. Author, book of poems; contributor to numerous magazines and newspapers.

KENNEDY, JOHN FITZGERALD (1917–1963) Thirty-fifth president of the United States, assassinated in 1963 while serving his first term. Author of *Profiles in Courage,* which won Pulitzer prize for biography.

KHRUSHCHEV, NIKITA SERGEYEVICH (1894–1971) Russian political leader. Named First Secretary of the Communist Party, 1953. Premier of Soviet Union, 1958; ousted, 1964, after de-Stalinizing Russia. Lived in seclusion from then until his death.

KIPLING, RUDYARD (1865–1936) English writer born in Bombay. Won Nobel prize for literature, 1907. Writings include *Captains Courageous, Kim, Plain Tales From the Hills,* and *Barrack-Room Ballads.*

KISSINGER, HENRY A. (1923–   ) Assistant to the president (Nixon) for National Security Affairs, 1969–75. Secretary of State, 1973–77. Author, *White House Years, Years of Upheaval,* others.

KNAPP, WILLIAM (1920–1990) Writer and editor for *New Yorker* magazine for thirty years. Was consulting editor at time of death. Graduated Harvard University; 8th Air Force, World War II.

KRUTCH, JOSEPH WOOD (1893–1970) American critic and essayist. Editor, *The Nation;* professor at Columbia University. Author of *Comedy and Conscience After the Restoration, Edgar Allan Poe—A Study in Genius,* and other works.

LAMB, CHARLES (1775–1834) English essayist and critic. At times confined to mental institution. Author, *A Tale of Rosamund Gray, John Woodvil,* and others.

LAND, EDWIN HERBERT (1909–1981) Inventor and corporate executive. Invented polarizing filter for cameras and the Polaroid camera.

LAO-TSE (or LAO-TZU) (604–531 B.C.) One of the great Chinese philosophers who lived under the Chou dynasty. Founder of Taoism, a liberal religion advocating the eternal spirit of righteousness and declaring that forms and ceremonies are useless. Differed greatly from Confucianism. Taoism degenerated into a system of magic.

LA ROCHEFOUCAULD, DUC FRANÇOIS DE (1613–1680) French writer. Author, *Reflexions ou Sentences et Maximes Morales.*

LEACOCK, STEPHEN BUTLER (1869–1944) Canadian economist, writer, and humorist. Head of Economics Department, McGill University. Author, *Nonsense Novels, My Remarkable Uncle.*

LEAHY, FRANK (Sylvester Francis) (1909–   ) Utilities executive who started at the bottom with Detroit Edison Co. (1931) and rose to vice-president for employee and union relations (1961). Also, director, Leahy Company.

LEONARD, HUGH (born John Keyes Byrne) (1926–   ) Irish playwright who wrote *Da, A Life, The Au Pair Man,* and others.

LEVENSON, SAM (1911–1980) Performer, teacher, author. Brooklyn high school teacher who became a performer when he found his wit to be in demand. Wrote *Everything But Money, Sex and the Single Child, In One Ear and Out the Other*, others.

LIEBLING, A. J. (for Abbott Joseph) (1904–1963) Author, journalist, and long-time staffer and foreign correspondent for the *New Yorker*.

LILLIE, BEATRICE (Lady Peel) (1894 or 1898–1989) Quick-witted vaudevillian and comic performer of stage, radio, TV. Produced one-woman show, *An Evening With Bea Lillie*. Ziegfield Follies, 1957–58. Films include *Exit Smiling, Around the World in 80 Days, Thoroughly Modern Millie*. Autobiography, *Every Other Inch a Lady*.

LINCOLN, ABRAHAM (1809–1865) Sixteenth president of the U.S. Little formal schooling. Storekeeper, rail splitter, postmaster, surveyor, lawyer. Issued Emancipation Proclamation declaring freedom of the slaves. Made immortal Gettysburg Address. Shot by John Wilkes Booth.

LINDSAY, JOHN VLIET (1921–   ) Mayor, New York City in mid-sixties. Republican Congressman from New York. Sought presidential nomination, 1972.

LIVY (Titus Livius) (59 B.C.–A.D. 17) Roman historian and writer. Under patronage of Emperor Augustus, wrote history of Rome from its foundation to 9 B.C. Younger brother of Emperor Tiberius.

LOEWI, OTTO (1873–1961) German-born pharmacologist. Shared with Sir Henry Hallett the 1936 Nobel prize for physiology and medicine.

LONGFELLOW, HENRY WADSWORTH (1807–1882) American poet and professor of modern languages. Author, *The Village Blacksmith, The Song of Hiawatha, The Courtship of Miles Standish*.

LOUIS XIV (also known as Louis the Great) (1638–1715) Acceded to French throne at age of five and reigned for seventy-three years. Inordinately ambitious, he established the most magnificent court in Europe. His idea of government was summed up in the words, *I am the state*. While the masses suffered great poverty, French art enjoyed its golden age during his reign.

MACAULAY, THOMAS BABINGTON, BARON (1800–1859) English writer and politician. Secretary of War. Wrote *History of England*, essays, speeches.

MACHIAVELLI, NICCOLÒ (1469–1527) Italian statesman and political philosopher. Author of *Il Principe (The Prince)*. Deprived of office by the Medici when they regained power in 1512. Imprisoned, then retired to write.

MACKLIN, CHARLES (1697–1797) Irish actor and playwright. Famous for his portrayal of Shylock. Wrote *Love à la Mode*, a farce; *Man of the World*, a comedy.

MacLEISH, ARCHIBALD (1892–1982) American poet, essayist, librarian. Assistant Secretary of State, 1944–45. Author of *Conquistador*, for which he won Pulitzer prize.

MACMILLAN, HAROLD (1894–1986) British publisher, economist, and politician. Prime minister, 1957–63. Wrote *The Middle Way*.

MAIMONIDES (also known as Rabbi Moses ben Maimon) (1135–1204) Jewish philosopher born in Spain. Emigrated and became physician to the Sultan of Egypt and Rabbi of Cairo. Believed in freedom of the will; condemned asceticism; taught care of body as well as soul. Wrote on logic, mathematics, medicine, law, and theology.

MALRAUX, ANDRÉ (1901–1976) French novelist. Author, *La Condition Humaine*, for which he was awarded the Goncourt prize. Translated into English as *Man's Fate*.

MAO TSE-TUNG (Zedong) (1893–1976) First chairman of the People's Republic of China. Son of a peasant farmer, he helped found the Chinese Communist Party. Defied attacks of Chiang Kai-shek's forces, resisted Japanese aggression, and proclaimed People's Republic in 1949. Author, *Little Red Book* of Chairman Mao's sayings.

MARC ANTONY (also called Marcus Antonius) (82 B.C.–30 B.C.) Roman orator, soldier. Related to Julius Caesar, whom he aided in Gaul. Succumbed to Cleopatra's charms, followed her to Egypt, and bestowed on her extravagant titles. Defeated at Actium, fled to Egypt, committed suicide.

MARDEN, ORISON SWETT (1906–   ) New York lawyer and civil rights activist associated with Vera Institute for Justice and Legal Aid associations.

MARSHALL, THOMAS RILEY (1854–1925) Twenty-eighth vice-president of the United States, 1913–21. Governor of Indiana. Opposed women's suffrage and prohibition. Made remark, "What this country needs is a good five-cent cigar."

MARX, GROUCHO (1890–1977) Comedian and zany ringleader of the Marx Brothers. His movies include *Animal Crackers, Duck Soup, Night at the Opera*. Host of radio-TV quiz show, "You Bet Your Life."

MASLOW, ABRAHAM HAROLD (1908–1970) Psychologist. Founder of humanistic psychology emphasizing positive features of man and his capacity for personal growth and achievement.

MASON, JACKIE (1931–   ) Borscht belt and nightclub comic and mimic. After a fading career in vaudeville, made major comeback with one-man Broadway show, *The World According to Mason.* Subsequent TV sitcom, "Chicken Soup," bombed, and Mason returned to Broadway with second successful one-man show.

MASSON, THOMAS LANSING (1866–1934) Humorist, editor, author, associate editor of the *Saturday Evening Post,* and managing editor of *Life* magazine. Author, *A Bachelor's Baby.*

McCARTHY, EUGENE J. (1916–   ) Writer, lecturer, syndicated columnist. Also senator from Minnesota, and Liberal who ran in presidential primaries in 1970s.

McGOVERN, GEORGE STANLEY (1922–   ) Democrats' unsuccessful presidential nominee against Nixon, 1972. Senator from South Dakota, history professor, author, *A Time of War, A Time of Peace.* Decorated DFC, WWII.

MEAD, MARGARET (1901–1978) American anthropologist. Made expeditions to Western Samoa, New Guinea, and Bali. Author, *Coming of Age in Samoa, Growing Up in New Guinea, Male and Female.*

MEDLICOTT, SIR FRANK (1903–   ) British solicitor who served with the Ministry of Health in 1943. Knighted, 1955.

MELBOURNE, 2nd VISCOUNT (né William Lamb) (1779–1848) English statesman. Whig, M.P.; lost seat because of support of Catholic emancipation. Irish Secretary, Home Secretary, Prime Minister. Adviser to young Queen Victoria.

MENCKEN, H. L. (Henry Louis) (1880–1956) American editor and satirist. Founded, with George Jean Nathan, and edited, the *American Mercury.* Author, *New Dictionary of Quotations.*

MENNINGER, WILLIAM W. (1931–   ) American psychiatrist who, with his brother Karl, practices in Topeka, Kansas, at the Menninger Clinic. Author, *Caution, Living May Be Hazardous.*

MERMAN, ETHEL (Ethel Zimmerman) (1909–1984) Broadway star, preeminently an entertainer in musical comedy. Made debut in 1930 in *Girl Crazy.* Best known for roles in *Gypsy, Annie Get Your Gun, Anything Goes,* and *Call Me Madam.* A reviewer said she had "a voice that might easily have tumbled the walls of Jericho."

MICHELANGELO, BUONARROTI (1475–1564) Italian sculptor, painter, architect, and poet of the High Renaissance. Studied Leonardo's art in Florence; summoned by Pope Julius II to Rome where he decorated the ceilings of the Sistine Chapel. Succeeded Sangallo as architect of St. Peter's in Rome. Among his sculptures are *Battle of the Centaurs, Madonna of the Steps, Bacchus, Pietà,* and a colossal figure of young David carved out of a single marble block.

MILTON, JOHN (1608–1674) English poet who wrote in both English and Latin. Studied classics and wrote *L'Allegro* and *Il Penseroso.* Wrote on religion, marriage, divorce. Went blind but continued to write, mostly sonnets, as well as *Paradise Lost* and *Paradise Regained.* Succumbed to gout.

MINOW, NEWTON NORMAN (1926–   ) Lawyer and chairman of the Federal Communications Commission, 1961–63.

MIZNER, WILSON (1876–1933) Dramatist, short-story writer, Hollywood scriptwriter and occasional real estate entrepreneur.

MORGAN, J. P. (for John Pierpont) (1837–1913) American banker and financier who formed J. P. Morgan & Co. in 1895. Best known for his government financing, his reorganization of important American railroads, and his industrial consolidations, especially his formation of United States Steel Corp. President, Metropolitan Museum of Art.

MORLEY, JOHN (Viscount) (1838–1923) English statesman and man of letters. Editor, *Fortnightly Review* and *Pall Mall.* Secretary of State for India, 1905–10. Author, *Edmund Burke, Life of Gladstone.*

MOSES, ROBERT (1888–1981) New York state and municipal official. As New York City Parks Commissioner, he landscaped the area with his personal vision of parks, bridges, and highways.

MUGGERIDGE, MALCOLM (1903–1989) British writer, social critic, and former editor of *Punch* magazine.

MURROW, EDWARD ("Ed") ROSCOE (1908–1965) American news commentator and pioneer in broadcast journalism. Television narrator of CBS's "See It Now" and "Person to Person." Head of U.S.I.A., 1961–64.

MUSKIE, EDMUND SIXTUS (1914–   ) Governor of Maine, U.S. Senator, unsuccessful candidate for the U.S. vice-presidency, 1968. Sought Democratic presidential nomination, 1972. Named Secretary of State under Jimmy Carter, 1980.

NADER, RALPH (1934–   ) Lawyer, author, and leader of the consumer movement of the 1960s and 1970s. Author, *Unsafe at Any Speed.*

NAPOLÉON BONAPARTE (1769–1821) French army commander known as The Little Corporal. Successfully occupied parts of Italy, Austria, and Syria and dissolved the Holy Roman Empire. Lost supremacy of the seas to England in defeat by Nelson at Cape Trafalgar. Eventually defeated at Waterloo and exiled to Elba.

NASH, OGDEN (1902–1971) American writer. Author of humorous verse as in *Hard Lines, The Primrose Path, I'm a Stranger Here Myself,* and *Good Intentions.*

NEHRU, JAWAHARLAL (1889–1964) First prime minister of India, 1947–64. Successor to Gandhi as leader of India's National Congress Party. Served five years in jail for his nationalist activities.

NELSON, (ADMIRAL) HORATIO (1758–1805) British naval hero who lost one eye and right arm in battle. Defeated Napoléon at Battle of Trafalgar but died of his wounds just as victory was completed.

NEUMANN, HANS H. (1917–1987) Director of preventive medicine for city of New Haven, Conn. Physician and popular lecturer and writer on problems of sexually transmitted diseases, drug abuse, and health care systems. Author, *Straight Story on V.D., Foreign Travel and Immunization Guide.*

NIXON, RICHARD MILHOUS (1913–   ) Thirty-seventh president of the United States, 1969–74. Resigned after Watergate revelations. Vice-president under Eisenhower, 1953–61. Also served in Senate and House of Representatives.

OGILVY, DAVID MACKENZIE (1911–   ) Founder, later chairman, Ogilvy & Mather advertising agency. Author, *Confessions of an Advertising Man; Blood, Brains & Beer; Ogilvy on Advertising.* Elected to Advertising Hall of Fame. Decorated, Commander, Order of British Empire.

OLIVER, ANDREW (1706–1774) American colonial political leader. Lieutenant governor of Massachusetts and Secretary of the Province. Unpopular, and hanged in effigy.

OPPENHEIMER, J. ROBERT (1904–1967) American physicist instrumental in development of the atom bomb. Associated with the Institute for Advanced Study at Princeton. Contributed to development of quantum theory.

OSBORN, HENRY FAIRFIELD (1857–1935) American naturalist and conservationist. President, N.Y. Zoological Society; chairman of the board, Conservation Foundation. Author, *Our Plundered Planet*.

OSLER, WILLIAM, M.D. (Sir) (1849–1919) Canadian physician. His teaching and personality strongly influenced the progress of medicine. A chance allusion in a public address relative to men over 60 was misinterpreted as a suggestion that all men over this age should be chloroformed, which brought him much undesirable notoriety. Author, *Principles and Practice of Medicine*.

O'TOOLE, JOHN E. President, American Association of Advertising Agencies. Thirty-one years with Foote, Cone & Belding Communications, where he rose from copywriter to chairman and CEO. Author, *The Trouble With Advertising* (Chelsea House, 1981).

PALMERSTON, HENRY JOHN TEMPLE (1784–1865) Viscount, English statesman. Prime Minister, Foreign Secretary, Secretary of War. Supported neutrality in American Civil War.

PARKER, DOROTHY (né Rothschild) (1893–1967) American writer. On staff of *Vogue*, *Vanity Fair*. Book reviewer for *New Yorker*. Member Algonquin Round Table with Benchley, Thurber, others. Known for acerbic wit. Authored verse and short stories and collaborated on four screenplays, including *A Star Is Born*.

PARKINSON, CYRIL NORTHCOTE (1909–   ) English historian and author. Wrote *Parkinson's Law*.

PERES, SHIMON (1923–   ) Israeli politician. Born Poland, emigrated to Palestine, 1934. Educated NYU and Harvard. Prime Minister of Israel, 1984–86. Member Knesset, Deputy-General, Ministry of Defense. Minister of Interior & Religious Affairs.

POE, EDGAR ALLAN (1809–1849) American poet and story writer. Dismissed as student at West Point for disobedience of orders. Wrote essays, short stories, critical reviews, in addition to poetry. Contributor to literary journals; associate editor, *Gentleman's Magazine*. Edited *Graham's Magazine* but was dismissed for irregular habits. Wrote "The Gold Bug," "Murders in the Rue Morgue," "The Raven," "Ulalume," "Annabel Lee," "The Bells." Suffered abject poverty and despondency aggravated by alcohol.

POWELL, JODY (Joseph Lester) (1943–   ) Presidential aide to Jimmy Carter, then press secretary to Carter 1976–81. Nationally syndicated columnist.

PRATT, THEODORE (1901–   ) Author and free-lance journalist.

Wrote novels, plays, short stories, motion-picture scripts, and articles. Author, *Escape to Eden, The White God.*

PRIESTLEY, JOHN BOYNTON (1894–1984) English novelist, critic, and playwright. Author, *George Meredith, Let the People Sing, The Long Mirror,* others.

QUAYLE, JAMES DANFORTH (1947–   ) Politician, vice-president under George Bush. Office of Attorney General in Indiana, Assistant to Governor of Indiana, Congressman, 1977–79. Senator from Indiana, 1981–88.

REAGAN, RONALD WILSON (1911–   ) Fortieth president of the United States, 1981–89. Motion-picture actor and sports announcer who aspired to the highest elected office in the land and achieved it in 1980 after failing to get the Republican nomination in 1976. Governor of California, 1967–74.

RICH, LEE. Entertainment-industry executive. CEO, MGM/UA Communications. Former president, co-owner, Lorimar Productions. TV producer "Dallas" series, "The Waltons," "Knots Landing," "Falcon Crest," others. Started in advertising. Also former president, Mirisch Rich TV.

RICHARDS, ANN (WILLIS) (1933–   ) Elected governor of Texas, 1990, with a victory over Republican Clayton Williams in narrow battle. Excellent debater. Delivered keynote address at 1988 Democratic National Convention.

RICHELIEU, Duc de, ARMAND-JEAN du PLESSIS (1585–1642) Known as the red eminence from the color of his habit, was a French statesman and cardinal. Chief Minister of Louis XIII, who was completely under his control.

RIVERS, JOAN (1937–   ) Entertainer. Guest hostess, "Tonight" show. Hostess, "The Late Show Starring Joan Rivers" and "The Joan Rivers Show." Syndicated columnist. Comedy albums. Coauthor, *Rabbit Test.*

ROBBINS, JEROME ("Jerry") (1918–   ) Choreographer; also dancer, director, and associate artistic director of New York City Ballet. Choreographed *High Button Shoes, The King and I, Two's Company, Pajama Game.*

ROCKEFELLER, DAVID (1915–   ) Banker. Director and chairman of the board, Chase Manhattan Bank. Chairman, Chase International Investment Corp.

ROCKEFELLER, JOHN DAVISON, III (1906–1978) Chairman, Board of Trustees, Rockefeller Foundation. Chairman, Board of Trustees, Population Council.

ROCKEFELLER, NELSON ALDRICH (1908–1979) Assistant Secretary of State; governor of New York, 1959–73. U.S. vice-president under Nixon.

ROCKWELL, WILLARD FREDERICK, Jr. (1914–1978) Manufacturing executive, and president and chief executive officer, Rockwell Manufacturing Co.

ROGERS, WILL (William Penn Adair) (1879–1935) Actor, lecturer, humorist, vaudevillian. Starred in motion pictures, wrote syndicated newspaper articles. Killed in plane crash.

ROOSEVELT, (Anna) ELEANOR (1884–1962) Author, lecturer, and delegate to the United Nations. Wife of President Franklin D. Roosevelt. Author, *On My Own, This I Remember,* and the column "My Day."

ROOSEVELT, FRANKLIN DELANO (1882–1945) Thirty-second president of the United States, and only president to be elected for a third term (1933–45). Known for his New Deal legislation. Author, *Whither Bound, Looking Forward.*

ROOSEVELT, THEODORE (1858–1919) Twenty-sixth president of the United States. Succeeded to the presidency on death of McKinley, 1901; elected president, 1904.

ROSTEN, LEO C. (pseudonym Leonard Q. Ross) (1908–   ) Author, political scientist, who wrote for motion pictures, magazines, government publications. Author, *Captain Newman, M.D., The Velvet Touch, The Joys of Yiddish, The Education of Hyman Kaplan.*

RUBICAM, RAYMOND (1892–1978) Advertising executive and co-founder of Young & Rubicam, Inc., advertising agency.

RUSKIN, JOHN (1819–1900) English art critic and sociological writer. Author, *The Art of England, Modern Painters, Ethics of the Dust.*

RUSSELL, BERTRAND ARTHUR WILLIAM (1872–1970) Third Earl of Russell. English mathematician and philosopher. Pacifist who opposed World War I.

SAHL, MORTON ("Mort") LYON (1927–   ) Stand-up comic known for his "little lectures" on the contemporary scene. Said to be the first important political satirist since Will Rogers. Disparages everything with nihilistic impartiality.

SAMUELSON, PAUL A. (1915–   ) American economist. Awarded Nobel prize in economic science in 1970. Wrote *Foundations of Economic Analysis* and *Economics: An Introductory Analysis.*

SANDBURG, CARL (1878–1967) American author, newspaperman, and magazine staffer. Wrote, lectured, sang folk songs, collected old ballads. Won Pulitzer prize for history, 1939; for poetry, 1951.

SANTAYANA, GEORGE (1863–1952) Poet and philosopher born in Spain. Emigrated to United States in 1872. Taught philosophy at Harvard; lived and wrote in France and Italy; authored several volumes of verse and philosophy.

SAROYAN, WILLIAM (1908–1981) American fiction writer and playwright. Author, *The Daring Young Man on the Flying Trapeze, The Time of Your Life, My Heart's in the Highlands.*

SCHOPENHAUER, ARTHUR (1788–1860) German philosopher and a chief expounder of pessimism.

SEAVER, THOMAS (1944–   ) Professional baseball pitcher, Cincinnati Reds. Began his career with the New York Mets. Vietnam antiwar speaker.

SELYE, HANS, M.D. (1907–1982) Canadian experimental psychologist. Born in Vienna, where he got his M.D. Known for his work and writings on stress. Wrote *Stress, The Stress of Life.*

SEN, A. K. (Amartya Kumar) (1933–   ) Professor of economics and philosophy at Harvard University and former professor of economics at Delhi University. Author, books and articles. Born in India.

SHAMIR, YITZHAK (1914–   ) Israeli politician, born Poland, emigrated to Palestine, 1935. Prime Minister, 1983–84. Exiled by British in 1946, given political asylum in France, returned to Israel, 1948. Member Knesset.

SHAW, GEORGE BERNARD (1856–1950) British playwright, novelist, and critic. Began writing plays in his mid-thirties and became the leading British playwright of his time. Authored *The Devil's Disciple, Caesar and Cleopatra, Man and Superman, Major Barbara, Pygmalion, Saint Joan.* Awarded Nobel prize for literature, 1925.

SHOR, "TOOTS" (Bernard) (1905–1977) New York saloon keeper whose Toots Shor Club was a famous watering hole in the 1950s for café society and theatrical celebrities. Walter Winchell is said to have picked up most of his gossip in this East Side club.

SIMON, NEIL (1927–   ) Comedy playwright with remarkable Broadway success. Wrote *Come Blow Your Horn, Barefoot in the Park, The Odd Couple, Sweet Charity, Plaza Suite, Sunshine Boys,* others. Awarded Pulitzer prize.

SMITH, ADAM (George Jerome Waldo Goodman) (1930–   ) Author, TV producer, editor, investment adviser. Editor in chief *Adam Smith's Money World*. Executive V.P., *Institutional Investor*. Portfolio Manager, Lincoln Fund. Associate editor, *Time* and *Fortune*.

SMITH, ALFRED EMANUEL (1873–1944) Politician, member New York state legislature. Governor of New York, 1919–20 and 1923–28. Democratic candidate for president of the U.S. in 1928 and first Roman Catholic to run for that office.

SOLERI, PAOLO (1919–) Italian-born architect, environmental planner, sculptor. Author, *The Bridge Between Matter and Spirit*.

STAFFORD, FRANK PETER, JR. (1940–) Economics educator, consultant, author. Chairman, Department of Economics, Stanford University Graduate School of Business. Special Assistant for Economic Affairs, U.S. Department of Labor. Formerly professor of economics, University of Michigan.

STEINEM, GLORIA (1934–) Writer, editor, lecturer, feminist. Editorial consultant, contributing editor, free-lance writer, various publications. Cofounder, contributing editor *New York* magazine. Cofounder, editor, *Ms.* magazine. Active civil rights and peace campaigns. Author, *The Thousand Indias, Marilyn: Norma Jean, Outrageous Acts & Everyday Rebellions* (NAL Books, 1984).

STEVENSON, ADLAI EWING (1900–1965) U.S. ambassador to the United Nations; governor of Illinois, 1949–53. Unsuccessful candidate for the presidency in 1952 and 1956.

STORY, JOSEPH (1779–1845) American jurist. Member U.S. House of Representatives from Massachusetts; U.S. Supreme Court; professor of law, Harvard. Prolific writer on legal matters.

STRAUSS, RICHARD (1864–1949) German composer, chief conductor of Berlin Court Opera. Head of Reich's music bureau. Considered the leader of the New Romantic School. Composed fifteen operas, including *Salome, der Rosenkavalier*, and *Die Frau Ohne Schatten*. Also wrote symphonies, ballets, chamber music, choral works.

STREEP, MERYL (Mary Louise) (1949–) Leading lady of stage, screen. *The Deer Hunter, Kramer vs. Kramer* (Academy Award), *Julia, Sophie's Choice, Silkwood*, others.

SULZBERGER, IPHIGENE OCHS (1893–1990) Central figure in history of the *New York Times*. Played important role in selecting successors to her father, Adolph S. Ochs, who acquired the *Times* in 1896. Influential in appointments of her husband, Arthur Hays Sulzberger; her son-in-law, Orvil E. Dryfoos; and her son, Arthur Ochs Sulzberger as *Times* publishers. Known as a woman of energy, social conscience, and impish humor. Worked on behalf of parks, the environment, education and libraries, and the welfare of animals.

SWANN, DONALD (1923–   ) British actor, composer, and performer in musicals. Appeared in *At the Drop of a Hat* and in productions with Michael Flanders.

SWIFT, JONATHAN (1667–1745) English satirist. Wrote on corruption in religion and education; ecclesiastical pamphlets; articles in the *Examiner, Tatler, Spectator*. Most famous work, *Gulliver's Travels*, a satire on courts, statesmen, political parties.

SZENT-GYÖRGYI, ALBERT (1893–1987) Hungarian-born chemist who won a Nobel prize in 1937 for physiology and medicine. Known for his work on biological combustion and for isolating vitamin C.

TALLEYRAND-PÉRIGORD, CHARLES-MAURICE de (1754–1838) French statesman. Ambassador to England. Abbé of Saint-Denis and bishop of Autun. Excommunicated by the Pope. Named Grand Chamberlain by Napoléon. Quarreled with Napoléon and, at his fall, instrumental in restoring Bourbons to power.

THACKERAY, WILLIAM MAKEPEACE (1811–1863) English novelist and journalist. Frequent contributor to *Punch*. Author, *Vanity Fair, Pendennis, Henry Esmond*.

THOMAS, LEWIS, M.D. (1913–   ) Physician and author. Wrote *The Hazards of Science; The Lives of a Cell: Notes of a Biology Watcher*, for which he won a National Book Award.

THOMAS, MARLO (Margaret) (1944–   ) Leading lady of Broadway, Hollywood. Also TV series, "That Girl." Author, *Free to Be . . . You & Me*. Daughter of Danny Thomas, wife of Phil Donahue.

THOMAS, NORMAN (1884–1968) American socialist politician and unsuccessful presidential candidate on Socialist ticket in five elections, 1928–44. Ordained a Presbyterian minister but resigned. Associate editor, *The Nation*.

THOREAU, HENRY DAVID (1817–1862) American writer and teacher. Born in Concord, Mass.; retired to a hut beside Walden Pond for two years; devoted his life to a study of nature and to writing.

THORNTON, CHARLES BATES ("Tex") (1913–1981) Electronics manufacturer and chairman of the board, Litton Industries. Former executive, Hughes Aircraft and Hughes Tool Co.

THURBER, JAMES (1894–1961) American artist and writer, famous for his cartoons in the *New Yorker*, of which he was managing editor. Author, *My Life and Hard Times, The Middle-Aged Man on the Flying Trapeze, Is Sex Necessary?*

TILLICH, PAUL J. (1886–1965) American theologian and philosopher. Born in Prussia, taught in German universities until barred by Nazis. Attempted to synthesize traditional Christianity and modern culture.

TOLLEY, W. P. (1900–   ) Formerly university chancellor, airline executive. Wrote *The Meaning of Freedom* and edited *Preface to Philosophy.*

TOLSTOY, COUNT LEV (Leo) NIKOLAYEVICH (1828–1910) Russian novelist, social and moral philosopher, and religious mystic. Founder of Tolstoyism. Author, *War and Peace, Anna Karenina.*

TOMLIN, LILY (1939–   ) Actress, TV and movies, who gained fame as a member of TV's comic show "Laugh-In."

TOYNBEE, ARNOLD (1852–1883) English sociologist and economist. Pioneer in social settlement movement. Toynbee Hall, in the district of Whitechapel, the first social settlement in the world, is named for him.

TRUEBLOOD, (David) ELTON (1900–   ) College professor, philosopher, writer. Associated with Harvard, Stanford, Swarthmore, Earlham College. Taught religion and philosophy. With U.S.I.A., 1954–55.

TRUMAN, HARRY S. (1884–1972) Thirty-third president of the U.S. Judge, senator, vice-president. Became president on death of FDR, 1945. Ordered atomic bombing of Hiroshima and Nagasaki. Elected president, 1948. Promulgated Truman Doctrine, Marshall Plan, NATO.

TUCHMAN, BARBARA W. (1912–1989) Historian who won Pulitzer prizes for *The Guns of August* and *Stillwell and the American Experience in China, 1911–45.*

TUCKER, B. R. (for Benjamin Ricketson) (1854–1939) American anarchist. Founded *The Radical Review* and *Liberty.* Author, *State Socialism and Anarchism.*

TUCKER, SOPHIE (1884–1966) Screen, stage, burlesque, vaudeville actress, and nightclub entertainer.

TURNER, RALPH HERBERT (1919–   ) Educator and sociologist. Editor, *American Journal of Sociology* and *Sociology and Social Research.* Author, *The Social Context of Ambition.*

TWAIN, MARK (pseudonym of Samuel L. Clemens) (1835–1910) American humorist and writer. Author, *The Adventures of Tom*

Sawyer, The Prince and the Pauper, Adventures of Huckleberry Finn, A Connecticut Yankee in King Arthur's Court.

VAN BUREN, MARTIN (1782–1862) Eighth president of the U.S., 1837–41. Vice-president 1833–37. Lawyer, attorney general of N.Y., U.S. Senator, governor of N.Y., Secretary of State.

VERNON, JACKIE (1920–1987) Stand-up comic. Known for his off-color jokes on the borscht circuit and at Las Vegas appearances.

VOLTAIRE (assumed name of François-Marie Arouet) (1694–1778) French satirist who was imprisoned in the Bastille where he wrote the tragedy *Oedipe*. Defender of victims of religious intolerance. Author, *Le Dictionnaire Philosophique.*

VON BRAUN, WERNHER (1912–1977) German-born engineer and rocket specialist. Responsible for development of V-2 long-range rocket. Chief, Guided Missile Development Division, 1950–56.

WARD, ARTEMUS (pseudonym of Charles Farrar Browne) (1834–1867) American humorist, newspaperman, and lecturer. Moved to England in 1866 and became an editor of *Punch*. Author, *Artemus Ward, His Travels.*

WEBSTER, NOAH (1758–1843) American lexicographer and author. Lectured on the English language; edited the *American Magazine*; practiced law; published *The Herald*. Published his first dictionary in 1806.

WEST, DAME REBECCA (pseudonym of Cicily Isabel Fairfield) (1892–1983) English critic and novelist. Author, *Henry James, The Birds Fall Down, Return of the Soldier*, and many others.

WEST, MAE (1892–1980) Hollywood leading lady and archetypal sex symbol of the 1930s. Vulgar, mocking, overdressed, seductive. Wrote most of her own stage plays and film scripts, full of double meanings.

WHITE, E. B. (for Elwyn Brooks) (1899–1986) Author, editor. Essays, sketches, poems, stories for *New Yorker* magazine. Wrote for *Talk of the Town* section, 1926–38. Columnist for *Harper's* magazine.

WILSON, (Thomas) WOODROW (1856–1924) Twenty-eighth president of the United States, 1913–21. Previously, governor of New Jersey. Awarded Nobel Peace prize, 1919.

WIRTZ, WILLIAM WILLARD (1912–1983) Government official and former Secretary of Labor. With War Labor Board, 1943–45. Chairman of National Wage Stabilization Board, 1946.

WRIGHT, FRANK LLOYD (1867–1959) American architect. Innovator of striking designs in private dwellings and public and quasi-public buildings. Among his best-known works was the old Imperial Hotel in Tokyo. Founder of the Taliesin Fellowship, a cultural experiment in the arts.

WRIGLEY, WILLIAM, JR. (1861–1932) American industrialist. Founder and president Wm. Wrigley, Jr. & Co., Chicago, manufacturers of chewing gum.

SUBJECT INDEX

How to Track Your Topic

This is more than an ordinary index, more than a mere listing of where to find what in the book—although it is that, too. It is a valuable tool to help you write a sharper and livelier talk.

In looking for interesting material with which to enliven your speech, first check the Contents for those sections that might have pertinent material. After selecting your items from those sections, check this Index for words that are the same as, or similar to, the heading. There's good reason for doing that. If, for example, you're writing a business talk and have excerpted from the section on Business what you want to use, you should then check the word *business* in this Index. Under that word, you will find page numbers for other business-related items scattered throughout the book. For example, you will be referred to business selections in the sections entitled Openers, Youth and Age, and, of course, Doctors, Lawyers, Industry Chiefs.

If you can still use additional material, run your eye down this entire Index to find key words that suggest related items. In the case of a talk on business, you will find in the Index the word *selling*. This will refer you to material in the sections entitled "The World of Advertising," "Facts, Figures, and Research," "Proverbs," "One-liners," and "Spellbinders"—all business-related items. Many of these may be pertinent to the subject of your talk. Depending upon what aspect of business you're addressing yourself to, you might also find relevant references under such Index words as change, cities, prophesying, women, problem solving, leadership, and many others.

Regardless of the subject of your talk, you should use the same procedure. If you're preparing a speech on a topic such as "The Feminist Movement" for which there is no specific section in this book, the Index will give you references under words such as women, achievement, success, action, children, marriage, knowledge, egotism, equality, and many more.

Were you readying a speech on the subject of travel, there might be helpful material for you in the references for the words conventions, wealth, skeptics, Englishmen, Frenchmen, Japanese, and so on.

So don't shortchange yourself. Use this Index. Browsing through it may suggest numerous categories of appropriate material that might not otherwise have occurred to you.

abortion, 40, 155
accomplishments, 8
achievement, 60, 163, 216, 218, 236
acting, actors, 92, 108, 121
action, 192, 219, 263
ad lib, 23
adolescence, 64
adversity, 219
advice, 157, 177, 178, 182, 253
after-dinner speeches, 9, 13, 162
age, aging, 54, 56, 57, 61, 114, 155,
    181, 214, see also section on
    Youth and Age
aggressiveness, 37
aim, 116
airplanes, 17
alcohol, alcoholism, 81, 103, 131,
    216, 231
ambition, 43, 99, 209
America, Americans, 70, 72, 107,
    120, 126, 148, 165, 191, 197,
    199, 201, 225
anger, 104, 169, 196, 213
appearances, 255
applause, 24
appreciation, 99
arrogance, 44, 115, 128, 133, 134,
    143, 156, 198, 209, 210, 232
art, artists, 104, 149, 156
aspirations, 53
astronauts, 37, 258
attention, 15
audience, 5, 6, 14, 66, 226, 229
awards, ix, 13, 17

beauty, 219
benefits, 129
bias, 237
birthdays, 10, 52
births, 86
boring, 199, 221
bosses, 25
Boy Scouts, 51, 234
bravery, 218

brevity, 12, 14, 18, 21, 22, 26, 70,
    224, 227, 236
brilliance, 133
burglary, 201

candidates, 45
careers, 41
cars, 52, 54
celebrities, 187, 199
challenges, 225
change, 69, 74, 77, 78, 82, 88, 91,
    97, 189, 200, 201, 223, 232
chaos, 126
character, 224
charity, 58, 210
church, 117
cities, 90, 140, 170, 259
civilization, 203
clairvoyance, 8
college, 58, 63, 84
commitment, 223
committees, 73, 74
common sense, 197, 200
communication, 64, 123, 132
Communism, 203
competition, 196, 253, 264
complacency, 69, 223
compromise, 184
computers, 87, 91
conceit, see arrogance
confidence, 105, 166, 226
congressmen, 37, see also section
    on Politics
consciousness, 96
conservation, 41
conservatives, 58, 200
consistency, 178
consultants, 262
consumerism, 66, 75, 79, 134, 256
contemplation, 211
contentment, 176
controversy, 14, 111, 222
conventions, 44, 89, 190
conversation, 11, 99, 106, 108, 230
cooperation, 118

courage, 7, 188, 224
courtesy, 177
cowards, 183, 222, 232
creativity, 111, 127, 129, 135, 180,
    226, 229, 234
credibility, 130
credit, 10
crime, 140, 141, 165
criticism, critics, 46, 96, 110, 163,
    195
customs, 165

danger, 41
death, 116, 120, 121, 160, 170, 174,
    177, 192, 196, 202, 210, 222
decisions, 58, 198
dedication, 72
defeat, 200, 201
democracy, 149, 194, 199, 202
dependability, 70
depression, 72
destiny, 118
determination, 211
dialogue, 198
dictators, 193
dictatorship, 149
differences, 144, 145, 203
diplomacy, 37
diplomats, 97
director, 1
disasters, 122
discipline, 194
diversity, 190
divisiveness, 62
doctors, 46, *see also* section on
    Doctors, Lawyers, Industry
    Chiefs
dreamers, 234
dreams, 65
drinking, 13, *see also* alcohol,
    alcoholism
drugs, 156

ecology, 223
economics, 40

economy, 40, 69, 82, 200, 218
education, 56, 59, 126, 210, 218,
    see also learning
efficiency, 74
effort, 188
eloquence, 101, 186
emphasis, 129
endurance, 37
enemies, 139, 148, 176, 177, 183,
    198, 252
engineers, 46
English, Englishmen, 53, 144, 145,
    153, 231
enlightenment, 211
entrepreneurship, 197
environment, 225
equality, 97, 182, 191
evil, 201
excellence, 71, 76
executives, 74, 167
experience, 141, 198
expertise, 16
extravagance, 218
eyeglasses, 11

facts, 94, 126, 163, 195, 222, 228,
    232
failure, 40, 100, 107, 109, 127, 163,
    188, 218, 219
faith, 213, 217
fallibility, 198
falsehoods, 213
fame, 125, 213
fanatics, 102
fate, 209
faults, 213
favors, 215
fear, 48, 57, 147, 217
feminism, 204
films, 145
flattery, 7, 12, 13, 15, 17, 18, 19,
    25, 26
flying, 142, 144, 170
fog, 143
fools, 11, 164, 175, 179, 215

football, 44
force, 195
fortune, 108, 214
France, French, Frenchmen, 19, 50,
    153, 177, 182, 188
freedom, 42, 51, 106, 188, 191, 195,
    201, 202
freedom of speech, 147, 148, 232
free enterprise, 67
friends, friendship, 64, 139, 148,
    176, 196, 217, 219, 252
frontiers, 225
future, 174, 189, 198, 199, 202, 223

gambling, 85
garbage, 39, 73, 87
generalists, 235
generations, 52, 56, 62, 64 134, 215,
    see also section on Youth and
    Age
generosity, 19, 101
genius, 8, 20, 72, 101, 210
ghostwriters, 22, 27
gifts, 10
global issues, 144, 145, 149, 199,
    see also section on Away From
    Home
goals, 57, 188, 233
golf, 21, 103
goodwill, 127, 131, 233
governing, 216
government, 38, 48, 188, 190, see
    also section on Politics
greatness, 48, 200, 212, 214
greed, 212
grief, 108

happiness, 61, 78, 98, 100, 216
harmony, 215
haste, 105
hate, 177
health, 110, 152, 155
heaven, 140
heroes, 51, 54, 101, 177, 179, 201,
    214

history, 188, 201, 202, 215
honesty, 101, 195, 210
honor, 41, 53, 80, 166
hope, 174, 226
hospitality, 217
hospitals, 159
humanity, 211
humility, 223, 232
humor, 109, 111
hunger, 217

idealism, 64, 96, 99, 198, 201
ideas, 25, 55, 68, 80, 100, 111, 123,
    126, 134, 192
ignorance, 46, 189, 215
illness, 153, 157
illusions, 101
image, 8, 188
imagination, 44, 109, 126, 256
immortality, 62
importance, 103, 107
impromptu talk, 7
improvement, 178
inequality, 145, 191
inferiors, 213
inflation, 107
information, 86, 92, 132
ingenuity, 256
inheritance, inheritors, 51
initiative, 224, 237
injustice, 196, 200
innovation, 78, 225, 234
insight, 199
inspiration, 7, 195, 202, 223
integrity, 80, 157
intelligence, 101, 199, 200
interviews, 29
introductions, 12, 13, 41, see also
    section on Openers
intuition, 129, 134
inventions, 228
invocations, 7

Japanese, 144, 145
journey, 184, 192, 202
judges, 19, 191

judgment, 80, 224
justice, 149, 161, 163, 164, 165,
    166, 195, *see also* section on
    Doctors, Lawyers, Industry
    Chiefs

kindness, 176, 212, 215
knowledge, 52, 53, 55, 56, 73, 91,
    92, 101, 126, 127, 189, 193,
    203, 208, 210, 219, 231, *see
    also* learning

language, 55
laughter, 12, 25, 221
laws, 162, 215, *see also* section on
    Doctors, Lawyers, Industry
    Chiefs
laziness, 45
leaders, leadership, 43, 68, 167,
    168, 193
learning, 109, 218, *see also*
    education
legality, 135
leisure, 106, 213, 228
liberal, liberals, 58, 200
liberation, 204
liberty, 42, 165, 190
lies, lying, 47, 48, 81, 128
life, living, 61, 63, 191, 198, 211,
    227
listeners, 226
longevity, 119
Los Angeles, 142, 143
love, 202, 223
loyalty, 211
luck, lucky, 109, 179, 217
lunch, 7, 224

managers, 146
marriage, 59, 110
materialism, 207, 228, 230
maturity, 57, 58
media, 132
medicine, 216, 226, *see also* section

on Doctors, Lawyers, Industry
    Chiefs
mediocrity, 68, 212
meetings, 75, 98
mercy, 194, 215
mergers, 81, 169
microphone, 11, 268
middle age, 64, 89, 226, *see also*
    section on Youth and Age
minds, 189, 193, 218
ministers, 7, 22, 44, 67, 117, 229
miracles, 117
misers, 176, 213
mistakes, 97, 128
misunderstandings, 222
modesty, 122, 199
money, 38, 53, 68, 72, 74, 76, 97,
    99, 100, 104, 105, 106, 107,
    110, 130, 144, 153, 159, 181,
    213, *see also* wealth
morale, 166
mothers, 52
music, 84, 110, 120

neighbors, 165
news, 235
newspapers, 39, 126
New York City, 140, 141, 143, 231,
    259
New York state, 93
Nobel prize, 86
nobility, noble, 180, 210
nonviolence, 207
nostalgia, 52

obligations, 215
opportunity, 227
optimism, 106
order, 127
originality, 20, 74, 101, 126, 131,
    221
outer space, 146, 200, 224, 230

painters, painting, 51
panic, 198

patience, 37, 58, 182
patriotism, 203
peace, 66, 108, 119, 175, 180, 182, 195, 203, 215
perfection, 214
performance, 74, 76
perseverance, 77
persistence, 43, 103
persuasion, 18, 128, 130
philosophers, 124, 226
philosophy, 184, 210
planner, planning, 169
policy, 118
politics, 128, 192, 215, 253, *see also* section on Politics
polls, 93, 94
population, 86, 88, 89, 90
poverty, 108, 109, 176, 191
power, 74, 105, 194, 199, 201, 204
pragmatism, 64, 206
prayers, 44, 180, 203
presidency, president, 37, 38, 39, 44, 45, 47, 58, 93, 107, 205
press, 3, 47, 98, 101, 189
prestige, 188
price, 67, 75, 76, 158
pride, 76, 127
problems, 98, 99, 104, 192, 222, 230
productivity, 126
products, 132
profits, 66, 82, 109, 182
progress, 80, 96, 195, 200, 211, 226
promises, 179
promptness, 257
prophesies, 194
prosperity, 100, 180
protectionism, 196
psychiatrists, 121, 154
psychology, 126
public, 126
publicity, 3, 125, *see also* section on Extra Mileage From Your Speech
public relations, 133
punishment, 164, 217, 224

purpose, 37, 188, 201

quality, 76, 124, 193
questions, 223, 224, 237

rapport, 5, 137
reality, 57
recession, 72, 73, 78
regrets, 8
regulations, 40
rehearsal, 35, *see also* section on Rehearsals
relativity, 94
reputation, 184
resistance, 234
respect, 62
responsibility, 75, 97
retirement, 26, 71, 79, 169
reunions, 60
roast, 9, 25
ruthlessness, 111, 201

sacrifice, 201
sales, selling, 67, 68, 71, 77, 128, 130, 209
salvation, 214, 229
sarcasm, 209
scholars, 215
science, scientists, 124, 159, 231, 260
security, 75, 202
self-assurance, 62
sense, 135
services, 69
sex, 40, 59, 71, 81, 145, 158
silence, 76, 175, 178, 181, 209, 217
simplicity, 20
skeptics, 187
sleep, 21
slogans, 42
software, 82
solutions, 222, 227, 255
sophistication, 141
sorrow, 193, *see also* grief
southerners, 141, 142, 237

space age, 90, *see also* outer space
speech, 210, *see also* talking
spending, 149
spirit, 214
sports, 229
status quo, 98
stock, 86
strength, 189, 202, 211
stress, 133
stubbornness, 174
stupidity, 104, 111, 132
suburbia, 89, 103, 109
success, 17, 39, 61, 70, 71, 72, 74,
    78, 107, 111, 113, 168, 219,
    226, 236
supermarkets, 86, 146
surrender, 194
suspicion, 183, 216

tact, 115, 232
takeovers, 68
talent, 9, 43, 100
talking, 209, 217, *see also* speech
tardiness, 257
taxes, 100, 109, 144, 170
taxis, 141
technology, 91, 121, 125
teenagers, 37, *see also* section on
    Youth and Age
telephones, 52, 100
television, 52, 53, 87, 93, 129, 130,
    134, 224
theater, 122
theories, 230
thievery, thieves, 117, 141, 219
thrift, 179
time, 104, 216, 228
toastmaster, 10, 16
tolerance, 7
trade, 66
tradition, 48, 81, 98, 202
travel, 105, 138
treachery, 210
trust, 109, 180, 212
truth, 37, 38, 41, 47, 51, 64, 73, 94,
    98, 104, 108, 110, 111, 120,

    126, 130, 152, 175, 177, 195,
    207, 210, 211, 218, 224, 227,
    230
tyranny, 191, 196

understanding, 102, 198
unemployment, 72
unity, 47
universality, 124

vacations, 52
valiant, 222
valor, 194
value, 67
vanity, 127, *see also* arrogance
VCRs, 82, 87
vice, 216
vice-presidency, 38, 43, 44
victory, 53
violence, 89, 195
VIPs, 67
virtue, 212, 216
voting, 48, *see also* section on
    Politics

Wall Street, 197
war, 47, 108, 180, 189, 191, 192,
    196, 203
weakness, 194, 202
wealth, 109, 176, 183, 209, 212
winning, 168
wisdom, wise, 52, 73, 80, 109, 117,
    164, 175, 178, 211
wishes, 45
women, 71, 74, 89, 199, 204, 257
words, 42, 102, 193, 204, 218, 226,
    233, 263
work, 76, 77, 102, 103, 106, 109,
    169, 181, 211, 212, 215, 226,
    236
writer's block, 27
writing, 98, 128, 129, 130, 131, 192,
    193

youth, 42, 181, 226, *see also*
    section on Youth and Age